Mystery of Creation

Mystery of Creation

Paul Haffner

GRACEWING

First published in 1995
by
Gracewing
2, Southern Avenue
Leominster
HerefordshireHR6 0QF
www.gracewing.co.uk

Second edition 2010, revised, updated and reset.

ISBN 978 085244 316 3

Cover: *Adam and Eve* (1526), oil on panel by Lucas Cranach the Elder, courtesy of Courtauld Institute Galleries.

Contents

Foreword

When did you last read a book with a whole chapter dedicated to angels? When did you last come across a balanced, serious, optimistic view on the rapport between theology and ecology? How many attempts have been made to provide a solid, interdisciplinary overview of the Catholic Church's teaching on creation? Rev Paul Haffner has entered this intriguing field with a sure hand. His excellent background, spanning the gamut of science, philosophy and theology has prepared him admirably for a task which today is usually dealt with in specific articles and monographs. His respectful approach to differing teachings and theories is never allowed to dissolve into relativism. He is familiar with the 'Big Bang' theory, with Albert Einstein and with recent theoreticians, as he shows himself blessed with the gift of explaining in accessible terms some of the more abstruse opinions in vogue today.

Rev Haffner is equally at ease with the scientific as with the theological approach. While embracing the basically positive assessment of human endowments, including the amazing abilities of mind and will, as held by the Catholic Church throughout the ages, he is able to combine the best of human achievement with the certainties of Christian revelation. The logical flow of his presentation, beginning with the Scriptures and passing on to the finest of Catholic tradition, gives ample space to the Church's teaching authority. The judiciously chosen teaching of the Magisterium, particularly that of our twentieth century, goes a long way to dispel every lingering suspicion that modern science and technology are in irremediable contrast with faith and revelation. Rev Haffner shows how the two can and should complement one another. With evident pride, he shows that modern science got its impetus in the 'Christian' Middle Ages. He does not dodge the thorny issues of Galileo or Copernicus, but does show a consistent Catholic search for the truth, a search which he readily admits—as the title of his work, *Mystery of Creation* states—will never be completely achieved.

Throughout the book the reader will find not only solid and reverent reasoning, but also some of the sapiential approach to theology which marks the writing and teaching of the Eastern part of Christendom. Rev Haffner provides meaningful citations from the poets, from the Eastern liturgies and often delves into the teaching of the Eastern Fathers, who made little or no distinction between dogmatic and mystical theology. The ecumenical dimension of this methodology is an added advantage. To appreciate the difference of approach between East and West is of immense value in the ecumenical urgency that has been voiced of late—and with much resonance—by none other than Pope John Paul II, who as might be expected, is often cited in this work. For those who have commented on the distinctly philosophical and theological setting of the present Pope's talks, even at Wednesday audiences, this book shows how relevant his teachings are for some of the most gripping problems of our times. The many citations from Pope John Paul II are included not so much as an argument from authority, but rather a good and even excellent way of expressing the Church's Catholic faith in this field.

This much-needed book will serve not only those who take up the study of theology, but also those who are involved in any sort of communication about the Catholic faith. How often Catholics are confronted with questions like: Is your Church opposed to the theory of evolution? Why? Why does your Church seem to put little store in the created things around us? Does your Church resist attempts by women to claim equal rights with men? Why? You keep speaking about the inherent goodness of nature and of nature's God, but then why all this suffering of the innocent, by natural catastrophes which too often snuff out the lives of thousands at a time? This book meets these and many other currently burning issues head on. By giving a brief description of various opinions, the Church's stand is put into better perspective. The Catholic position is seen to be an avoidance of the extremes of utopia on the one hand and of a disdain for material things on the other, while stressing the basic need of mankind to use the things of this world in such a way as not to jeopardize one's eternal destiny. Grace does build on nature, but this very statement means that gratuitous grace from God has as its foundation the natural goods of His creation. The Catholic Church, buffeted on many sides, has staunchly defended the radical goodness of our human nature, even while acknowledging its obviously wounded and imperfect state.

Even when redeemed by Christ and made holy in the depths of its being by the powerful action of the Lord's

Spirit, the treasures of God are contained in vessels of clay, which daily must take radical measures to avoid break-up. Every day of creation is a risk, but also a promise that 'the best is yet to come'. The basically positive thrust of this book goes a long way in showing that the Catholic Church, often accused of neglecting, depreciating or even despising earthly realities in favour of what communists label 'a pie in the sky', has consistently taken another path: that of valuing all the gifts of nature. Among numerous examples which bear witness to this are the art treasures that the Church fostered and preserved, and the deep involvement of its sons and daughters in modern means of social communication. The gifts of nature are thus seen as glorious anticipations of an even more splendid enhancement of which the author writes movingly in the final chapter.

A final characteristic of this much-to-be-commended book is its attention to a contemporary preoccupation: that of avoiding the study of a subject in 'splendid isolation', but rather taking the more difficult and more objective path of an interdisciplinary study. Again, taking his cue from the Eastern Fathers, the author sees the Creator as God in Three Persons Who reveals Himself, creating through His Son the Word in the power of His Holy Spirit. Time after time he shows that Catholic theology must in the end be viewed in its integrity, as one truth illustrates and deepens our understanding of some other facet of our faith. How much richer is theology when both the personal or individual aspects of revelation are completed and enhanced by its communal dimension. The marvellous consistency between protology and eschatology puts into even sharper evidence the fact of the basic goodness of creation: the one thing God cannot do is to create something bad or evil. And the more God is allowed to be Himself in creation's regard, the better it will inevitably become. Since God is simply infinite, the possibilities of creation are relatively endless. Far from reining in the explosively dynamic dimension of creation, God's intervention is a challenge to delve ever deeper into the depths of creation in order to discern how much of Himself He has left mirrored there.

This book will not only provide much information about creation and about creation's God, but will issue in a paean of praise and thanksgiving in the contemplation of so much good that gives us a taste and yearning for the Good that will finally satisfy and fulfil all the outreach of our spirits for truth and goodness and beauty.

Redemptus Maria Valabek, O.Carm.
Dean, English Section Pontifical Institute *Regina Mundi*
Apostolic Examiner of the Clergy of Rome

Preface to Second Edition

Nearly fifteen years have now elapsed since the publication of the first edition of this work dealing with the mystery of creation. During the last twenty years or so, interest in the theology of creation has greatly flourished, whether it be in the interpretation of cosmology or in discussions on evolution. Scarcely a week passes without some important issue being aired in the media, touching at least obliquely upon questions which are treated in this book. Above all, during the Pontificate of Pope John Paul II of holy memory, and that of Pope Benedict XVI, the Church herself has taken a vivid interest in the realm of creation theology in general and in that of Christianity and science in particular.

The text has now been considerably expanded, especially in those areas where students have expressed an interest in further elaboration. These topics include the treatment of evolution, the problem of evil, and the Christological vision of creation. Some errors have also been eliminated, and the notes and bibliography have been updated. In commending this volume to the next generation of readers, I express my gratitude to John and Ashley Noronha who kindly read this text and made helpful suggestions.

Rome, 17 January 2010

Feast of Our Lady of Peace

Preface

I believe that this work fills a gap which has been evident for some years, namely the need for a general introduction to the Catholic theology of creation. Cardinal Ratzinger pointed out recently that faith in the Creation and its correct interpretation is of fundamental importance, because God has a real relationship with the world. If this relationship is not understood as an integral part of God's plan, then faith loses its foundations and slips away into mere vague feeling. He is not alone in voicing this concern.

Some of the books on creation written over the past few years have furnished only a partial vision; they have omitted an account of how angels came into being and how some fell, and they have been sketchy on the issue of original sin. Others have been written solely from the standpoint of the dialogue between science and religion or of ecology. The present book seeks to redress a balance lacking in other works and at the same time outline the interface with the issues in science and technology. Above all, this work seeks to show the link between the theology of creation and other branches of theology, and to discuss the dialogue between theology and the natural sciences. The layout followed is a progressive unwrapping of the economy of creation. The first six chapters furnish some basic themes concerning the theology of creation. Thus, chapter one outlines the rational and revealed sources of this study. Chapter two deals with the creation of the invisible realm of pure spirits, while the third chapter covers the creation of the material universe. This paves the way for a discussion of the creation of the human person in chapter four. Chapter five deals with God's Providence towards what He has created, illustrating a link between creation and salvation history. Only in chapter six is the Fall of angels and man and woman dealt with, after a solid understanding of creation has already been proposed. Chapter seven seeks to examine the link between creation and Christ the Saviour and Redeemer, so as to unfold the specifically Christian flavour of creation, and to point out the connections between the theology of creation and Christology and ecclesiology. Chapter eight deals in a particular way with some of the questions in the relationship between science and religion, while chapter nine treats of some of the practical ecological applications of this area. Finally, chapter ten attempts to draw the threads together of a relation between protology, the study of the 'first things' and eschatology which looks at 'the last things'. Thus, the present work should help the student of theology appreciate a deeper relation between the various branches of this sacred science.

This book has been written with undergraduate university students in mind, but it may also be of service outside the university context, in adult education schemes and discussion groups. I am grateful to many people for their help in the gestation of this volume. Fr Redemptus Valabek O.Carm kindly supplied the Foreword. Discussions with my students at the Pontifical Gregorian University and the Pontifical Institute Regina Mundi sowed the seed for some of the ideas which it contains. Thanks are due to Fr Willibrord Welten SJ of the Pontifical Gregorian University for his suggestions concerning the philosophical parts of this text and to Dr Stephen Dingley for his comments on the scientific portion. I am grateful to Frank and Philomena Whitesell and Larry and Ester Wong for their help. Above all I express my thanks to Mr Thomas Longford the publisher who has helped bring the book to birth. The book is dedicated to my mother, to my sister Christine and to Martin, her husband.

Rome, 24 September 1995
Feast of Our Lady of Ransom

Abbreviations

AAS	*Acta Apostolicae Sedis. Commentarium officiale.* Rome: Vatican Polyglot Press, 1909– .
CCC	*Catechism of the Catholic Church* Dublin: Veritas, 1994.
DP	*Discourses of the Popes from Pius XI to John Paul II to the Pontifical Academy of Sciences. 1936–1986.* Vatican City: Pontifical Academy of Sciences, 1986.
DS	H. Denzinger and H. Schönmetzer. *Enchiridion Symbolorum, Definitionum et Declarationum de rebus fidei et morum.* Barcelona/Freiburg im Breisgau/Rome: Herder, 1976.
IG	*Insegnamenti di Giovanni Paolo II.* Vatican City: Vatican Polyglot Press, 1978–2005.
IP	*Insegnamenti di Paolo VI* Vatican City: Vatican Polyglot Press, 1963–1978.

ND	J. Neuner and J. Dupuis, *The Christian Faith in the Doctrinal Documents of the Catholic Church.* London: Collins, 1983.
OR	*L'Osservatore Romano*, daily Italian edition.
ORE	*L'Osservatore Romano*, weekly English edition.
PG	J.P. Migne. *Patrologiae cursus completus, series graeca*. 161 vols. Paris: 1857–1866.
PL	J.P. Migne. *Patrologiae cursus completus, series latina*. 221 vols. Paris: 1844–1864.
SC	*Sources Chretiennes*. Paris: Cerf, 1942– .

The Scriptural quotations and abbreviations in this work are generally from the New Jerusalem Bible.

1

Creation in Reason and Revelation

For the bright firmament
shoots forth no flame
So silent, but is eloquent
In speaking the Creator's name.

William Babington, *Nox Nocti Indicat Scientiam*

The mystery of creation is of considerable relevance to the world of today. From the very earliest times, the external universe has aroused within the human person a sense of wonder and a search for solutions to questions about the origins of man and the cosmos. Man's investigations into the universe have evoked a corresponding interior journey which has sometimes been a pilgrimage leading to the very threshold of faith in a Creator; at other times man's reflection on creation has resulted in idolatry, an effect of the original tragedy which weakened man's will and obscured his intellect to a certain degree. History indicates how many pre-Christian and non-Christian cultures approached creation in ways which were not conducive to belief in the Creator and which were also detrimental to human and scientific development.[1] At the present time, with the widespread diffusion of popular scientific and technological information concerning man and the universe, there is a special need for Christians to understand the doctrine of creation in as much breadth and depth as possible, in order to be able to give reasons for our faith and hope (1 P 3:15). Key issues at the forefront of a dialogue between Christian faith and modern science include the origin of the universe, the beginning and structure of life, as well as the origin and nature of man and woman. The theology of creation also touches on practical questions like ecology and bioethics.

It is therefore becoming more necessary than ever to shed a specifically Christian light upon creation, defined as God's action in making the cosmos as well as in terms of the product of His work, namely the created reality. God's work of creation is to be distinguished from procession, emanation and transformation. Procession occurs when, without division of substance, an immutable nature is completely given to several persons: this is the case in the Mystery of the Most Holy Trinity. Emanation takes place when a being draws forth from its own substance another similar or analogous substance as a separate reality, or else produces within itself a new manner of being, which is distinct from itself. Transformation occurs when an external agent causes a change of state within another being. The Christian idea of creation is neither procession, emanation, nor transformation, but rather involves God's absolute power bringing into being outside of Himself something which in no way existed before. The question of *why* man and the cosmos are here at all is also most important, in order to appreciate how the drama of salvation history unfolds within the theatre of what God has created.

1.1 *A realist perspective*

An access to the true nature of the universe is needed in order to reflect properly on God's handiwork. Reality is rather like a mine in which understanding, like precious metal, has to be quarried at the cost of great effort. Christian tradition has always held that man is truly capable of understanding creation and gradually uncovering its meaning, within a realist perspective. In the prelude to his monumental profession of faith, Pope Paul VI stated:

> It is of the greatest importance to recognize that over and above what is visible, the reality of which we discern through the sciences, God has given us an intellect which can attain to *that which is*, not merely the subjective content of the 'structures' and developments of human consciousness.[2]

Reality speaks to us, communicating its message through the senses of our human nature, shaped from flesh and spirit. A realist approach to the cosmos is essentially based on the Thomist axiom: 'the being of a thing, not its truth, is the cause of truth in the intellect.'[3] Common-sense realism involves a true partnership between man as a knower and the world and contrasts with an idealist, a positivist, an existentialist or a nihilist position.

Moderate realism is the 'cement' in any synthesis of faith and reason; it stipulates the real existence of the external world independent of the mind of the observer, yet with a mutual relation between the mind and reality. An analogy with art may be a useful way of making clearer what we understand by *moderate realism*. The basis for this analogy is inspired by the words of the great Doctor of the Alexandrian School, St Gregory of Nyssa:

> As painters transfer human forms to their pictures by means of certain colours, laying on their copy the proper and corresponding tints, so that the beauty of the original may be accurately transferred to the likeness, so I would have you understand that our Master also, painting the portraits to resemble His own beauty, by the addition of virtues, as it were with colours, shows in us His own sovereignty.[4]

In the epistemological problem it is the relation between thinker, reality and thought that is being considered; the analogy in art concerns the relation between the painter, the model and the painting. Let us consider various attempts by different artists to portray a model. *Naïve epistemological realism* would correspond to the photographic approach in art, either simply an enlarged photograph or a painting which is just like a photograph, in which there would be no attempt at interpretation by the painter. The model would be merely copied with no mutual interaction between the painter and the model. This the approach of some of the realistic schools of art. In the equivalent of *idealism*, the reality of the model being portrayed would not be acknowledged as independent of the artist. All would come from the mind and feelings of the painter, which he would impose on the canvas. This corresponds to the art of the expressionist movement of the early twentieth century, a movement which saw the destruction of the idea of art being a 'mirror of nature'; the autonomy of art was stressed.

In *existentialism*, the philosopher would tend to destroy the unity of being, and hence distinct yet related entities are seen as totally disconnected one from another. In the equivalent in art, the separate parts of the body of the model would be shown as completely independent; also an attempt would be made to say that there was no connection between this model and any other human person, any idea of human nature or essence being denied. This corresponds in some ways to Dadaism and surrealism which sought to undermine meaning in art as it had been traditionally understood. In the equivalent in art of *positivism and empiricism*, the painter would allow what he sees from his model to be his 'input'; he would exclude other factors such as what he knows of the character and personality of the model from his artistic considerations. The model may be interpreted in a more or less abstract way. This corresponds to impressionism (as exemplified in such figures as Monet), which sought to oppose the 'idealist' tendencies of expressionism. The *nihilist* denies any meaning at all in man and the world. Some modern artists (for example, the exponents of abstract expressionism) are also nihilist to the extent that their work denies any relation at all between the model and the painting.

In the situation which corresponds with *moderate realism*, the painter attempts to gather all the various aspects of his model which he can, including what he knows of the personality. Then, in accordance with the true nature of the model and taking into account his own interpretation and the qualities of his artist's materials, he attempts to project onto the plane of his canvas, the multi-dimensional nature of his model and the surroundings including the light patterns. Thus the artist has truly interacted with nature, and he respects what is proper to his model, to his own artistic skill, to his materials and to his surroundings. Various artists could be said to have typified this approach, including Giotto (thirteenth to fourteenth century), P. Breughel (sixteenth century), J. Vermeer (seventeenth century), Canaletto (eighteenth century) and Sir J. Reynolds (eighteenth century). P. Duhem manifests, in his art, that perception of reality which is congruent with his essentially realist approach to the universe.[5] An appreciation of moderate realism is needed so as to do full justice to the cosmos approached through reason, and also to promote a true relation between revelation and reason concerning creation.

1.2 *Reason and Revelation*

Creation theology is one area where the interface between human thought and Christian belief stands out in bold relief. Through reason, man studies creation in search of its Creator. Through revelation, God enters His own creation in search of man. Through faith and theology, God and man meet within the setting of the universe. Even the understanding of the cosmos obtained through reason alone in scientific investigation, is imbued with mystery. Scientific endeavour remains always incomplete and has not completely unravelled the riddle of the universe.[6] It is not certain that rational research will ever get to the point of completely solving all the enigmas in the cosmos despite the claim of some scientists, such as Stephen Hawking:

> However, if we do discover a complete theory, it should in time be understandable in broad principle by everyone, not just a few scientists. Then we shall all, philosophers, scientists, and just ordinary people, be able to take part in the discussion of the question of why it is that we and the universe exist. If we find the answer to that, it would be the ultimate triumph of human reason—for then we would know the mind of God.[7]

Even though humanity does make progress in its scientific understanding of the universe and despite the fact that man by his nature transcends the material world, a great sense of mystery always remains. The concept of cosmic mystery is not the same as that of a detective novel, where at the beginning there is a crime to be solved, a culprit to be found, and at the end of the book all is clear. In other words, the sense of mystery diminishes as time goes on. However, as humanity turns the pages of the book of nature, the cosmos does not appear to become progressively less mysterious; the history of this past century's science has demonstrated quite the opposite: namely that as our knowledge increases, we are overwhelmed by the beauty and complexity of the universe. While, on the one hand, cosmic enigma discourages an excessive sense of pride in the achievements of science to date, on the other hand, it should not make us feel insignificant and incapable of knowing the universe. It should rather arouse a poetic sense of wonderment, akin to that expressed by Alfred Noyes:

> I look up
> And out, beyond our Milky Way, and see
> Those twisting nebulae, like coils of mist
> Where suns as vast as our whole universe
> Are less than atoms. Then, beneath my feet
> I see the dust, of which each molecule now,
> Rends open, in its infinitesimal heart,
> Unfathomable gulfs of suns and stars.[8]

Scientific investigation of the cosmos is filled with metaphysical presuppositions such as the realist perspective and the idea of the universe as a totality.[9] These philosophical presuppositions are, at the same time, not alien to science, but rather are supported by its findings. However, a shroud of mystery remains even at the level of metaphysics, for we are still not clear from philosophy alone, for example, *why* God created the cosmos.

It would be a mistake, however, to confuse wonderment at the cosmos with a quasi-religious instinct, as if God were to be *directly* accessible through the creation. This is the problem with *ontologism*, which holds that human reason knows God by a kind of immediate natural intuition, and seems to presuppose that part of human reason is divine.[10] Rather, our knowledge of God is mediated by created things and operates by analogy. This avoids any confusion between God and His creation, which generally slides into pantheism. Within Eastern Christendom, the distinction between God and His creation is protected by the further distinction between the divine energies and the divine essence. According to St Basil and St Gregory of Nyssa, in the world only the Divine energies, the active forces of the Divine goodness, are manifested and operate; and it is only these energies which are comprehensible and accessible to us in our relations with God.[11] Yet, *these energies are God Himself.* The depths of the essence of God, dwelling in inapproachable light, are closed to us for ever. However, what is comprehensible of Him, God has revealed *by His operations* in the world. By them we can contemplate His eternal Divinity and power (Rm 1: 19-20). Nevertheless the *nature* of God is ineffable and inaccessible—it is only accessible to God Himself.[12]

Appreciation for and amazement at the material creation is also to be distinguished from that type of false mysticism where complex aspects of material reality are endowed with a pseudo-religious quality. Attempts to read mystical significance into certain patterns observed in elementary particle physics fall into this category.[13] A similar problem is found in the writings of the French Jesuit Pierre Teilhard de Chardin (1881–1955). He attempted to create a fusion of Christianity and evolutionary theory, but taught not so much Catholicism as New Age pantheism. His error starts with a confusion between matter and spirit, whereby even material entities are endowed with spiritual properties: 'We are logically forced to assume the existence in rudimentary form of some sort of psyche in every corpuscle, even in those whose complexity is of such a low or modest order as to render it imperceptible.'[14] This error of panpsychism is followed by a confusion between God and His creation, leading to pantheism. Teilhard described his view of reality as a 'superior form of pantheism' or as an 'absolutely legitimate pantheism'.[15] He admitted to being 'essentially pantheist', and as having dedicated his life to promoting a true 'pantheism of union'.[16] Teilhard goes even further when he denies the immutability of God: 'As a direct consequence of the unitive process by which God is revealed to us, he in some way "transforms himself" as he incorporates us... I see in the World a mysterious product of completion and fulfillment for the Absolute Being himself.'[17] The concept of Creation is no longer applied in a biblical sense, and Teilhard explicitly stated: 'I find myself completely unsympathetic to the Creationism of the Bible... I find the Biblical idea of creation rather anthropomorphic.'[18] Teilhard stresses instead the mutual complementarity of the Creator and His creation: 'Truly it is not the notion of the contingency of the created, but the sense of the mutual completion of God and the world that makes Christianity live.'[19] God's freedom to create is not clear enough; the cosmos seems to be necessary rather than contingent. Moreover, man's freedom is not clear.

Teilhard proposed a new cosmic Christology in which Christ remains too immanent and does not transcend the evolutionary process; furthermore, Teilhard does not take original sin and the Cross into sufficient consideration. In this understanding, man's cooperation is missing; that is, man is not seen as bringing redemption to all of creation. The Incarnation and Redemption are thus reduced to the natural order, and become necessary rather than gratuitous: 'God cannot appear as the Prime Mover toward the future without becoming Incarnate and without redeeming, that is without Christifying Himself for us.'[20] The Incarnation seems to be a fruit of the evolutionary process: 'Christ is the end–

product of the evolution, even of the natural evolution of all beings; and therefore evolution is holy.'[21] Teilhard's conception of evil as a failing and not a condition leads to serious problems with his approach to original sin.[22] This leads to a false idea concerning the Cross and the Redemption wrought by Christ. Briefly, according to Teilhard, the concept of a Cross of expiation is replaced by the notion of a 'cross of evolution' with Christ conceived as the apex of man's spiritual evolution.[23] The angelic world seems to have no place in Teilhard's system. His eschatology is vague to say the least, and tinged with an evolutionist and Hegelian ideology. The term of his continuous creation in Christ is the *Pleroma,* the final state of the world, the consummation of all things in Christ. God's continuous creation is directed to 'the quantitative repletion and the qualitative consummation of all things... the mysterious Pleroma in which the substantial One and the created many fuse without confusion into a whole which, without adding anything essential to God, will nevertheless be a sort of triumph and generalization of Being.'[24] As a result of these errors and ambiguities, the Church has on several occasions drawn attention to the problems and advised vigilance on the part of the faithful.[25]

The concept of supernatural mystery must be reserved for what is truly the supernatural realm. While it may be possible to unravel many of nature's puzzles here on this earth (even if we do not reach the solution of the totality of the cosmos), a supernatural mystery lies in the revealed order and is more profound still than any rational enigma. For the revelation of a truth concerning God the Creator tells us much, but still leaves us with mystery, for God transcends us completely. We can understand our relationship with Him by increasing degrees, according to the graces of understanding which we are granted in this world; the lives of saints and mystics are transparent examples of this. However, even in the life to come in paradise, when we see God face to face, His Trinity will still be a mystery to us in the sense that He is infinitely greater than we are.[26]

Christian theology teaches us that there are many truths known to us only through Christian revelation, such as the fact that the Creator of all is the Most Holy Trinity. However, some of what revelation tells us concerning creation has already been at least glimpsed by the power of reason. On the basis of well-known Scriptural passages (Wisdom 13:1–9 and Romans 1:19–20), the Church has always held that it is possible to arrive at the existence of God through a consideration of His creation. The First Vatican Council defined this solemnly by stating:

> The same Holy Mother Church holds and teaches that God, the beginning and end of all things, can be known with certainty from the things which were created through the natural light of reason.[27]

In the course of the centuries many proofs of the existence of God have been developed, the most famous being the classical five ways of St Thomas Aquinas.[28] The first way is an argument from motion, the second from considerations of efficient causality, the third from possibility and necessity, the fourth from the gradation to be found in beings, and the fifth from purpose and design.[29] All these ways involve a reflection on created reality in order to arrive at God. Man is capable of seeing that creation is good, notwithstanding original sin. He can also perceive that there is a unity within creation. Noting the truth, goodness, and unity of the cosmos, man appreciates beauty within the universe in its different forms in the various wonders of nature. It is also expressed in art, literature, music and painting. Above all in our human experience, we perceive it in other persons, not simply in their physical appearance but also in beauty of spirit and of noble deeds.

Man does not create all this beauty but rather he receives and unveils it, and thus cooperates in its revelation. However, more than this, man can arrive, via a reflection upon creation, at the fact that beauty is not able to explain its own existence, it is not here by chance, but rather it is *created*. We realize that there is always something more beautiful than what we have experienced or uncovered, and so we are led by degrees to Uncreated Beauty. It is as if God has left a kind of trade-mark upon creation which can thus be traced back to its Creator. Hence, man fully discovers and admires beauty only when he refers it back to its source, the transcendent beauty of God. While philosophical demonstrations of God's existence are real proofs they are not intended to be the same as mathematical or scientific formulae. In other words, 'to desire a scientific proof of God would be equivalent to lowering God to the level of the beings of our world, and we would therefore be mistaken methodologically in regard to what God is.'[30]

Christian revelation confirms the truth of God's existence but goes much further, furnishing a perspective of God the Creator as the Most Holy Trinity, which could not have been obtained by human thought alone. Similarly, we can perceive through reason that the human person has some spark of the immortal within him; Christian revelation confirms this natural truth stating that man is a unity of body and soul whom we see in a new and deeper way in the light of Christ's human nature. The confirmatory power of revelation is necessary because often man's appreciation of natural truths is clouded by the after-effects of the Fall. Clearly, revelation is above reason, but there can be no discord between the two orders of knowledge. This is because the same God bestows the light of reason on the human mind, then reveals mysteries and infuses faith. God can never deny Himself nor can truth contradict truth: 'Like two streams from the same source, the truths of reason and the truths of faith descend to man. There is never a quarrel between them, they are sisters of unequal beauty.'[31]

In Christian tradition, therefore, it has been customary to speak of two books as sources of our knowledge of God the Creator, namely the Book of the Scriptures and that of the universe. The fact that creation reveals something of the Creator can be called natural revelation as distinct from supernatural revelation:

> 'Let the earth bring forth the fruit tree yielding fruit.' Immediately the tops of the mountains were covered with foliage: paradises were artfully laid out, and an infinitude of plants embellished the banks of the rivers. Some were for the adornment of man's table; some to nourish animals with their fruits and their leaves; some to provide medicinal help by giving us their sap, their juice, their chips, their bark or their fruit. In a word, the experience of ages, profiting from every chance, has not been able

> to discover anything useful, which the penetrating foresight of the Creator did not first perceive and call into existence. Therefore, when you see the trees in our gardens, or those of the forest, those which love the water or the land, those which bear flowers, or those which do not flower, I should like to see you recognising grandeur even in small objects, adding incessantly to your admiration of, and redoubling your love for the Creator.[32]

Creation and revelation are intertwined, for creation reveals something of God and His plan, while revelation invites us to an intimate relationship with God against the backdrop of what He has made. While God reveals Himself both through creation and through His Son, the ways and degrees of this revelation are different. By gazing at creation, we can learn something of the contours of Him who made all. The glory of God is in the first place essentially in Himself, as the Most Holy Trinity, the Father, the Son and the Holy Spirit. The act of creation is the beginning of the revelation of God's glory, for through this work, God's interior which springs from the very mystery of His Divinity, is manifested 'outside' to the creatures of the visible and invisible world, in proportion to their various degrees of perfection.[33] However, God only reveals Himself fully in and through His Son, through Whom He made all things, His Son Who comes to us in human form so vesting Himself in the very creation for which He was responsible. Creation is therefore the medium through which God reveals Himself, even though having created the cosmos, God was free not to have shared His inner life with us. Hence creation is a natural gift and divine revelation in Christ is a further gift, but in the supernatural order. Current Catholic theology considers the supernatural dimension not simply as an addition to the natural order, as icing is put on a cake. Instead, grace is seen as conspiring with nature to produce a new organic unity.[34]

1.3 *Tradition, Scripture and the Magisterium*

Divine revelation, given once and for all to the Church by Christ, is handed down in the same Church through Scripture and Tradition and these two sources have much to say about creation. The Church in its faith and theology does not derive the fullness of the content of revelation and the certainty concerning this deposit of faith from Scripture alone, but also from all that is contained within the Tradition of the Church. An example from the theology of creation lies in the fact that although the doctrine of creation out of nothing is indicated in the Scriptures (2 Maccabees 7:28 and Romans 4:17), the complete doctrine and its certainty is contained in Tradition as taught by the Church's teaching office or Magisterium.

The guidance of the Papal teaching office on creation and other topics is especially important in this rapidly-changing scientific age. St Peter's successor as 'the perpetual and visible source and foundation of unity both of the bishops and of the whole company of the faithful'[35] is not merely a static focus of unity, but one which leads to still greater unity. Despite the ebb and flow in the tide of the Church's fortunes in history there is nevertheless a prophetic direction in the rôle of Peter's successor. The work of each Pope is woven into the tapestry of salvation history as a whole, since the Holy Spirit is guiding the Church into all truth (cf. Jn 16:13). The organic relationship of the Pope within the Church is beautifully illustrated by Bernini's 'Glory' in St Peter's basilica in Rome. From above, the Holy Spirit shines upon the Chair (*Cathedra*) of Saint Peter, divinely guiding each of his successors in their Magisterium. From below, the chair is supported by four saints, who are also bishops and theologians: St Ambrose and St Augustine (of the Latin Church) and St Athanasius and St John Chrysostom (of the Greek Church). This illustrates in a marvellous way how St Peter's successor, infallibly guided by the Spirit, acquires his theological formulations with the help of the bishops and the faithful and is in close touch with the sense of faith (*sensus fidei*)[36] of the entire People of God.

Each of the various layers of meaning in the Scriptures needs to be uncovered by the Church so as to illustrate the treasures contained therein. This is particularly pertinent as regards the book of Genesis, whose evocative source of teaching on creation has been the object of scholarly investigation over the centuries, in many attempts to discern the revealed truth which it contains. However, when Scripture has been separated from its vital matrix of Tradition and the teaching office of the Church, exegetes have not always been able to avoid those possible pitfalls known as *concordism, fundamentalism* and *liberalism*.

Concordism relates to the efforts whereby 'numerous commentators of Genesis 1 tried to establish its concordance with cosmogonies taken for the last word in science.'[37] The danger of this stance is clear, for when a scientific position changes, as it necessarily must for science is in continual development, faith in the word of God as revealed in Scripture may be jeopardized. It is all too easy to be amused by the concordist exegesis of Archbishop Ussher which, in a seventeenth-century attempt to reconcile the six-day creation account with Newtonian physics, fixed the time of creation in the year 4004 B.C. on Sunday 23rd October at 9 o'clock in the morning! Nevertheless, concordism is still a possible trap for the Christian today who attempts to read into the book of Genesis too close a connection with the Big Bang theory.

The fundamentalist approach 'starts from the principle that the Bible, being the word of God, inspired and free from error, should be read and interpreted literally in all its details. But by "literal interpretation" it understands a naïvely literalist interpretation,…, which excludes every effort at understanding the Bible that takes account of its historical origins and development. It is opposed, therefore, to the use of the historico-critical method, as indeed to the use of any other scientific method for the interpretation of Scripture.'[38] While the fundamentalist approach is right to uphold the divine inspiration of Scripture and the inerrancy of the Word of God, it fails to see the full consequences of the Incarnation, ignoring the historical, cultural and human aspects of biblical revelation.[39] It often goes hand in hand with the 'Scripture alone' approach to theology, which was one of the characteristics of the Protestant reformation. Fundamentalism 'accepts the literal reality of an ancient, out-of-date cosmology, simply because it is found expressed in the Bible.'[40] This renders difficult any dialogue between science and faith today, as can be seen in the fundamentalist rejection of any rôle played by evolution within creation.

On the other hand, the liberal or modernist approach to Scriptural interpretation exaggerates the rôle of human techniques in the formation of the Bible and in its exegesis. In a rationalist way it seeks to reduce to merely symbolic or mythological meanings that which in fact Scripture teaches as true at the deepest level. Both Catholic and Protestant theologies have at various times suffered the effects of modernist reductionism. Liberal approaches to exegesis have sought to emphasize the similarity between the content of the book of Genesis and that of ancient near-Eastern myths, so undermining the uniqueness of biblical revelation. This is far from the truth as can be seen from the radical difference between Genesis and accounts from the Babylonian neighbours of the Jewish people of old. In the ancient Babylonian myth, *Enuma Elish,* there are various generations of divine beings and 'creation' is effected by means of a struggle between them. In Genesis, there is only one God and therefore no struggle between various divinities. In the Babylonian myth, matter exists before the formation of the world, while in Genesis, there is no pre-existent material. The vision of Genesis is of a linear cosmos with respect to time, while that of *Enuma Elish* is cyclical. The cosmos of the Babylonian myths is neither good nor rational. Genesis teaches a world which is good (Gn 1:25) and its rationality is implied because God created man and woman in His own image (Gn 1:27) commanding them to fill and conquer it (Gn 1:28):

man and woman would have to understand creation in order to rule it.

An interesting realist approach to the interpretation of the book of Genesis (and in particular of Genesis 1) has been proposed by S. L. Jaki. Instead of loading his study with theological, allegorical or mystical interpretations, Jaki focuses on the tent-model of the cosmos which permeated the mentality of the ancient Hebrews, as the simple way to understand the message of the first book of the Bible.

> The world-tent, like any tent structure, has easily identifiable essential parts: the roof and the base, or the ground. Anything else is accessory but still part of the whole. This makes possible its use for the purposes of conveying the idea of totality in two ways: either by referring to the whole as such, or by enumerating first its essential parts and then what are principally accessory to each of them.[41]

A statement of totality through a listing of its composite parts is often seen in many books of the Old Testament. In this perspective, the main thrust of the first chapter of Genesis is the doctrine that God is the Creator of the dynamic *all* or totality of the cosmos. This good, ordered and intelligible whole is a home for man and woman.

1.4 *A synthetic approach*

Just as the cosmos, in the order of nature, is a unified whole, so also, in the realm of grace, the several aspects of the Christian faith make up a single hymn of praise in response to God the Creator who reveals Himself in Christ. Faith is a response to the *content* of what God reveals, an example being the profession that God created the whole cosmos out of nothing. Faith is also understood as the trust or confidence we have in God who works His purpose out through creation and divine Providence.[42] Without faith and its various aspects we cannot form a Christian theology of creation, which is based upon faith seeking a global or synthetic understanding. In this picture, theology is like a large castle in which each stone has a value in the whole edifice: indeed if one brick is removed, damage is done to the whole building (see Ep 2:20). Theology can also be compared to a seamless garment of many colours forming a unified whole. In a world where intense specialization leads to a fragmentation in many disciplines, including theology, it is more necessary than ever to see the unitary nature of this sacred science. Although the mystery of creation is examined here from many facets, it remains a seamless whole. Just as by dismantling a car, a mechanic may better understand how it works, so also the analytic process in theology furnishes a clearer perspective of the unified whole.

The point of departure for a unified approach to theology is that, according to the analogy of faith, all truths or dogmas are intimately linked with each other and with the entire economy of the deposit of revelation. Moreover, the doctrine of creation is the logical and ontological basis of all other doctrines: 'Without Creation, and a Creation by God who is Father, there is no possibility of a discourse about Incarnation, Redemption, and final consummation in a New Heaven and Earth.'[43]

Three types of synthesis can be specified. The first is the kind belonging to one particular natural science or the interdisciplinary relations between a group of such sciences. The aim here is to have a unified view of a particular science, and difficult though this is, it is the object of reason. The second type of synthesis is that existing between mysteries which are accessible to faith alone, where the synthesis is a gift from God, and the aim is the contemplation of God Himself. This is the privileged domain of the mystic. The third variety of synthesis is the one relating truths which are the object of faith with those which are the object of reason. This work is theological, in which faith and grace guide reason.

A synthetic theological picture has the clear advantage of helping perception of the organic unity of all theology, so indicating the one mystery revealed by Christ:

> The individual theological disciplines are to be taught in such a way that, from their internal structure and from the proper object of each as well as from their connection with other disciplines, including philosophical ones and the sciences of man, the basic unity of theological instruction is clear, and in such a way that all the disciplines converge in a profound understanding of the mystery of Christ, so that this can be announced with greater effectiveness to the People of God and to all nations.[44]

A unified approach also has the advantage that it is satisfying to student and scholar alike, furnishing them with a sense of the relatedness of all truth. A synthesis differs from a mere system, where theological truths are organized for convenience or pragmatic pedagogical reasons; it respects the nature of the theological truths in themselves and never forces *a priori* relations between them where they are not appropriate. Syncretism is markedly different from synthesis, in that the former mixes together with Christian theology elements which may be alien and even opposed to it. Indeed many types of philosophy are incompatible with Christian faith and thus cannot be used in a synthesis of Catholic theology.[45] In fact, it is precisely the realist philosophy which has been mentioned above that constitutes the metaphysics and epistemology germane to the construction of an organic vision of Catholic theology of which an important part is a most specifically Christian treatment of creation.

These observations are very pertinent to the theology of creation where it is all too easy to mingle together many elements from various religions, philosophical systems and scientific opinions and thus end up with confusion. 'It is important to emphasize that when theology employs the elements and conceptual tools of philosophy or other disciplines, discernment is needed. The ultimate normative principle for such discernment is revealed doctrine which itself must furnish the criteria for the evaluation of these elements and conceptual tools and not *vice versa*.'[46] A profound synthesis is necessary in order to avoid the one-sidedness in some recent theological approaches to creation spirituality which bypass considerations of the Fall and the Redemption and the rôle of Christ the Redeemer in order to make way for an over-optimistic, and not specifically Christian world-picture. The present work seeks to relate creation to other important aspects of Christian theology precisely in order to avoid this kind of imbalance.

A renewed interest in creation should be helpful not only to specialists but also to all Christians in an ecumenical spirit, for denominational differences often touch upon the dogma of creation or at least upon its philosophical and theological consequences.[47] The theology of creation is a theme which so far has not been explored in great detail within ecumenical dialogue; it is a topic in which Eastern and Western Christendom could mutually enrich each other. The Western approach starts with a reflection upon creation and proceeds to Christ who has revealed the mystery of the Holy Trinity. The Eastern approach starts beyond time with the divine mystery of the Holy Trinity and arrives at the unfolding of the economy of creation and of salvation. The ecumenical exchange, as well as that carried out with scientists, could foster a deeper understanding of the theology of creation. Development of this kind is not to be understood as a change in the content of dogmas and doctrines, but rather a more profound penetration into the mystery revealed once and for all in Christ:

> Therefore, let there be growth and abundant progress in understanding, knowledge and wisdom, in each and all, in individuals and in the whole Church, at all times and in the progress of ages, but only within the proper limits, namely, with the same dogma, the same meaning, the same judgment.[48]

A progressive and systematic unfolding of the mystery of creation now begins with a description of how the invisible spirit world came into being.

Further Reading

Congregation for the Doctrine of the Faith, *Instruction on the Ecclesial Vocation of the Theologian* (Vatican City: Libreria Editrice Vaticana, 1990)

Pontifical Biblical Commission, *The Interpretation of the Bible in the Church* (Vatican City: Libreria Editrice Vaticana, 1993)

E. Gilson, *Methodical Realism* translated by P. Trower (Front Royal, Va.: Christendom Press, 1990)

S. L. Jaki, *Genesis 1 Through the Ages* (London: Thomas More Press, 1992)

J. H. Newman, *An Essay on the Development of Christian Doctrine* Edited with an introduction by J. M. Cameron (London: Pelican, 1974)

Notes

1 In the present work, we cannot go into great detail on this point. The reader is referred to S. L. Jaki, *Science and Creation: From Eternal Cycles to an Oscillating Universe* (Edinburgh: Scottish Academic Press, 1986),which describes the views of creation prevailing in ancient China, India, Egypt, Mesopotamia, Greece as well as among the Aztecs, Incas, Maya and the medieval Arabs; he shows how science was stymied as a result of these world-pictures. We will also touch upon this question again on pp. 19–20, 37, 85–86, 206–207, 235–236 below.

2 Pope Paul VI, *Credo of the People of God* (30 June 1968), 5.

3 St Thomas Aquinas, *Summa Theologiae*, I, q.16, a.1: '… esse rei, non veritas eius, causat veritatem intellectus.'

4 St Gregory of Nyssa, *De Hominis Opificio*, 5.1.

5 See S. L. Jaki, *The Physicist as Artist: The Landscapes of Pierre Duhem* (Edinburgh: Scottish Academic Press, 1988). The book contains 235 illustrations in half-tone and ten colour plates.

6 As regards the incompleteness of science, see S. L. Jaki, *The Relevance of Physics* (Edinburgh: Scottish Academic Press, 1992) and my *Creation and Scientific Creativity: A Study in the Thought of S.L. Jaki* (Leominster: Gracewing, 2009), pp. 32–42; 230-232.

7 S. W. Hawking, *A Brief History of Time. From the Big Bang to Black Holes* (London: Bantam Press, 1988), p. 175.

8 A. Noyes, *The Torch-Bearers*, vol. III, 'The Last Voyage' (Edinburgh/London: William Blackwood and Sons, 1930), p. 68.

9 Metaphysics investigates principles of reality transcending those of any particular science. The word derives from the Greek words μετά (meaning 'beyond' or 'after') and φυσικά (meaning 'physical'). Metaphysics is thus concerned with explaining the fundamental nature of being and the world.

10 See, for example, an error of Bl A. Rosmini Serbati, which was condemned in the year 1887 by the Holy Office and which can be found in DS 3201. English translation in ND (141): 'In the order of created things there is immediately manifested to the intellect something divine in itself, such that it belongs to the divine nature.' See also Congregation for the Doctrine of the Faith, *Note on the Force of the Doctrinal Decrees Concerning the Thought and Work of Fr Antonio Rosmini Serbati* (1 July 2001), §7, which indicated that the meaning of the proposition, 'as understood and condemned by the Decree, does not belong to the authentic position of Rosmini, but to conclusions that may possibly have been drawn from the reading of his works.' At the same time 'the objective validity of the Decree *Post obitum* referring to the previously condemned propositions, remains for whoever reads them, outside of the Rosminian system, in an idealist, ontologist point of view and with a meaning contrary to

Catholic faith and doctrine.'

11 See St Basil, *Adversus Eunomium* 1:32: 'δυναμεως γαρ, και σοφιας, και τεχνυς, ουχι δε της ουσιας αυτης ενδεικτικα εστιν ποιηματα.' St Gregory of Nyssa, *In Canticum canticorum* II, in *PG* 49, 1013: 'την θειαν φυσιν ακαταληπτον ουσαν παντελως και ανεικαστον, δια μονης ενεργειας γινωψκεσθαι.'

12 See St Basil, *Adversus Eunomium* 1:14.

13 An example of this approach would be F. Capra's *The Tao of Physics* (London: Flamingo, 1985) which seeks close parallels between modern physics and Eastern mysticism.

14 P. Teilhard de Chardin, *The Phenomenon of Man* (New York: Harper & Row, 1961), p. 301.

15 *Ibid.*, pp. 294, 310.

16 P. Teilhard de Chardin, Letter cited in Philippe de la Trinité, *Rome et Teilhard de Chardin* (Paris: Fayard, 1964), p. 168.

17 P. Teilhard de Chardin, *The Heart of Matter* (London : Collins, 1978), pp. 52–54.

18 P. Teilhard de Chardin, Letter cited in Philippe de la Trinité, *Rome et Teilhard de Chardin* (Paris: Fayard, 1964), p. 168.

19 P. Teilhard de Chardin, 'Contingence de l'univers et goût humain de survivre' (1953) unpublished essay, p. 4.

20 See C. Cuénot, *Teilhard de Chardin* (London: Burns Oates, 1965), p. 293.

21 P. Teilhard de Chardin, *Hymn of the Universe* (London: Collins, 1965), p. 133.

22 P. Teilhard de Chardin, *Letters from a Traveller* (New York: Harper, 1962), p. 269.

23 See P. Teilhard de Chardin, *Christianity and Evolution* (New York: Harper, 1971), pp. 216f..

24 P. Teilhard de Chardin, *The Divine Milieu* (New York: Harper & Row, 1960), p. 122.

25 See *L'Osservatore Romano* (1 July 1962 , n.148), which refers to the *Monitum* (dated 30 June 1962 in *AAS* 54 (1962), p. 166) directed at the errors of P. Teilhard de Chardin. The text

runs as follows: 'Several works of Fr Pierre Teilhard de Chardin, some of which were posthumously published, are being edited and are gaining a good deal of success. Prescinding from a judgment about those points that concern the positive sciences, it is sufficiently clear that the above mentioned works abound in such ambiguities, and indeed even serious errors, as to offend Catholic doctrine. For this reason, the eminent and most revered Fathers of the Supreme Sacred Congregation of the Holy Office exhort all Ordinaries, as well as Superiors of Religious institutes, rectors of seminaries and presidents of universities, effectively to protect the minds, particularly of the youth, against the dangers presented by the works of Fr Teilhard de Chardin and of his followers.' A year later, in 1963, the Vicariate of Rome required that Catholic booksellers in Rome should withdraw from circulation the works of Teilhard de Chardin, along with any other books which supported his views. In 1967, the Apostolic Delegation in Washington affirmed that the *Monitum* was still in place. In 1981, this same affirmation was repeated, this time by the Vatican itself. The following is the text of the 1981 statement (see *L'Osservatore Romano*, 20 July 1981): 'The letter sent by the Cardinal Secretary of State to His Excellency Mgr Poupard on the occasion of the centenary of the birth of Fr Teilhard de Chardin has been interpreted in a certain section of the press as a revision of previous stands taken by the Holy See in regard to this author, and in particular of the *Monitum* of the Holy Office of 30 June 1962, which pointed out that the work of the author contained ambiguities and grave doctrinal errors. The question has been asked whether such an interpretation is well founded. After having consulted the Cardinal Secretary of State and the Cardinal Prefect of the Sacred Congregation for the Doctrine of the Faith, which, by order of the Holy Father, had been duly consulted beforehand, about the letter in question, we are in a position to reply in the negative. Far from being a revision of the previous stands of the Holy See, Cardinal Casaroli's letter expresses reservation in various passages—and these reservations have been passed over in silence by certain newspapers—reservations which refer precisely to the judgment given in the *Monitum* of June 1962, even though this document is not explicitly mentioned.'

26 See R. Latourelle, *Theology of Revelation* (New York: Alba House, 1966), p. 430: 'The ineffability of God will become the very object of our vision, but never, even in final revelation, will our understanding of this mystery be perfectly exhaustive… Vision will be an unceasing initiation into the mystery of God.'

27 Vatican I, Dogmatic Constitution *Dei Filius* on the Catholic Faith, Chapter 2 'On Revelation' in DS 3004. English translation from ND 113.

28 See my work, *The Mystery of Reason* (Leominster: Gracewing, 2001), chapter 7 'Proofs for the Existence of God'.

29 St. Thomas Aquinas, *Summa Theologiae*, I, q.2, a.3.

30 Pope John Paul II, *Discourse at General Audience* (10 July 1985), §2. English translation from *ORE* N.28 (15 July 1985), p. 1.

31 Pope Pius XII, *Address to University Youth* (20 April 1941), in *AAS* 33 (1941), pp. 157–158. English translation from M. Chinigo, *The Teachings of Pope Pius XII* (London: Methuen,1958), p. 147. See also Vatican I, Dogmatic Constitution *Dei Filius* on the Catholic Faith, Chapter 4, 'Faith and Reason' in ND 133.

32 St Basil, *The Hexæmeron*, Homily V, 9.

33 See Pope John Paul II, *Discourse at General Audience* (12 March 1986), §3. English translation in *ORE* N.11 (17 March 1986), p. 1.

34 On this question, modern theology has been greatly influenced by H. de Lubac, *The Mystery of the Supernatural* (New York: Herder and Herder, 1967), who wished to avoid an overly extrinsic vision of the supernatural order. However care must also be taken to preserve the gratuity of this order and its difference from, as well as its relation to, the order of creation.

35 Vatican II, *Lumen Gentium*, 23.1.

36 Cf. *ibid.*, 12.1.

37 S. L. Jaki, *Genesis 1 Through the Ages* (London: Thomas More Press, 1992) p. 43.

38 Pontifical Biblical Commission, *The Interpretation of the Bible in the Church* (Vatican City: Libreria Editrice Vaticana, 1993), pp. 69–70.

39 See Vatican II, *Dei Verbum*, 12.

40 Pontifical Biblical Commission, *The Interpretation of the Bible in the Church*, p. 72.

41 Jaki, *Genesis 1 Through the Ages*, p. 279. See also p. 296, where Jaki states that 'for a proper interpretation of Genesis 1 no small help could have been derived from biblical references to major constructions. In three such cases,—the ark, the tabernacle, and the new Jerusalem of Ezekiel—the product themselves could be and were indeed seen as typified already in God's erstwhile construction of the universe.'

42 See Vatican I, *De fide*, 1 in DS 3008; Vatican II, *Dei Verbum*, 5.

43 S. L. Jaki, *Cosmos and Creator* (Edinburgh: Scottish Academic Press, 1980), p.56. Cardinal Ratzinger made the same point when he states: 'It is not accidental that the Apostles' Creed begins with the confession: "I believe in God the father Almighty, Creator of heaven and earth." This primordial faith in the Creator God (a God who really is God) forms the pivot, as it were, about which all the other Christian truths turn. If vacillation sets in here, all the rest comes tumbling down.' J. Card. Ratzinger and V. Messori, *The Ratzinger Report* (Leominster, England: Fowler Wright Books, 1985), p.78.

44 Pope John Paul II, Apostolic Constitution *Sapientia Christiana* (1979), 67 §2. See Vatican I, Dogmatic Constitution *Dei Filius* Chapter IV 'Faith and Reason' in DS 3016 (English translation ND 132) which describes 'the connection of these mysteries with one another.'

45 See, for example, the discourse of Pope John Paul II to the American bishops (15 October 1988) in *OR* 248/128 (16 October 1988), p. 4: 'Not every philosophy is capable of providing

that solid and coherent understanding of the human person, of the world, and of God which is necessary for any theological system that strives to place its knowledge in continuity with knowledge of faith.'

46 Congregation for the Doctrine of the Faith, *Instruction on the Ecclesial Vocation of the Theologian* (Vatican City: Libreria Editrice Vaticana, 1990), 10.4.

47 See my *Creation and Scientific Creativity*, p. 240.

48 Vincent of Lerins, *Commonitorium primum*, 23 in *PL* 50, 668. Quoted in Vatican I, Constitution *Dei Filius* on the Catholic Faith, Chapter 4, in DS 3020. English translation from ND 136.

2

The Spirit World

Christian thought is not satisfied with the merely ministerial rôle of the heavenly spirits; the angels are more than ministers and messengers, they are, above all, a portion of the universe, they are its noblest portion.

Anscar Vonier, *The Angels*

The angels 'appear' as the first aspect in the mystery of creation. Leaving aside, for the moment, whether or not they were created before the material cosmos, there is a good case for treating these pure spirits first, since, at least in the order of creation, they are considered to be superior to the human person within the hierarchy of being. This follows the teaching found in St Paul that 'visible things last for a time, and the invisible things are eternal' (2 Co 4:18). The tradition of the Eastern Churches tends to start with the invisible creation before moving to what is visible, in contrast to the Western approach which begins with what is seen and then proceeds to the unseen.

2.1 The existence of the angels

2.1.1 Old Testament

The presence of a realm of pure spirits is to be noted both in the Old and New Testaments. In the Old Testament, the beings whom we commonly term angels are called messengers, spirits, sons of God, guardians, heavenly hosts. In Hebrew the principal term for 'angel' is *malak* literally meaning a messenger.[1] Angels make up the 'heavenly household' of God, who sends them to minister to human beings in the history of salvation. Often, in the Old Testament, the distinction between God and His angel is not very clear (for example Gn 16:7–14; Ex 3:2–6; Jg 2:1–5; 13:3–22). In particular, the angel of the Lord, appearing in a dream to Jacob says: 'I am the God of Bethel where you poured oil on a monument, and where you made a vow to me' (Gn 31:13). Furthermore, Hosea identifies God, with whom Jacob wrestles, as an angel (Ho 12:4–5; cf. Gn 32:25–31). In other texts, the distinction between God and His angel is very clear, such as when, after the episode of the adoration of the golden calf, God no longer wishes to guide His people in person but intends to entrust them to His angel (Ex 32:33–34; 33: 1–3; cfr Is 63:9). Despite various exegetical theories, it is very difficult to delineate exactly the precise spheres of influence of Yahweh and of His angel. However, this lack of clear definition has a double value. It affirms the reality of the angel as a messenger of God and the efficacious presence of Yahweh, who cannot be enclosed in that reality, but always lies beyond it. In this way, the salvific presence of the Lord and His transcendence are stressed at one and the same time, precisely through the figure of the angel who is distinct from God, but closely linked to Him.[2]

The first appearance of good angels in the Old Testament occurs when God drives our first parents out of the garden of Eden, and places two cherubim with flaming swords to guard the tree of life (Gn 3:24). Two heavenly messengers accompany the Lord when He tells Abraham that Sodom and Gomorrah are to be destroyed (Gn 18) and they guide Lot out of the city. They blind those who try to get into Lot's house, so that they are unable to find the door. The two messengers have the task of destroying the two cities, because of the sins of those who dwell therein (Gn 19). The angel of the Lord prevents Abraham from sacrificing his only son (Gn 22:11f.). In a dream, Jacob sees angels descending from and ascending to heaven (Gn 28:12). The angel of the Lord appears to Moses from the middle of the burning bush (Ex 3:2). The angel of the Lord accompanies and protects Israel during the Exodus (Ex 14:19). God promises that He would send His messenger to bring His chosen people to their destination (Ex 23:20–23). Outside Jericho, Joshua sees a heavenly spirit with a sword in his hand, who introduces himself as sent by the Lord and encourages him to take the city (Jos 5:13ff.). An angel accuses the people of Israel of infidelity and tells of divine punishment (Jg 2:1ff). The angel of the Lord calls Gideon (Jg 6:11ff.); he appears to the wife of Manoah and foretells the birth of Samson (Jg 13:3ff). However, when asked what his name is, the heavenly being replies: 'Why ask my name? It is a mystery' (Jg 13:18).

During the period before the exile, the understanding concerning angels deepened and the concept of their rôle widened. In the period of the Kings, the hosts of angels and heavenly beings express the power and majesty of God, but are distinct from God. While Elijah was fleeing from Jezebel, an angel came to nourish him for the long journey ahead (1 K 19:5ff). The apparition of the angel (vv.5–8) is clearly distinguished from that of God (vv.9–11). A further feature of this period was the building of the Temple as the fixed abode of God upon earth, and the place of worship. At this point the liturgical activity of the angels is seen in terms of adoring God and interceding for man at prayer, so glorifying the Lord. Two groups of angels are seen, each with a different rôle. The first group are the *cherubim*.[3] In Solomon's temple images of the cherubim were to be found in the Holy of Holies (1 K 6:23–28); they are the bearers of God in theophanies and reveal his presence (2 Sam 22:11). The other category consists of the *seraphim*.[4] These feature in Isaiah's vision:

> I saw the Lord Yahweh seated on a high throne; His train filled the sanctuary; above him stood seraphs, each one with six wings: two to cover its face, two to cover its feet and two for flying. And they cried out to one another in this way, Holy, Holy, Holy is Yahweh Sabaoth. His glory fills the whole earth (Is 6:1–3).

One of the seraphim purified Isaiah using a burning coal taken from the altar, so preparing the prophet for his ministry (Is 6:1–3). These angels are seen gathered around the Lord's throne as the heavenly army and their action is totally referred to God and to his sovereignty.

During the period after the exile, the Israelites' understanding of angels was considerably enriched, partly through contact with Babylonian culture, and with the Persian and Graeco-Roman religions as can be seen in the books of Job, Daniel, and Tobit, as well as in the apocryphal and deutero-canonical books. However, as has been remarked earlier in another context[5], despite an apparent similarity, there is a fundamental difference between biblical faith and extra-biblical conceptions. This applies also to angels, and so the two visions cannot be seen as continuous. The biblical vision is essentially free from superstition, and the angelic beings of the Old Testament are mere creatures, infinitely below God. In biblical revelation, man deals essentially with God, and the angels are merely God's servants in the order of salvation. On the other hand, in extra-biblical angelology there is much superstition and strange detail; often also the angels are regarded as divine. As a matter of fact, during the period of the exile and thereafter, it seems that the biblical authors speak more about the rôle of the angels, precisely because monotheism itself is more firmly rooted and so the sovereignty of God would not be threatened.[6]

One of the rare occasions when an angel is mentioned by name in the Old Testament occurs when the Archangel Raphael is sent to heal Tobit and to give Sarah as bride to Tobias. Afterwards he reveals himself as follows:

> I am going to tell you the whole truth, hiding nothing from you... So you must know that when you and Sarah were at prayer, it was I who offered your supplications before the glory of God and who read them; so too when you were burying the dead.

> When you did not hesitate to get up and leave the table to go and bury a dead man, I was sent to test your faith, and at the same time God sent me to heal you and your daughter-in-law Sarah. I am Raphael, one of the seven angels who stand ever ready to enter the presence of the glory of the Lord... As far as I was concerned, when I was with you, my presence was not by any decision of mine, but by the will of God; it is He whom you must bless throughout your days, He that you must praise (Tb 12:11–15, 18).

The name Raphael means 'healing of God' and the names of only two of the other archangels are seen in Old Testament revelation. Michael (whose name means 'Who is like God') is the great patron and protector of the people of Israel (Dn 10:13, 21; 12:1). Gabriel (whose name signifies 'strength of God') is God's messenger (Dn 8:16; 9:21; see also Lk 1:19, 26).

In the Old Testament, it is interesting to observe that the angels are intermediaries between God and mankind, in both a descending and an ascending sense.[7] Among the 'descending' category, coming from God to man, some angels are destroying angels (see Ex 12:23; 2K 19:35; Ezk 9:1; Ps 78:49), while others are guardian angels either of individuals or nations (see Ex 23:20; Dn 10:13). Generally appearances of angels last only so long as the delivery of their message requires, but frequently their mission is prolonged, such as when they are constituted as the guardians of the nation during some particular crisis (Ex 14:19; Ba 6:6). During the struggle of Judas Maccabaeus for the freedom of the Jewish people, warrior angels appear several times who protect the sacred treasury of the temple (2 M 3:25–26) and who help the forces of Israel in their battles (2 M 10:29–30; 11:8). In the 'ascending' sense, angels bring man's prayers before God (Jb 33:23ff.) and intercede for men (Tb 12:15).

Angels also have a certain mediatory rôle in Old Testament prophecy. In particular, the angel of the Lord is seen to enjoy a great importance in the book of the prophet Zechariah, and his rôle is made clearer. He has other angels under his direction (Zc 1:8–11), intercedes for the people (Zc 1:12), hands the word of the Lord on to the prophet and to the high priest (Zc 1:14; 3:6); he carries out justice in God's name (Zc 3:1–2), and purifies the sinner (Zc 3:4–5). In the book of Zechariah, the angel acts as a type of lieutenant for God and is clearly distinct from Him. In the book of Ezekiel (Ezk 1:4–14), there is a description of angels which has to be interpreted with care. The various aspects which the prophet outlines are not to be used to try and give a complete description of the spirits, rather they are a way of showing that the angelic nature transcends human conception of it. In the book of Daniel, there is a strong apocalyptic element and here angels are also seen to reveal the meaning of the heavenly world and of the last things. An incalculable number of angels surrounds God's throne (Dn 7:10). Michael, who is one of the princes of the heavenly court, is the protector of Israel (Dn 10:13–21); it is he who defends the people of God at the end of the ages (Dn 12:1). Gabriel gives the explanation of the visions to the prophet Ezekiel (Dn 8:16ff.): 'Son of man, understand this: the vision shows the time of the End… I shall tell you what is going to happen when the Retribution is over, about the final times.'

2.1.2 *New Testament*

The New Testament picture of the nature and rôle of angels abstains from abstract or fantastic speculations, and presents them essentially as the spirits at God's service, in His economy of salvation on man's behalf. Their work consists of being God's messengers, of being intermediaries between God and man, and of revealing God's glory.[8]

As regards the Incarnation and Birth of the Messiah, the rôle of the angels is always subordinate to God's plan of salvation. In St Luke's Gospel, the birth of John the Baptist was announced by an angel, who is later seen to be Gabriel (Lk 1:11, 19). The archangel Gabriel announces to the Blessed Virgin Mary that she is to become the Mother of the Messiah. The archangel faithfully hands on the word of God, in such a way that Mary is able to respond freely and say: 'I am the handmaid of the Lord, let what you have said be done to me' (Lk 1:38). Later, an angel of the Lord announces to the shepherds the birth of Christ, and together with the angel 'there was a great throng of the heavenly host praising God' (Lk 2:13). In St Matthew's Gospel, an angel of the Lord appears in a dream to St Joseph, to explain that Mary has 'conceived what is in her by the Holy Spirit' (Mt 1:20) and to encourage him to take her home as his wife. The angel of the Lord appears a second time in a dream to Joseph to warn him about Herod and tell him to take Mary and the infant Christ and 'escape into Egypt until I tell you' (Mt 2:13). The angel then appears to Joseph again in a dream to tell him when it is safe to return to Israel (Mt 2:19–20).

In the earthly life, passion and glorification of Christ, the angels appear at certain specific moments. After the temptation of Christ in the wilderness, 'angels appeared and looked after Him' (Mt 4:11). Jesus makes some references to angels in his preaching. They rejoice when sinners are converted (Lk 15:10); they look upon the face of God (Mt 18:10); they lead the dead into the next life (Lk 16:22); as immortal and spiritual beings, they make up part of the Kingdom of God (Mk 12:25). The mediation of the angels is expressed when Christ says: 'I tell you most solemnly, you will see heaven laid open and, above the Son of Man, the angels of God ascending and descending' (Jn 1:51). Before His passion, Christ speaks of twelve legions of angels who would come to His aid if He requested (Mt 26:53). An angel from heaven comforts Jesus during His agony in the garden of the Mount of Olives (Lk 22:43), which Newman describes poetically as follows:

> It needs that very Angel, who with awe
> Amid the garden shade,
> The great Creator in His sickness saw,
> Soothed by a creature's aid
> And agonized, as victim of the Law
> Which He Himself had made.
> For who can praise Him in His depth and height,
> But he who saw Him reel amid that solitary fight?[9]

Angels are present at the Resurrection and Ascension of Christ. They are the first witnesses of the Risen One and prepare the promulgation of the news of His rising from the dead. An angel of the Lord comes down from heaven, rolls away the stone closing the tomb and says of Jesus: 'He is not here, for He has risen, as He said He would' (Mt 28:6). The angel then sends the women who came to the tomb to the disciples, who are then sent out into the world by Christ Himself (Mt 28:19). Thus in the economy of revelation and of salvation, angels, men and women all have their important place. At the Ascension of Christ, two men in white tell the Apostles: 'Jesus, who has been taken up from you into heaven, this same Jesus will come back in the same way as you have seen Him go there' (Ac 1:11). The angels appear as interpreters of this event and encourage the hearts of the Apostles to do God's will; their action also looks forward to Christ's second coming and is thus extended across the ages in the life of the Church.

After the Ascension of Christ, the angels continue their salvific rôle on behalf of man in and through the Church. An angel of the Lord frees the Apostles from prison and encourages them in these words: 'Go and stand in the Temple, and tell the people about this new Life' (Ac 5:20). After being freed from prison by an angel on another occasion, St Peter expresses the faith of the early Church in the aid brought by these spiritual beings: 'The Lord really did send His angel and has saved me from Herod and from all that the Jewish people were so certain would happen to me' (Ac 12:11). The work of angels in favouring the mission of the Church is clearly seen when an angel of the Lord sends Philip along the road to Gaza where he baptizes the eunuch from the court of the queen of Ethiopia (Ac 8:26). An angel of God appears to St Paul and encourages him in these words: 'Do not be afraid, Paul. You are destined to appear before Caesar, and for this reason God grants you the safety of all who are sailing with you' (Ac 27:24).

In this way the angel is at the Apostle's side to help him stay faithful unto the supreme sacrifice of martyrdom. The prayers of all the saints are presented before God's throne and offered to Him by the angels (Rv 8:3f.). The Church's worship participates in the heavenly Jerusalem 'where the millions of angels have gathered for the festival' (Heb 12:22).

The consummation of salvation history is brought about by God, with the cooperation of His angels. The definitive act of Christ in bringing this about is marked by the command of one angel to another: 'Put your sickle in and reap: harvest time has come and the harvest of the earth is ripe' (Rv 14:15). The sound of the trumpets of the seven angels produces manifold and serious disasters (Rv 8:1–10:11; 11:14–19). Seven other angels with seven plagues are at the ready to pour out upon the earth the seven golden bowls filled with God's wrath (Rv 15:5–16:21). History will be brought to its close by the Second Coming of Christ. The angels accompany Christ in this great moment, as illustrated in the painting of the Last Judgment in the Sistine Chapel in Rome. Christ will come down from heaven at the voice of the archangel and the sound of God's trumpet (1 Th 4:16). He will be seen coming in power with His angels (2 Th 1:7; cf. Mt 16:27, 25:31). The Son of Man will send His angels to carry out His judgment and separate the subjects of the kingdom from those of the evil one, like the reapers at the harvest: 'the harvest is the end of the world; the reapers are the angels' (Mt 13:39). The angels form a heavenly court, where all men are judged by Christ according to faith and good works: 'If anyone openly declares himself for me in the presence of men, the Son of Man will declare Himself for him in the presence of God's angels. But the man who disowns me in the presence of men will be disowned in the presence of God's angels' (Lk 12:8–9).

The New Testament continually refers the nature and action of the pure spirits to Christ and His work of Redemption which is actualized in the Church until the close of the ages. Through Christ 'were created all things in heaven and on earth: everything visible and everything invisible, Thrones, Dominations, Sovereignties, Powers - all things were created through Him and for Him' (Col 1:16). The letter to the Hebrews emphasizes that redemption was wrought by Christ and not by angels for God 'did not appoint angels to be rulers of the world to come' (Heb 2:5). Christ did not take angelic nature to Himself but was 'for a short while made lower than the angels' (Heb 2:9); however He has now been exalted and is 'now as far above the angels as the title which He has inherited is higher than their own nature' (Heb 1:4). Christ in His divinity is already infinitely above the angels, so it is the glorification of the human nature of Christ that we are talking about and its exaltation above the angels. St Paul emphasizes that the Christian who is a partaker in Christ's divine nature has also, in this sense, been exalted above the angels (Col 2:9–15). The Apostle mentions that human beings 'are also to judge angels' (1 Co 6:3). This reverses the order of the creation, where man was lower than the angels. St Paul warns the Colossians against the false worship of angels (Col 2:18), an admonition which is possibly directed against flirtation with gnosticism. At the same time, the second letter of St Peter and the letter of Jude correct a lack of due respect for the angels: 'Such self-willed people with no reverence are not afraid of offending against the glorious ones, but the angels in their greater strength and power make no complaint or accusation against them in front of the Lord' (2 P 2:10–11; see Jude 9). The angels, in fact, are 'all spirits whose work is service, sent to help those who will be the heirs of salvation' (Heb 1:14).

In the Scriptures, the angels are not just a metaphor to indicate the action of God, but real beings with personhood, whose nature was more clearly understood over the centuries of theological reflection.

2.1.3 *The teaching of the Church*

The Symbol of Constantinople, which confirmed the faith of Nicaea, states: 'We believe in one God, the Father almighty, maker of heaven and earth, of all things visible and invisible.'[10] This implies a spiritual order of beings created by God. At the Fourth Lateran Council, in the year 1215, a more detailed statement on the angelic order was made in the context of belief in one true God the Father, the Son and the Holy Spirit:

> The Creator of all things, visible and invisible, spiritual and corporeal,… by His almighty power from the beginning of time made at once out of nothing both orders of creatures, the spiritual and the corporeal, that is, the angelic and the earthly, and then the human creature, who as it were shares in both orders, being composed of spirit and body.[11]

This passage from the Lateran Council was quoted once again at the First Vatican Council in 1870.[12] Pope Paul VI in his profession of faith for 1968, the Year of Faith, affirmed: 'We believe in one God, Father, Son and Holy Spirit, Creator… of things invisible—such as the pure spirits which are also called angels.'[13] Pope John Paul II has noted that the angels fully belong to and are inseparable from the central content of the revelation of God and the salvation of men in the person of Christ.[14] Thus Christian tradition teaches that the existence of spiritual, incorporeal beings, which Holy Scripture usually calls angels, is a truth of the faith.[15]

Right from New Testament times when the Sadducees denied the existence of angels (Ac 23:8), materialists through the ages have denied the existence of the spirit world. Rationalists have also tried to explain away angels in various ways by saying that they are personifications of divine attributes or activities or expressions of the forces of nature, or symbols of virtue (in the case of the good angels). A recent author maintained: 'When all is analysed and written, the hidden meaning of angels remains that they are an *inseparable part of each one of us;…* the angel is one of our inner and most magical aspects… If you really want to see an angel don't look for one outside: they reside within.'[16] Against all these false views, the Church teaches the objective and personal existence of angels and her liturgy in both East and West bears witness to her faith.[17]

The fact of angels is also reasonable, even if the whole mystery of the angelic order could not have been discovered by man without revelation. In a sense, creation is a hierarchy, in which there is purely material creation, then the composite material-spiritual creation of man and woman. It seems then in keeping with a kind of harmony in the universe that there should also be purely spiritual and invisible beings. A further argument, proceeding from the synthesis of all the truths of faith maintains that it would be impossible to explain original sin and thus the origin of evil in the world, if our first parents had not been tempted by a superior but evil spiritual being. There is also concrete evidence for the existence of pure spirits. Angels have appeared throughout the ages and also in our own times, not only to great saints, but also to ordinary people as has been documented by recent authors.[18]

2.2 *The creation of the angels*

The spirit world was created by God out of nothing, and so the angels are not, as the Gnostics thought, emanations from the substance of God, like steam evaporating from water. The angels were created 'from the beginning of time' according to the definition of the Fourth Lateran Council. It is not so clear precisely *when* they were created, a difficult question considering that the angels exist beyond time. Since the angels were not created from all eternity (*ab aeterno*), the possibilities remaining are before, during or after the creation of the material cosmos. In particular, they would seem to have to have been created before man and woman. The opinion that the angels were created *before the material creation* was commonly held by many Greek Fathers including St Basil and St Gregory Nazianzen as well as some Latin Fathers such as St Jerome and St Ambrose. St John Damascene followed St Gregory Nazianzen, taking the position that the angels were created before heaven and earth, because the spiritual creation must precede the visible creation and the creation of man. St John Damascene placed the angels neither within the perfect eternity (*aeternitas*) of God, nor within the physical time of man (*chronos* or *tempus*), but rather within the *aevum*, which, following an Aristotelian conception was a type of 'imperfect eternity' and measured the complete duration of a being.[19] Thus the angel was finite and contingent, not eternal and yet above any form of physical temporality.

St Augustine seemed to take the position that the angels were created simultaneously with the material world, interpreting the expression 'heaven and earth' (Gn 1:1) as denoting the spiritual and material worlds respectively.[20] St Gregory the Great held that the angels were created at the same time as matter, and cited a classical biblical argument supporting this position: 'He who lives for ever created all the universe at once' (Si 18:1).[21] The opinion of simultaneous creation became more common, especially after the Fourth Lateran Council in 1215, in which it was stated that God created 'at once' (*simul*) from the beginning of time the angels and the material world and then (*deinde*) created man. By 'at once' (*simul*) is meant a kind of moral simultaneity[22], which demonstrates the common unity of all creation. St Thomas simply regards as less probable the opinion according to which the angels were created before the material world. The Angelic Doctor would say that the works of God are perfect, and so He created everything at the same time, in one universe. However, if one takes the contrary position, it would not be erroneous, because many Fathers taught that the creation of the angels preceded that of the material cosmos.[23] Each member of the spirit world was an immediate result of God's creative act in the total number that He willed. In the realm of spirits, unlike the case of human beings, there are no material bodies, no sexual differentiation and hence no reproduction. In order to counteract the idea of sexual differentiation among the angels, Theodoret of Cyrus taught that, in the beginning, God did not create just two angels as in the case of human beings, but as many as He wished. Since angelic nature is not subject to corruption, there is no need for the angels to reproduce after their creation.[24] Pope Benedict XII, in his condemnation of certain errors imputed to the Armenians, refuted the notion that angels reproduced from one another.[25]

2.3 *The nature of the angels*

The word 'angel' is often used in a broad sense to designate purely spiritual beings. To be more precise, as St Augustine remarked, those spiritual beings who are *messengers* of God are called angels by reason of that office, and are termed spirits because of their immaterial nature.[26] The spiritual nature of the angels is presupposed by Scripture, even though it is not clearly described there. They are called spirits (Heb 1:14) and Jesus affirms that a spirit has 'no flesh or bones' (Lk 24:39). In the Scriptures, however, angels appeared with a kind of visible form. Most of the Fathers including St Augustine attributed some type of light bodily form to the angels. The reasoning behind this was often founded on a Platonic conception of the world. Only God is an immaterial Spirit. All creatures participate in His being in a gradually descending way from angels to men and thus are increasingly material. St Gregory the Great was one of the first to maintain the pure spirituality of the angels but asserted that 'compared with our body, they are spirits; however compared with the supreme and unlimited Spirit, they are bodies.'[27] The doctrine that the angels are pure spirits became general about one hundred years after Peter Lombard. The Scholastic writers of this period understood that it was not necessary for every finite being to have extension. The continuing tradition of the Catholic Church makes it clear that the angels are 'incorporeal' and are 'purely spiritual.'[28]

From the spiritual nature of the angels follows the fact that, like the human person but at a higher level, they are endowed with intellect and free will. They are personal beings and so are made in the image and likeness of God. Although in the order of creation the angel is a more perfect being than man and woman, nevertheless human nature is more complete since it is a microcosm of all creation both material and spiritual. As regards the angelic knowledge, since they have no sensory perception, they cannot know the external world alone, but when God created the angels He infused into their intellects the ideas of things. Their ideas are innate rather than acquired like ours. It is not possible to determine the extent of this knowledge, but the fact that angels have a wide knowledge is symbolized by their many eyes (Rv 4:6–8). When Christ affirms that the 'angels of heaven' are ignorant of the time of His Second Coming (Mt 24:36), it indicates that their knowledge is limited, but nevertheless the statement also implies that they enjoy a considerable breadth and depth in their knowledge. It is certain that the pure spirits are not omniscient and they do not know the future, nor the secrets of men's hearts. They may acquire knowledge of the open expressions of man's thoughts and desires. The angels do not know supernatural mysteries, which are above every created intellect, by their natural knowledge. Rather, they know supernatural truths by the supernatural knowledge which they have in the beatific vision.

Corresponding to their great knowledge, the angels have a free and powerful will. Owing to the intuitive penetration of their intellect, the angels make immediate and irrevocable decisions of the will, which explains why the angelic sin is final and irredeemable. However, the angelic power should not be exaggerated, they are simply creatures and depend absolutely on God: 'Who in the skies can compare with Yahweh? Which of the heaven-born can rival Him?' (Ps 89:6). The fact that the angels are free leaves a possibility open that they may turn away from God. Such a possibility became a reality, which was foreseen by God in view of a greater good, and will be treated later as the fall of the angels. The natural immortality of the angels is a further consequence of their purely spiritual nature. On the other hand, man's original state of immortality is a *preternatural gift*.[29]

Very often, in art and literature, angels are depicted in human form. Perhaps what is most interesting is how iconography has portrayed them in terms of their gender or lack of it. Following the Scriptures, where the angels generally appeared in the form of a male human being[30], much art represents the angels in the form of a young or ageless man. In some cases there has been a tendency to represent angels in a more feminine form, but the best iconography has sought to present them as above any differentiation of gender, so emphasizing the fact that they are by nature without bodies.

> From the sixth century onwards, the angelic type is fixed. With the exception of the Seraphim of Isaiah, who have always been the despair of draughtsmen, angels are given asexual lineaments of body and their garments flow in dignified folds. The alternative forms of winged heads are expressions of beauty which is neither masculine nor feminine.[31]

God permitted some angels to assume physical form so that they could be seen by human beings, not for themselves, but on our account. Moreover the fact that angels assumed bodies in the Old Testament was a prefiguration of the Word of God Who would take a human body; all the apparitions in the Old Testament were ordained to the appearance of the Son of God in the flesh.[32]

2.4 *The number and hierarchy of the angels*

It is clear from the Scriptures that there are many angels, for example from the book of Daniel where one may read: 'A thousand thousand waited on Him, ten thousand times ten thousand stood before him' (Dn 7:10). The writer of the Letter to the Hebrews speaks of millions of angels 'gathered for the festival' (Heb 12:22). Curiosity, sometimes exaggerated, down the centuries has wished to discover more. An interesting example is given by St Cyril of Jerusalem, who wished to explain the creed and, within that context, the Last Judgement.

We will be judged before a vast multitude of persons. Hence the human race would be a small number in comparison with the angels. St Cyril notes that Christ taught that there would be more rejoicing in heaven over one sinner who repents than over ninety-nine just persons who have no need of repentance (Lk 15:7; Mt 18:13). The only sinner is the whole of the human race; the ninety-nine 'just ones' are the angels, whose number is therefore ninety-nine times as great as the total number of human beings.[33] St Gregory the Great interpreted the parable of the lost drachma (Lk 15:8–10) in a similar way. The woman's ten drachmas symbolize the ten types of rational creatures God has created, of which one, man, has fallen into sin. The other nine remaining represent the nine choirs of pure spirits. St Thomas affirmed that there must be a great number of angels because God wished the universe to be perfect, and it would therefore be appropriate to have the greatest possible number of perfect beings.[34] Another approach may be based on the idea that each human person has their own guardian angel, which would not be passed on to someone else when the person died. Now, since only some spirits would have the specific task of being guardian angels, it is likely that the total number of spiritual beings far exceeds that of human persons.

According to St Thomas, each angel is a separate species, and the only one of its kind and each one differs from the other specifically as a man differs from a dog, not simply as a man differs from another man. Other theologians such as St Albert the Great taught that all the angels together make up one species only, while others of the Franciscan school maintained that the individual hierarchies or choirs form particular species. Among the spirits there are some which are greater in the extent of their knowledge and the power of their will. This fact lies at the basis of an *angelic hierarchy*. Already in the Old Testament we have encountered cherubim and seraphim. In the Pauline letters there is a mention of principalities (or sovereignties), powers, virtues (or authorities), dominations and thrones (Col 1:16; Ep 1:21). To these levels of heavenly spirits should be added angels (1 P 3:22) and archangels (1 Th 4:15). The principalities and powers are also mentioned in a negative context as fallen spirits by St Paul (Ep 3:10; 6:12). This could refer to the fall involving some spirits who formerly belonged to those choirs. Moreover, some exegetes find it difficult to determine precisely whether St Paul uses these names to refer to the angelic hierarchy or just to stress the supremacy of Christ over every creature.[35] Nevertheless, the one option does not exclude the other and so St Paul could well describe the angelic hierarchy as well as affirm Christ's supremacy over it. It was Pseudo-Dionysius who developed the traditional classification of the spirit world. According to him there are nine choirs of spirits divided into three triads. In the first triad there are the seraphim, the cherubim and the thrones; although they differ among themselves they have in common the immediate contemplation of the divine splendour, which they hand on to the lower levels. The second triad consists of dominations, virtues and powers, and these enter into their relationship with God through the first level. The third level consists of principalities, archangels and angels.[36] In the spirit world, the higher orders communicate divine illumination to the lower ones and also direct them. St Gregory the Great proposed a slightly different hierarchy. The first rank is the same as in Pseudo-Dionysius. Then, in the second and third ranks, he inverted the positions of the virtues and principalities.[37] Pope Gregory the Great also maintained that the higher ranks of spirits contemplate God and perform no external service; the lower orders carry out actions for mankind.[38]

The Church has held this classification in high esteem for centuries, which shows that it does not contain anything contrary to the faith. In describing the angelic hierarchy, Pope John Paul II affirmed that the topic might seem rather distant from the mentality of the present day. Nevertheless, he pointed out that the Church 'in proposing with frankness the whole truth about God Who is the Creator of the angels, believes *that she is rendering a great service to man ...The religious encounter with the world of purely spiritual beings* becomes a precious revelation of his being not only body but also spirit, and of the fact that he belongs to a truly great and efficacious economy of salvation, within a community of personal beings who, for man and with man, serve God's providential plan.'[39]

Among the seven archangels implied in the book of Tobit (12:15), only three are named in the bible, Michael, Gabriel, Raphael. The Church, in her tradition, has been very wary of naming other angels. In 745, a Council at Rome under Pope Zacharias forbade the use of extra-biblical angelic names, and stated that the only permissible names to be used are those of Michael, Gabriel and Raphael. Later, during the time of Charlemagne, a local council at Aachen in 789 not only forbade the use of non-biblical angel's names, but also excommunicated with severe penalties those who adored Uriel, whose name had been obtained from sources outside the canonical Scriptures. Recent statements by the Congregation for the Doctrine of the Faith confirm a ban on invoking angels by name, if these names are not to be found in the Scriptures or the Tradition of the Church.[40]

2.5 *The elevation of the angels*

In order to explain fully the Scriptural description of the angels it is necessary to take account of the fact that they are not merely pure spirits, but are filled with the Holy Spirit and living in intimacy with the Most Holy Trinity. They are in the presence of God, contemplate His face (Is 6:2; Dn 7:10; Mt 18:10) and offer Him perpetual worship (Rv 4:4–11). St Thomas followed Augustine and taught that the angels were created in a state of sanctifying grace which was gratuitous but which they needed in order to turn to God; each spirit was endowed with grace according to its natural gifts.[41] St Thomas would therefore propose only one step in angelic development, namely a single act in which the angels merited to move from grace to glory. Peter Lombard, St Bonaventure and Blessed Duns Scotus differ from the Angelic Doctor and specify that the angels were sanctified with grace at some 'time' after their creation. Thus for the latter school of thought the spirits would proceed through two steps before they arrived at the beatific vision. To summarize, 'theologians would say that the first act of the angels was self-consciousness, the second act a full co-operation with the grace that was in them, and the third act the clear Vision.'[42] Many theologians have proposed a Christological vision in which the mystery of the Divine Incarnation was revealed to the angels at their probation. They saw that a nature lower than their own was to be hypostatically united to the Person of God the Son, and that all the hierarchy of heaven must bow in adoration before the majesty of the Incarnate Word; and this, it is supposed, was the occasion of the pride of Lucifer.[43] The advocates of this view seek support in certain passages of Scripture, notably in the words of the Psalmist as they are cited in the Letter to the Hebrews: 'Again, when he brings the First-born into the world, he says: Let all the angels of God pay him homage.' (Heb 1:6; cf. Ps 97:7). Whichever way one conceives this mystery, the elevation of the angels forms the basis for a discussion of the original test which they had to undergo before they ever reached the Beatific Vision, and thus helps us a little to understand the fall of some angels.

Notwithstanding the beatitude in which the angels live, they are subordinate to the Mother of God, who is the Queen of the Angels in the words of the Litany of Loreto. The Oriental Churches refer to Mary with the praises:

> Hail, O Depth, even beyond the sight of angels.
> Hail, O sacred Chariot of the One above the Cherubim;
> hail, perfect Dwelling of the One above the Seraphim![44]

It is interesting that in the Orthodox tradition the angels are subordinated not only to Christ, but also to Mary, who is for these spirits a Mediatrix of graces.

2.6 *The guardian angels*

The Old Testament already contains the idea that each individual and each community has an angel who is a protector or guardian. The Psalms proclaim that God 'will put you in His angels' charge to guard you wherever you go' (Ps 91:11; see also Ps 34:7). The people of God of the Old Testament were protected by a guardian angel (Ex 23:20), who was sometimes St Michael the archangel (Dn 10:13; 12:1). Christ teaches that each human being is protected by an angel: 'See that you never despise any of these little ones, for I tell you that their angels in heaven are continually in the presence of my Father in heaven' (Mt 18:10). According to the literal interpretation of the book of the Apocalypse, angels were assigned to each of the seven churches (Rv 1:20).

A measured devotion to and veneration of the angels is encouraged by the Church, since from birth to death human beings are aided by their protection and intercession and indeed the whole Church benefits from the mysterious and powerful help of the angels.[45] The tradition of the Church has developed an understanding of this faith. In the words of Richard of Saint Victor:

> The ministry of the angels is for us not only temporal but eternal, since with the aid which they give us now, we can obtain the inheritance of everlasting life, and with them enjoy their happiness for ever.[46]

The Angelic Doctor taught that every human being has a guardian angel who accompanies him while a wayfarer upon this earth.[47] Not only do individuals have guardian angels, but also entire peoples and countries.[48] The guardian angel is one expression of God's merciful

Providence to assist people on their way to salvation, and to protect them from all evils both material and spiritual.[49] Of particular importance therefore is the fact that every member of the Mystical Body has a guardian angel, who brings his prayers unto the throne of God, who protects him and accompanies him to the judgment seat of God, as is graphically illustrated by the words of the angel in Newman's *Dream of Gerontius*:

> How should ethereal natures comprehend
> A thing made up of spirit and clay,
> Were it not task'd to nurse it and to tend,
> Link'd one to one throughout its mortal day?
> More than the Seraph in his height of place,
> The Angel-guardian knows and loves the ransom'd race.[50]

Twelve theorems concerning angelic nature[51]

1. Angels have a beginning, but they cannot perish; they remain everlastingly the same.
2. Angels are not subject to the laws of time, but have a duration measure of their own.
3. Angels are completely superior to space, so that they could never be subject to its laws.
4. Angelic power on the material world is exerted directly through the will.
5. Angelic life has two faculties only, intellect and will.
6. In the sphere of nature an angel cannot err, either in intellect or in will.
7. An angel never goes back on a decision once taken.
8. The angelic mind starts with fullness of knowledge, and is not, like the human mind, subject to gradual development.

9. An angel may directly influence another created intellect, but he cannot act directly on another created will.
10. Angels have free will; they are capable of love and hatred.
11. Angels know material things and individual things.
12. Angels do not know the future; they do not know the secret thoughts of other rational creatures; they do not know the mysteries of grace, unless such things be revealed freely, either by God or by the other rational creatures.

Further Reading

J. Daniélou, *The angels and their mission* (Manchester, NH: Sophia Institute Press, 2009)

P. Kreeft, *Angels and Demons: What Do We Really Know About Them?* (San Francisco: Ignatius Press, 1995)

P. P. Parente, *The Angels: The Catholic Teaching on the Angels* (Rockford, Illinois: Tan Books, 1994)

H. Price, *Angels: true stories of how they touch our lives* (London: Macmillan, 1993)

A. Vonier, *The Angels* (London: Burns Oates and Washbourne, 1934)

Notes

1 The Hebrew expression מַלְאָךְ is derived from a Semitic root, meaning 'to send'.

2 Cf. R. Lavatori, *Gli angeli* (Genova: Marietti, 1991), pp.23–24.

3 The Hebrew expression is כְּרוּב (*kruv*). The name is obtained in its turn from the Assyrian root *karâbu* meaning 'to be near', hence it means near ones, familiars, personal servants,

bodyguards, courtiers. The expression also signifies 'to be gracious' or 'to bless'.

4 The Hebrew expression is שָׂרָף. The name is derived from the Hebrew *saraph* meaning 'to burn'.

5 See chapter one, p. 12 above where it was noted that there was an essential difference between Genesis and the ancient near-Eastern myths.

6 See M. Flick & Z. Alszeghy, *Il Creatore* (Libreria Editrice Fiorentina, 1967), p. 531.

7 This would go some way to explain the passages in Scripture where angels are considered as ascending and descending. See for example Jacob's dream (Gn 28:13) and Christ speaking about angels ascending and descending upon the Son of Man (Jn 1:51).

8 See Lavatori, *Gli angeli*, pp. 30–35.

9 J. H. Newman, *The Dream of Gerontius*, §5.

10 Symbol of Constantinople as found in ND 12.

11 Fourth Lateran Council, Chapter 1: On the Catholic Faith, in DS 800: 'creator omnium visibilium et invisibilium, spiritalium et corporalium: qui sua omnipotenti virtute simul ab initio temporis utramque de nihilo condidit creaturam, spiritualem et corporalem, angelicam videlicet et mundanam: ac deinde humanam, quasi comunem ex spiritu et corpore constitutam.' English translation from ND 19.

12 Vatican I, Section III, Dogmatic Constitution *Dei Filius* on the Catholic faith, Chapter 1: God Creator of All Things, in ND 412.

13 Pope Paul VI, *Profession of Faith*, §8 in ND 39/1.

14 See Pope John Paul II, *Discourse at General Audience* 9 July 1986, in *IG* 9/2 (1986), pp. 226–227.

15 See *CCC* 328.

16 M. Godwin, *Angels. An endangered species* (New York: Simon and Schuster, 1990), p. 252.

17 See, for example, the Cherubic Hymn of the Byzantine Rite which expresses the faith of the Eastern Churches:

'Let us, who here mystically represent the Cherubim in singing the thrice-holy hymn to the life-giving Trinity, now lay aside every earthly care so that we may welcome the King of the universe Who comes escorted by invisible armies of angels.'
See also part of the Roman Canon which manifests the faith of the Western Churches:
'We pray that Your angel may take this Sacrifice to Your altar in heaven. Then as we receive from this altar the Sacred Body and Blood of Your Son, let us be filled with every grace and blessing.'

18 See, for example, H. Price, *Angels: true stories of how they touch our lives* (London: Macmillan, 1993). Current renewed interest in the spirit world is shown in numerous other recent books on the matter as well as in films like *Angels* (USA: Walt Disney, 1994).

19 *Aevum* has a beginning but no end, while *tempus* is marked by both a beginning and an end. *Aeternitas* has neither beginning nor end.

20 See St Augustine *The City of God* Book 11, chapter 9 in *PL* 41, 323–325. However, in his work *De Genesi ad litteram: Imperfectus Liber* chapter 3, nn.7–8 (*PL* 34, 222–223) Augustine considered the possibility that the angels could have been created before time began, at the beginning of time or again after the beginning of time.

21 See St Gregory the Great, *Moralium*, Book 32, chapter 12 in *PL* 76, 644–646. In the classic version of the Vulgate, the passage from Ecclesiasticus reads 'Qui vivit in aeternum, creavit omnia simul', but nevertheless the Scriptures simply teach that all creation is equally the work of God.

22 See I. M. Dalmau and I. F. Sagüés, *Sacrae Theologiae Summa* Volume II (Madrid: BAC, 1958), p. 569.

23 See St Thomas Aquinas, *Summa Theologiae* I, q.61, a.3.

24 Theodoret of Cyrus, *Haereticarum Fabularum Compendium*, Book 5, chapter 7, *PG* 83, 468–469.

25 See Pope Benedict XII, Libellus ad Armenios *Cum dudum*, 5

in DS 1007.

26 See St Augustine, *Enarratio in Psalmum 103*, Sermon 1, n.15 in *PL* 37, 1348–1349.

27 St Gregory the Great, *Moralium*, Book 2, chapter 3, in *PL* 75, 557.

28 See *CCC* 328 and 330.

29 See p. 117 below.

30 This is clear, for example from the context of Genesis 19:4–11, where the homosexual residents of Sodom are punished for having wished to abuse the angels sent to Lot. See also Mk 16:5, Ac 1:10.

31 A. Vonier, *The Angels* (London: Burns Oates and Washbourne, 1934), p. 16.

32 See St Thomas Aquinas, *Summa Theologiae* I, q.51, a.2.

33 See St Cyril of Jerusalem, *Catechesis* 15, n.24, *PG* 33, 904.

34 See St Thomas Aquinas, *Summa Theologiae* I, q.50, a.3.

35 Cf. Flick & Alszeghy, *Il Creatore*, p. 585.

36 Pseudo-Dionysius, *De coelesti hierarchia* chapters 7–9 in *PG* 3, 205–212, 237–242, 257–262.

37 See St Gregory the Great, *Homilia 34 in Evangelia*, 7 in *PL* 76, 1249–1250. St Thomas Aquinas in the *Summa Theologiae* I, q.108, a.6 states that there is no essential difference between the hierarchies of Dionysius and of St Gregory the Great.

38 See St Gregory the Great, *Homilia 34 in Evangelia*, n.12 in *PL* 76, 1253–1254. His description (*Homilia 34 in Evangelia*, nn.7–14 in *PL* 76, 1249–1255) of the 'tasks' of each choir can be summarized as follows:
The angels deliver ordinary divine messages.
The archangels deliver divine messages of special importance.
The virtues work miracles.
The powers fight back the tempter demons.
The principalities guide the other spirits in their actions.
The dominations are the superior chiefs of the heavenly armies.

The thrones judge along with God.
The cherubim enjoy the fullness of knowledge.
The seraphim enjoy the most perfect vision of God, and are the most ardent in charity.

39 Pope John Paul II, *Discourse at General Audience* (6 August 1986), in *IG* 9/2 (1986) pp. 327–328.

40 See Congregation for the Doctrine of the Faith, Letter to Cardinal Höffner of 24 September 1983 in *AAS* 76 (1984) pp. 175–176; and Idem, Decree of 6 June 1992 concerning certain practices of the *Opus Angelorum* (Engelwerk) in *AAS* 84 (1992), pp. 805–806.

41 See St Thomas Aquinas, *Summa Theologiae* I, q.62, a.6.

42 Vonier, *The Angels* pp. 63–64.

43 See F. Suarez, *De Angelis*, liber VII, xiii.

44 *Acathist hymn*, first and fifteenth chants.

45 See *CCC* 334 and 336.

46 Richard of Saint Victor, *Commentary on the Song of Songs*, chapter 4 in *PL* 196, 417.

47 See St Thomas Aquinas, *Summa Theologiae* I, q.113, a.4.

48 For example, Portugal keeps a liturgical memorial of its guardian angel on 10 June each year.

49 See St Thomas Aquinas, *Summa Theologiae* I, q.113, a.2.

50 J. H. Newman, *The Dream of Gerontius* §2.

51 These theorems are taken from Vonier, *The Angels*, pp. 26–27.

3

The Material Cosmos

The creation of the world is the work of Love: the universe, a created gift, springs from the Uncreated Gift, from the reciprocal Love of the Father and the Son, from the Most Holy Trinity.

Pope John Paul II, *Discourse at General Audience,* 5 March 1986

After the invisible world of pure spirits, it is now appropriate to consider the creation of the visible, material world out of nothing at the beginning of time.

3.1 *Creation out of nothing*

Creation out of nothing is a truth accessible to human reason, which can grasp unaided that God must be responsible for all that has been created; any vision proposing pre-existent material has an easy tendency to drift into pantheism. However, a production from nothing is outside human experience which knows only the making of things from pre-existent material. Hence divine revelation not only confirms the truth of creation out of nothing, but also provides a view far beyond that obtained by reason alone.

The Scriptures already indicate a belief that God created the entire material world out of nothing. The classic text is from the second book of Maccabees where a Jewish woman exhorts her son to remain faithful to the Law during the persecutions at the time of Antiochus Epiphanes (168 BC), in the words: 'I implore you, my child, observe heaven and earth, consider all that is in them, and acknowledge that God made them out of what did not exist, and that mankind comes into being in the same way' (2 M 7:28). This affirmation is not just an isolated case but rather expresses the climate of thought which was present in Israel even earlier on. Nevertheless care must be taken in the interpretation of certain key words in Genesis 1. Considering the passage, 'In the beginning, God created the heavens and the earth' (Gn 1:1), particular attention should be paid to the sense of the expressions 'in the beginning' (in Hebrew *bereshit*) and 'created' (in Hebrew *bārā*). The essential meaning of the word *bārā* is 'to cut' and 'to slash'; by the time of the exile, the word had become reserved to God's action alone apart from the five cases in which the word seems to indicate a purely human action.[1] The meaning which it seeks to convey is that God creates with supreme ease and effortlessness. Moreover, 'throughout its entire Old-Testament usage, a specific meaning accrues to *bārā* only in terms of a broader message about God's exclusive sovereignty over all.'[2]

In the whole account of creation in the book of Genesis, God's action is the sole principle through which the various elements of the universe are created. In the first chapter of Genesis, as well as the work of creation out of nothing in the strict sense (Gn 1:1) known traditionally as the *opus creationis*, there is also a description of the further work (the *opus distinctionis*) of ordering and dividing the matter created at the beginning (Gn 1:4, 7, 9) as well as the yet further work (*opus ornamenti*) of adornment (Gn 1:12, 16ff, 21, 25; 2:1). The use of the expression 'God said, "Let there be light", and there was light' (Gn 1:3) should be compared with the expression 'God said, "Let the earth produce vegetation"' (Gn 1:11). In the latter case God produces a further creation from something already created; the immediacy with which God does this is notable. On this basis, if the cosmos itself were created from some pre-existent material, then it should be expected that this substance would be described. However, God creates the light from nothing else. This argument would indicate that the idea of creation from nothing is implicit in Genesis 1.

The Scriptures teach incisively that God is responsible for the entire creation of *all* the cosmos. In the prophet Isaiah, we find the words 'I, myself, Yahweh made all things, I alone spread out the heavens. When I gave the earth shape, did anyone help me?' (Is 44:24). The author of the book of Wisdom affirms that *all* the world is the work of God: 'God of our ancestors, Lord of mercy, who by Your word have made all things' (Ws 9:1; cfr.1:14). The writer of Ecclesiasticus points out: 'By the words of the Lord all His works come into being' (Si 42:15). It is apparent that nothing can exist apart from the will of God: 'And how, had you not willed it, could a thing persist, how be conserved if not called forth by You?' (Ws 11:25).

In the New Testament, St John in his prologue to the Gospel affirms that *all* without exception was created through the Word: 'Through Him all things came to be, not one thing had its being but through Him' (Jn 1:3). St Paul asserts that God is the origin of all things (Rm 11:36) and 'calls into being what does not exist' (Rm 4:17). The Letter to the Hebrews states that 'it is by faith that we can understand that the world was created by one word from God, so that no apparent cause can account for the things we can see' (Heb 11:3).

In their opposition to heresy, especially gnosticism,[3] on the one hand and to paganism on the other, the Church Fathers gradually clarified the basic terminology in which the doctrine of creation was conveyed. In Christian times, the Greek and Latin forms of the verb 'to create' both underwent a development somewhat analogous to that of the word *bārā* in the Old Testament. It was necessary to attach to the word 'create' a more precise and specific meaning with which it was not initially endowed, in order to convey the special nature of God's action in creation. The word *creare* had, 'as a derivative of *crescere*, only the meaning of making something to grow.'[4] Yet the Latin expressions *creare* and *facere* and the Greek *poiein*, heavily used by the Church Fathers, did not exclude the sense of creation taught by the Christian Gospel. The original meaning of the word *creare* (and its ancient Greek and Latin synonyms) had in fact to be radically qualified in order to teach 'concisely the difference between non-being and being.'[5]

A semantic enrichment was thus in store for the word 'to make' as, in itself, it would not specify that the formless void (Gn 1:2) was also created from nothing. As S. L. Jaki explains: 'The thread which helped Christian orthodoxy out of the etymological labyrinth was provided by the now all too well-known expression *ex nihilo* (out of nothing) which was attached to the words *facere* (to make), *condere* (to establish), and *creare* (to make grow).'[6] Inspired by the expression 'God made them (i.e., heaven and earth) out of what did not exist' from the Second Book of Maccabees, the author of the *Shepherd of Hermas* stated of God the Creator that 'He made everything from what was not existing to exist.' The author of the *Shepherd of Hermas* (and Aristides and Saint Theophilos of Antioch) used the Greek expressions *ek tou me ontos* ('from the non-existing') and *ex ouk onton* ('from those not being'). It was Tertullian, however, who first used the concise Latin form *de nihilo* (from nothing).[7]

The definition, at the Fourth Lateran Council in 1215, of the dogma that the world was created out of nothing and with time confirmed a long-standing climate of Christian reflection on creation:

> We firmly believe and confess that there is only one true God, … the Father, the Son and the Holy Spirit, … the Creator of all things, visible and invisible, spiritual and corporeal, who by His almighty power from the beginning of time made at once out of nothing both orders of creatures.[8]

Theologians further clarified the meaning of the divine action by speaking of creation with the more precise formula: 'Creation is the production of the entire substance of a thing into existence from a state of non-existence' (*Creatio est productio totius substantia ex nihilo sui et subjecti*). In every kind of production the specific effect has no previous existence as such, and may therefore be said to have been made *ex nihilo sui*—from a state of non-existence—so far as its specific character is concerned (like making a computer out of its component parts). However what is peculiar to creation is the entire absence of any prior subject-matter—*ex nihilo subjecti*. In the act of creation, God is the exclusive and direct principle of the new being, to the exclusion of any pre-existing matter. As Creator, God is in a certain sense 'outside' of created being and what is created is 'outside' of God. At the same time the creature fully and completely owes to God its own existence and its own essence, because the creature has its origin fully and completely from the power of God.[9]

The First Vatican Council reiterated this teaching[10] and the Catholic doctrine that the visible and invisible cosmos was created by God out of nothing is clearly taught in the Catechism.[11] Pope John Paul II remarked that 'the Church *explains* and thoroughly *examines* this truth by making use of the philosophy of being, and she defends it from the distortions that arise from time to time in human thought.'[12] Amongst these distortions are materialism, the error that only matter exists, condemned at the First Vatican Council in the following terms: 'If anyone is not ashamed to assert that nothing exists besides matter, let him be anathema.'[13] This error has existed from antiquity and continues today in all the various forms of communism and, in practice, within certain expressions of capitalism.[14]

Christian teaching on creation out of nothing also excludes the error of pantheism, which fails to hold that God is distinct from His creation. The First Vatican Council first of all condemned pantheism in general terms: 'If anyone says that the substance and essence of God and of all things is one and the same, let him be anathema.'[15] The words 'substance' and 'essence' were then used to specify the various types of pantheism:

> If anyone says that finite beings, the corporeal as well as the spiritual, or at least the spiritual ones, have emanated from the divine substance; or that the divine essence becomes all things by self-manifestation or self-evolution; or lastly that God is the universal or indefinite being which, by self-determination, constitutes the universality of beings differentiated into genera, species and individuals, let him be anathema.[16]

In the first variety, substantial pantheism, finite beings are an emanation from the divine substance. Such was the case in the early centuries with gnosticism and the various other heresies proposing emanationism which held that creatures were not essentially distinct from the divine substance but emanated from God. In the second form, essential pantheism (for example the pantheism of Schelling), there exists a single essence and all things result from an evolution of that one divine essence. In the third kind of pantheism (which could be termed differential pantheism), there exists a single being which differentiates and becomes all beings. Various types of pantheism are also present in world religions including Hinduism and Buddhism. If God is not distinct from what He has made, the creation is no longer a free gift from Him but rather is a necessary form of existence. In pantheist world views the cosmos is in fact often considered to be necessary and eternal, and spirit is perceived as a dimension of matter or matter is viewed as a dimension of spirit. If one holds pantheism, the coming of God in human flesh adds nothing new to God's relationship with His creation. It remains to be seen that the Christian doctrine of the Incarnation is in fact the only effective shield against pantheism.[17]

The meaning of creation out of nothing implies that God did not use pre-existent matter to make the cosmos. Thus, the act of Creation is not a motion, since between being and non-being there can be no real succession. The doctrine of creation out of nothing maintains that God is the sole cause of all of the cosmos, which has a relation of total dependence on God. In other words, God is the only Creator. Gnosticism effectively undermined this truth by affirming that the material world was created by a lower being who had emanated from God. Various forms of dualism maintained that God created only 'the good part' of the cosmos or only 'the spiritual part', while an equally powerful but evil being was responsible for creating the material or 'bad' part. History furnishes us with many different examples of this tendency, including Manichaeism.[18] In the year 561, the Council of Braga (in Portugal) condemned certain errors of the Priscillianists,[19] whose ideas reflected a Manichaean and Gnostic flavour. According to the Priscillianists, the devil, who was not created good by God but emerged from darkness, is the creative principle of matter and evil. Around the year 1180, the Albigensians resurrected the old Manichaean errors and taught that matter was created out of nothing by the devil. Around the same time, the Cathars and the Waldensians despised the material part of the creation and tended to a similar dualist error. Pope Innocent III prescribed a profession of faith to the Waldensians in the year 1208, which asserted the creation of all things by

God.[20] Against all dualist currents of thoughts, the Fourth Lateran Council in 1215 defined the revealed truth concerning God the only Creator of all things. Belief in God as the only Creator also involves a rejection of polytheism, which held that many gods were responsible for creation. Polytheism is to be found in the ancient religions of Babylonia, Egypt, Greece and Rome, in current world religions such as Hinduism and in tribal cults.

3.1.1 The work of the Most Holy Trinity

Although in the Creed the act of creation is attributed especially to God the Father Almighty, 'it is also a truth of faith that the Father, the Son and the Holy Spirit are the unique and indivisible "principle" of creation.'[21] Thus it is said that there is One Creator, referring to the divine nature, and at the same time it is stressed that the creation is the work of the whole Trinity. The passage in Genesis where the Spirit of God hovered over the waters (Gn 1:2), inspired the Fathers to think in terms of the creative power of the Holy Spirit. In the Old Testament, personified Wisdom is seen to play a rôle in the act of creation (Pr 9:1; Ws 7:27) and can be seen to indicate the work of the Son and the Holy Spirit. St Augustine developed St Paul's expression that 'there is one God, the Father, from Whom all things come..., and there is one Lord, Jesus Christ, through Whom all things come' (1 Co 8:6), and provided the classic formula in which everything is created by the Father, through the Son, in the power of the Spirit.[22] St Thomas Aquinas elaborated the traditional teaching concerning the *appropriation* of the work of the creation to the Persons of the Holy Trinity.

To the Father power is attributed, which is particularly manifested in the creation, so that the Father is given the name of Creator. To the Son is appropriated Wisdom, the intellective agent in the act of creation and hence it is said that the creation is carried out through the Son. To the Holy Spirit is attributed goodness and with Him is associated the bringing of things to their proper ends, giving them life, and hence one can say that the world was created in the Holy Spirit and subsists in Him.[23] A more recent approach to the appropriation of actions to the Persons of the Most Holy Trinity attributes creation to the Father, the renewal of creation to the Son (re-creation), and the transformation of creation to the Holy Spirit (trans-creation). The act of creation, like all external acts of the Blessed Trinity is a reflection and revelation of the inner life of Personal relations within the same Holy Trinity.

3.1.2 Continuing creation

After the initial creation, does God create anything else? Apart from human souls which are created out of nothing every day, does God make new beings from nothing? Of course, He is free to do so, but the meaning of the seventh day rest (Gn 2:2) is that God's creative act is complete after the beginning. Furthermore, the author of the Letter to the Hebrews remarks: 'God's work was undoubtedly all finished at the beginning of the world' (Hb 4:3). The Angelic Doctor elaborates the following solution to the question:

> Nothing entirely new was afterwards made by God, but all things subsequently made had in a sense been made before in the work of the six days… He made

> nothing afterwards that had not existed previously, in some degree, in the first works.[24]

Hence even the creation out of nothing of human souls each day is not 'new' in the absolute sense since these are of the same nature as the souls of Adam and of Eve made in the beginning. God's providential care of what He has made is, in some sense, a continuing creation. A theological discussion on evolution may perhaps be considered in the light of continuing creation.[25] When the Scriptures refer to God 'creating something new on earth' (Jr 31:22) they look forward to the new creation of grace or of glory.

3.2 *Creation with time*

Related to the *ex nihilo* element in the dogma of creation is the assertion that the universe was created with time (*cum tempore*). The expression 'with time' is preferable to the use of the phrase 'in time', since the latter implies that the cosmos is placed into a type of 'receptacle' where time already exists. In fact, time only begins with the creation of matter.[26] The use, in the book of Genesis, of the words 'In the beginning' (Gn 1:1; *bereshit* in Hebrew) is not, of itself, a proof of the creation of the universe at a finite time in the past. However, as was remarked for the expression *bara* above, the whole thrust of the first chapter of Genesis refers to events at the beginning of time. In many other passages from the Scriptures, the sacred authors speak of the pre-existence of God over and above His creation. In the Old Testament, several texts stress that nothing is antecedent to God: 'Before the mountains were born, before the earth or the world came to birth, you were God from all eternity and for ever' (Ps 90:2). The Wisdom of God existed before all things (Pr 8:22-26). The writer of the book of Ecclesiasticus states that 'God created His works in the beginning' (Si 16:26). Qoheleth issues a warning against perceiving too easily the beginning of God's work for 'though He has permitted man to consider time in its wholeness, man cannot comprehend the work of God from beginning to end' (Qo 3:11). Yet other books of the Old Testament seem to be more optimistic: 'It was He who gave me true knowledge of all that is,... the beginning, end and middle of the times' (Ws 7:17-18). In the New Testament, Jesus asks the Father to glorify Him with the glory He had before the world existed (Jn 17:5) and desires that the disciples see the glory God gave Him, because He loved Him before the foundation of the world (Jn 17:24). St Peter affirms that Christ was 'known since before the world was made' (1 P 1:20). St Paul reminds us that we have been chosen in Christ before the creation of the world (Ep 1:4).

Christian tradition stressed the fact that the cosmos had a beginning and so rejected Plato's concept of the unbegotten, eternal universe. However, Christianity could not attach the word 'begotten' to the universe, since this term had already been used to express the relation of God the Son to God the Father. So the Christian idea of creation could not be tied on to the words 'to generate' and 'to beget'; this was fortunate, because the Gnostics regarded the world as an emanation from God and thus used the expression 'to beget the world'. Tellingly, the Arians, paralleling neo-Platonist emanationism, also relied on expressions like 'to generate' and 'to beget' in their conception of the relation between God and creation.

In reaction to the pagan and heretical views of the eternity of the world, Christian thinkers of the early centuries, such as St Augustine, tried to prove the temporal nature of the cosmos.[27] St Athanasius argued against the Arians that the Word is eternal, therefore He is not created, and by the same token, the creature could not be eternal.[28] In the Middle Ages, there was much discussion concerning the eternity of the world,[29] and two basic positions became apparent. St Bonaventure followed St Augustine and St Athanasius, and maintained that there was an intrinsic contradiction in the notion of an eternal world: in other words the affirmation of the eternity of the world was tantamount to denying that it was created. St Bonaventure proposed six proofs to show that the created world could not be eternal. First, time can increase in steps from its beginning, but to the infinite nothing can be added. The second and third proofs deal with the fact that earthly time is characterized by measure and order, and these qualities are uncharacteristic of eternity, which cannot be measured. Fourth, the finite cannot contain the infinite, but the world contains itself. In other words, there is an incompatibility between a finite world and infinite time. Fifth, the world exists for man and an eternal world would presuppose an infinite number of men, which would be impossible. Sixth, creation out of nothing means to have being in succession to non-being (*habere esse post non esse*), first not to be and then to be, and so the universe cannot have existed from all eternity. There is thus an intrinsic contradiction between creation out of nothing and creation from eternity.[30] St Albert the Great followed Bonaventure's line in his youth, but then later changed to the other opinion, according to which the temporality of the world can only be known from revelation. Holding this latter position were Peter Lombard, Saint Thomas Aquinas and Blessed John Duns Scotus. The Angelic Doctor taught that creation with time was an object of faith alone:

> By faith alone do we hold, and by no demonstration can it be proved, that the world did not always exist, as was said above of the mystery of the Trinity (q.32, a.1). The reason for this is that the newness of the world cannot be demonstrated on the part of the world itself… Hence that the world began to exist is an object of faith, but not of demonstration or science. And it is useful to consider this, lest anyone, presuming to demonstrate what is of faith, should bring forward reasons that are not cogent, so as to give occasion to unbelievers to laugh, thinking that on such grounds we believe things that are of faith.[31]

St Thomas believed that reason could not prove the temporal character of the universe either from the nature of the cosmos or from the relation of the world to God. The starting point of such a proof would be the essence of the world and yet essence by definition prescinds from space and time, so it cannot be proved from the concept of the world that it did not always exist. The free will of God is the effective cause of the world and this can be known by divine revelation alone. While St Thomas thought that the beginning of the world with time could not be proved by any philosophical demonstration,[32] nevertheless he used 'arguments of convenience for a temporal beginning of creation' and so acknowledged 'the appropriateness of the truth that the faith teaches', and showed 'by various examples how faith and reason complement each other.'[33]

The doctrine of creation with time is the pivot upon which hang all the other articles of the Christian creed, and it is in this context that the link is forged between creation and salvation history:

> Whenever the meaning of creation in time is weakened, let alone eliminated, the meaning of all other tenets of the Christian creed become weakened or eliminated. Those tenets—Fall, Incarnation, redemption, the growth of the Kingdom of God, eschatology, final judgment—presuppose not only creation but also a creation in time because all those tenets refer to events in time which alone can constitute that sequence which is salvation history.[34]

3.3 *The freedom of the Creator*

In the first chapter of Genesis, 'God said, 'Let us make man in Our own image, in the likeness of Ourselves'' (Gn 1:26). This anthropomorphic expression shows God almost consulting Himself about the creation, and is a way of expressing the divine freedom. In the psalms, God's freedom in creation finds various expressions: 'In the heavens, on the earth, in the ocean, in the depths, Yahweh's will is sovereign' (Ps 135:5). The book of Wisdom makes clear the dependence of the creation on the will of God: 'And how, had You not willed it, could a thing persist, how be conserved if not called forth by You?' (Wis 11:25). St Paul speaks of the 'predetermined plan of the One who guides all things as He decides by His own will' (Eph 1:11).

On many occasions in the history of Christianity, it was necessary for the Church to teach God's freedom in creation. In the year 543, a provincial council of Constantinople condemned the Origenists, who exaggerated Origen's theology under the influence of Platonist philosophy and so effectively denied the absolute freedom of God's creative act:

> If anyone says or holds that God's power is finite, or that He has created all that He could comprehend and think, or that creatures are co-eternal with God, let him be anathema.[35]

In the year 1140, the Council of Sens condemned several errors of Peter Abelard, among which some denied God's freedom.[36] Similarly, the proscription of certain errors of Eckhart in 1329 touched upon the freedom of God to create.[37] The Council of Florence in 1442 affirmed that God was free in making all of the creation:

> (The Holy Roman Church) most firmly believes, professes and proclaims that the one true God, Father, Son, and Holy Spirit, is the Creator of all things, visible and invisible, who, when He so willed, out of His bounty made all creatures, spiritual as well as corporeal.[38]

The First Vatican Council in 1870, stressed once more that God created 'with absolute freedom of counsel'.[39] When the Second Vatican Council stated that 'the eternal Father, in accordance with the utterly gratuitous and mysterious design of His wisdom and goodness created the whole universe,' it implied a total freedom in that gratuity.[40] The Catechism makes it clear that the world has its origin in God's absolutely free will, and is not a necessary form of existence.[41]

God was free, both from internal necessity and from external coercion, either to create the cosmos or not to create it. Furthermore, He was not bound to create this particular form of the cosmos, but could have created one of an indefinite number of other possible universes. Thus this particular form of the cosmos, as well as its very existence, is contingent or dependent on a particular choice on the part of God. One consequence of the non-necessary character of the current cosmos, is the question of whether this is the best of all possible worlds. Several philosophers were proponents of absolute optimism, including Abelard, Malebranche and Leibniz. In particular, Leibniz contended that God was morally bound to create the best of all possible worlds:

> One may say that as soon as God has decreed to create something there is a struggle between all the possibles, all of them laying claim to existence, and that those which, being united, produce most reality, most perfection, most significance carry the day. It is true that all this struggle can only be ideal, that is to say, it can only be a conflict of reasons in the most perfect understanding, which cannot fail to act in the most perfect way, and consequently to choose the best. Yet God is bound by a moral necessity, to make things in such a manner that there can be nothing better: otherwise not only would others have cause to criticize what he makes, but, more than that, he would not himself be satisfied with his work, he would blame himself for its imperfection; and that conflicts with the supreme felicity of the divine nature.[42]

Leibniz's affirmation that God, in His wisdom is bound to produce the best of all possible worlds, starts from the false concept that God must act in His creation according to all the possibilities that it offers. However, it is characteristic only of a creature with a capacity to develop towards perfection, to have a tendency to choose the best. Hence the creature gradually arrives at increasing perfection through these choices. On the other hand, in His act of creation, God cannot receive an increase of being, happiness or perfection from outside of Himself.

Leibniz speaks of God's moral responsibility to create the best out of a number of possible worlds, each of which is more or less good. This is an inversion of reality: God did not choose this world because it is best; rather, it is best because God chose it. God's choices are not determined by anything or anyone outside Himself. Leibniz's view also tends to eliminate man's responsibility for sin by representing sin as little more than a misfortune that has befallen him.

Moreover, the idea of the best possible world is an objective which cannot be reached, because for every world that exists, a better one could be imagined, unless it were absolutely perfect and thus like God Himself. Only the *act* of creation, once it has been freely made, must be perfect, because it is entirely divine. God's action is always perfect, but the object resulting from the action, inasmuch as it is finite, is by the same token imperfect.[43] The Christian vision does however involve a relative optimism with respect to the world that God has actually created. Since it is a work of God, it is clear that it corresponds perfectly to what God willed to make, because there can be no obstacle to God's sovereign Will. The world is on a pilgrimage to that perfection which God wills to communicate to it. Sin cannot impede this, because when God has permitted sin and evil, He has done so with a view to drawing forth a greater good.[44] In fact, God has created the world to reveal His perfection and give to His creatures a share in His goodness. The world was thus created for the glory of God, as can be seen from its unity, goodness, rationality and beauty.

3.4 *The unity in creation*

The universe by its very definition implies a single entity which is united within itself. The fact that God created all the cosmos goes some way to indicate that it is a unity. St Thomas affirmed the unity of the world, since the 'very order of things created by God shows the unity of the world.'[45] The inherent unity within all of creation is thus a manifestation of the perfection and wisdom of God who created it; this unity lends itself in turn to the unfolding of God's economy of salvation. The cosmos is not only a unity, but is also unique as G. K. Chesterton affirmed:

> The universe is a single jewel, and while it is a natural cant to talk of a jewel as peerless and priceless, of this jewel it is literally true. This cosmos is indeed without peer and without price: for there cannot be another.[46]

S. L. Jaki defines the cosmos as the 'true and specific totality of all coherently and consistently contingent interacting beings.'[47] The unity within the cosmos is not merely visible but also resides in the unseen spiritual world: 'The ensemble of creatures constitutes the universe: the visible and invisible cosmos, in the totality and parts of which there is reflected eternal Wisdom and expressed the inexhaustible Love of the Creator.'[48] Cosmic unity has not been destroyed by the after-effects of original sin, though it has been disfigured. Moreover, man's perception of this unity has been rendered more difficult by the effects of the Fall.

The cosmos is ordered in *hierarchical* unity, as has already been seen in the case of the spirit world. The human person is the apex of the whole visible creation, and even among human beings there is a gradation of being and action. In the animal kingdom there are also different levels of differentiation, higher and lower grades. The cosmic hierarchy in nature and in grace finds its focal point in Christ, the King of the whole cosmos, both visible and invisible (Col 1:16).

3.5 The goodness of creation

The goodness of God's creation is stressed six times in the first chapter of Genesis (Gn 1:4, 10, 12, 18, 21, 25), but only after the creation of man and woman is the creation described as 'very good' (Gn 1:31). The reasons for this distinction will be made clear in the next chapter, but for now the repeated affirmation that what God has made is good is highly significant. It implies that the whole of the cosmos is good in its entirety as well as its various parts. What is being spoken of here is a goodness in the order of being (an ontological goodness) rather than a goodness in the order of action (a moral goodness).

As has already been mentioned above in relation to dualism, God created all of the universe as good. Thus evil enters the world later as a result of a free choice on the part of rational creatures. Any idea that a kind of demiurge is responsible for the material part of creation is rejected in the Judaeo-Christian perspective: 'Death was not God's doing, He takes no pleasure in the extinction of the living. To be—for this He created all; the world's created things have health in them, in them no fatal poison can be found, and Hades holds no power on earth' (Ws 1:13–14). Outside this tradition, it was often difficult to maintain a perspective in which the cosmos was regarded as good. In the early Christian centuries, the Fathers of the Church had to fight vigorously against the Gnostic and Manichaean heresies, which were systems proposing the essentially pessimistic view that matter was evil as it was not created by God.

The wholesomeness and homeliness of the cosmos as seen in the book of Genesis sets this account apart from all mythological descriptions of creation, be they from the ancient Near East or elsewhere. For example, the 'Sumerians, Babylonians, and Assyrians were convinced that every part of nature had a will of its own, often capricious and standing in continual conflict with one another. Such parts of nature, or forces of nature, could in their belief be pacified only by prayer and sacrifice.'[49] Among the Aztecs of pre-Columbian America, man was reduced

> to the status of flotsam and jetsam, and his interests appeared to be best served if he plunged headlong into the cyclic, rhythmic, and basically violent transformations of nature that surrounded him... The supreme aim of Aztec life was a participation in the rhythm of that violent action whereby their own gods lived.[50]

The Sabbath day rest is also of key importance in this context, for it is absent from cosmogonies outside the

Old Testament. Most significant is 'the idea of a God who works for six days and does an obviously perfect work, conveyed by the systematic reassertion of the goodness of what God had done.'[51]

Essentially it is the Incarnation in which God the Son takes on human nature that safeguards and reinforces the doctrine that material creation is good. Creation was carried out in the power of the Holy Spirit who endowed the cosmos with goodness. This goodness of the creation makes it attractive to the human person, who can perceive such goodness and refer this back to the good God who was responsible for it.

3.6 *The rationality of creation*

Creation reflects the supreme rationality of the God who made it. Since creation is a unity, then *all* of created reality must participate in this rationality in various ways. The Old Testament wisdom literature illustrates that God's handiwork is imbued with the intelligibility of His Wisdom:

> It was He who gave me knowledge of all that is,
> who taught me the structure of the world
> and the properties of the elements,
> the beginning, end and middle of the times,
> the alternation of the solstices and the succession of the seasons,
> the revolution of the year and the positions of the stars,
> the natures of the animals and the instincts of wild beasts,
> the powers of spirits and the mental processes of men,
> the varieties of plants and the medical properties of roots.
> All that is hidden, all that is plain, I have come to know
> instructed by Wisdom who designed them all (Ws 7:17-21).

The intelligibility of creation flows from the fact that God 'ordered all things by measure, number and weight' (Ws 11:20), and moreover that this order and harmony can be perceived by man's investigation in a realist perspective, and thus be referred to the supreme rationality of God. Fundamentally it is because the universe was created through the Word, the eternal Son of the Father, that it has the imprint of rationality left upon it.

Another aspect of cosmic rationality is that God created the universe, not in a blind way, but rather according to His wise plan, which is described by some authors as the eternal idea of the creation, or the exemplary idea (*idea exemplaris*). From all eternity God has 'imagined' or 'invented' the idea of the creature. God has constituted the creature in *His idea—from all eternity*. Yet *it was not yet the creature itself*. It was *only* an image, a sketch, a plan, a proposition of the creature. St John Damascene explains how God contemplated everything before creation, thinking outside time; and everything comes to pass in its time according to His timeless volitional thought, which is predetermination and image and pattern.[52] These 'images' and 'patterns' constitute the eternal and immutable counsel of God, in which all that is foreordained by God and is being unfailingly realized, is eternally figured.[53] This 'counsel' of God is eternal and has no beginning (αναρχος), because everything is immutable in God. With time itself the creature was brought out of nothingness into existence, or rather the new existence has been posited; the chain of times began. The creature, or rather the creatures, had to be realized according to the Divine Plan and to the Divine prototypes. God knows Himself and His perfections perfectly and similarly knows the possibility of impressing the image of these perfections upon created things. 'All things were known to Him before they were created' (Si 23:20). Since the world is created, we observe everywhere the manifestations of the Holy Trinity, *vestigia Trinitatis*. The fact that creation is part of God's plan excludes any idea that the universe had come about in a random, chance or chaotic way. Rather, the universe manifests evidence of its design and a purpose.[54] This purpose is not simply restricted to some inner harmony, but relates to God's providential care of His creatures. God's plan as revealed in His creation involves an economy of revelation and salvation in Christ.[55]

The unity, goodness and intelligibility of the created reality together lead to the beauty of all that God has made; this created beauty finds its apex in the human being whose creation as man and woman will be dealt with in the next chapter.

Further Reading

S. L. Jaki, *Is There a Universe?* (New York / Liverpool: Wethersfield Institute / Liverpool University Press, 1993).

Notes

1 See S. L. Jaki, *Genesis 1 Through the Ages* (London: Thomas More Press, 1992), p. 4ff. Jaki notes that the texts of Joshua 17:15, 18 and Ezekiel 23:47 clearly describe human actions while the readings of 1 Samuel 2:23 and Ezekiel 21:24 are uncertain.

2 *Ibid.*, p. 6.

3 Gnosticism, derived from the Greek word *gnosis* (knowledge) claimed a superior secret understanding of things. It was a system based on philosophical knowledge rather than on faith, where the distinction between the eternal uncreated Supreme Being and all other beings was blurred or erased. The production of matter was conceived of in terms of a downward emanation from God.

4 S. L. Jaki, *Cosmos and Creator* (Edinburgh: Scottish Academic Press, 1980), p. 70.

5 S. L. Jaki, 'Creation and Monastic Creativity' in *Monastic Studies* (Toronto) 16 (Christmas 1985), p. 79.

6 Jaki, *Cosmos and Creator*, p. 71.

7 See Tertullian, *De praescriptione haereticorum*, chapter 13, in *PL* 2, 26.

8 Lateran IV, *Symbol of Lateran* Chapter 1: On the Catholic Faith in DS 800; English translation in ND 19.

9 See Pope John Paul II, *Discourse at General Audience* (15 January 1986).

10 See Vatican I, Dogmatic Constitution *Dei Filius*, chapter 1 in DS 3002. See also canon 5 on chapter 1 in DS 3025.

11 See *CCC* 296–298.

12 Pope John Paul II, *Discourse at General Audience* (29 January 1986), §6. English translation in *ORE* N.5 (3 February 1986), p. 8.

13 Vatican I, *Dei Filius* chapter 1, canon 2 in DS 3022. English translation from ND 415.

14 See the condemnation of communism by Pope Pius XI in his Encyclical *Divini Redemptoris* (1937), 9: 'The doctrine of modern Communism, which is often concealed under the most seductive trappings, is in substance based on the principles of dialectical and historical materialism previously advocated by Marx, of which the theoricians of bolshevism claim to possess the only genuine interpretation. According to this doctrine there is in the world only one reality, matter, the

blind forces of which evolve into plant, animal and man. Even human society is nothing but a phenomenon and form of matter, evolving in the same way… In such a doctrine, as is evident, there is no room for the idea of God; there is no difference between matter and spirit, between soul and body; there is neither survival of the soul after death nor any hope in a future life.' For a critique of the materialism found in certain expressions of capitalism see Pope John Paul II, *Sollicitudo rei socialis* (1987), 28: 'All of us experience firsthand the sad effects of this blind submission to pure consumerism: in the first place a crass materialism, and at the same time a radical dissatisfaction, because one quickly learns—unless one is shielded from the flood of publicity and the ceaseless and tempting offers of products - that the more one possesses the more one wants, while deeper aspirations remain unsatisfied and perhaps even stifled.'

15 *Idem*, canon 3 in DS 3023. English translation from ND 416.

16 *Idem*, canon 4 in DS 3024. English translation from ND 417.

17 See chapter seven, pp. 207–208 below.

18 Manichaeism is the name given to ideas linked with the dualist sect founded by Mani (216–276) who was born in Babylonia but then lived in Persia in the third century. The system consisted of a hybrid mixture of many religious elements, teaching that at the beginning of the cosmos there were two equal and opposite principles, good and evil or light and darkness. Through their fight for supremacy, the world was created. There were two levels of believers, and the fact that the members of the higher level (the 'elect') were forbidden to marry, to consume meat or wine and were not allowed to work indicated a belief that the material realm was evil. St Augustine was a follower of the Manichaean sect in his youth and after his conversion to Christianity refuted it in his writings.

19 For the text of the some of the condemned errors of the Priscillianists, see ND 402/5–9 and ND 402/11–13.

20 The text of Pope Innocent III's Profession of Faith prescribed to the Waldensians in the part concerning creation reads:

'We believe with our heart and confess with our tongue that Father, Son, and Holy Spirit are one God... Creator, Maker, Ruler and Provider of all things, corporeal and spiritual, visible and invisible.' Text from DS 790, English translation from ND 403.

21 Pope John Paul II, *Discourse at General Audience* (5 March 1986), §4. English version from *ORE* 10(10 March 1986), p. 1.

22 See St Augustine, *De Trinitate* Book 1, chapter 6, n.12 in *PL* 42, 827.

23 See St Thomas Aquinas, *Summa Theologiae* I, q.45, a.6.

24 St Thomas Aquinas, *Summa Theologiae* I, q.73, aa.1 and 2.

25 For a treatment of evolution, see chapter eight, pp. 251–270 below.

26 See St Augustine, *The City of God* Book 11, chapter 6 in *PL* 41, 322: 'The world was not made in time, but with time.' See also St Thomas Aquinas, *Summa Theologiae* I, q.46, a.3: 'Things are said to be created at the beginning of time, not as if the beginning of time were a measure of creation, but because together with time heaven and earth were created.'

27 See St Augustine, *The City of God*, Book 11, chapters 4–6, and Book 12, chapters 15–16 (in *PL* 41, 319–322 and 363–366) for a summary of those arguments. See also *Confessions* Book 11 (*PL* 32, 805–826) for Augustine's notion of creation with time.

28 See St Athanasius, *Oratio I contra Arianos*, 29 in *PG* 26, 71–74.

29 See C. Vollert et al., *On the Eternity of the World* (Milwaukee, WI: Marquette University Press, 1964) and also L. Bianchi, *L'errore di Aristotele. La polemica contro l'eternità del mondo nel xiii secolo* (Firenze: La Nuova Italia, 1984).

30 See St Bonaventure, *Commentarius in II Librum Sententiarum Petri Lombardi*, Distinction 1, article 1, question 2 in *S. Bonaventurae Opera Omnia* (Quaracchi: Collegio San Bonaventura, 1885) Volume II, pp. 20–22. See also F. Copleston, *A History of Philosophy*, (New York: Image, 1985) vol. II, pp. 262–265.

31 St Thomas Aquinas, *Summa Theologiae* I, q.46, a.2.

32 See St Thomas Aquinas, *Quaestio Disputata De Potentia Dei*, 3,

17; and Copleston, *A History of Philosophy*, vol. II, pp. 366–368.

33 L. Scheffczyk, *Creation and Providence* (London / New York: Burns and Oates / Herder and Herder, 1970) p. 146. Cf. St Thomas Aquinas, *Summa Theologiae*, I, q.46, a.1 ad 6; Idem, *Summa Contra Gentiles*, II, 38.

34 S. L. Jaki, 'From Scientific Cosmology to a Created Universe' in *Irish Astronomical Journal* 15(1982), p. 259.

35 Council of Constantinople, *Anathematisms against the Origenists* (543) in DS 410. English translation in ND 401/8.

36 See Council of Sens, in DS 726–727.

37 When Eckhart was 'asked why God did not create the world sooner, he replied that God could not create the world sooner because nothing can act before it exists; therefore God created the world as soon as He existed.' See John XXII, Constitution *In agro dominico* (27 March 1329) in DS 951. English translation from ND [406/1].

38 The General Council of Florence, *Decree for the Jacobites*, in DS 1333. English translation in ND 408.

39 Vatican I, Dogmatic Constitution *Dei Filius* Chapter 1, in DS 3002. English translation in ND 412.

40 Vatican II, *Lumen Gentium* 2.

41 *CCC* 295.

42 G. W. Leibniz, *Theodicy. Essays on the Goodness of God, the Freedom of Man and the Origin of Evil*, 201.

43 See St Thomas Aquinas, *Summa Theologiae* I, q.25, a.6.

44 See St Thomas Aquinas, *Summa Theologiae* I, q.48, a.2, where he quotes St Augustine (*Enchiridion* 11, 3 in *PL* 40, 236) as saying that 'God is so powerful that He can even make good out of evil.' Cf. *CCC* 310–311.

45 St Thomas Aquinas, *Summa Theologiae* I, q.47, a3.

46 G. K. Chesterton, *Orthodoxy* (New York: Image, 1959), pp. 64–65.

47 See S. L. Jaki, *God and the Cosmologists* (Edinburgh: Scottish Academic Press, 1989), pp. 84, 94, 104. See also Idem, *Is there a Universe?* (New York: Wethersfield Institute, 1993).

48 Pope John Paul II, *Discourse at General Audience* (12 March 1986), §8, in *ORE* 11(17 March 1986), p. 1.

49 S. L. Jaki, *Science and Creation* (Edinburgh: Scottish Academic Press, 1986) p. 94.

50 *Ibid.*, p. 52.

51 Jaki, *Genesis 1 Through the Ages*, p. 8.

52 See St John Damascene, *On the Orthodox Faith*, 1, 9.

53 See St John Damascene, *On Holy Images*, 1, 10.

54 For the meaning of design and purpose in the universe see S. L. Jaki, *The Purpose of It All* (Edinburgh: Scottish Academic Press, 1990).

55 These themes will be explored in more detail in chapters five and seven below.

4

Man and Woman

When God at first made man,
Having a glass of blessing standing by;
Let us (He said) poure on him all we can:
Let the world's riches, which dispersed lie,
Contract into a span.

George Herbert, The Pulley

So far, discussion of the mystery of creation has dealt with the spiritual world and the material world. Now, it is to treat that microcosm of the universe which comprises both the material and the spiritual, the human person who is at one and the same time visible and invisible, who is body and soul in unity.

4.1 *The creation of man and woman*

The sub-human world reaches its full significance only in relation to man and woman. On six occasions in the first chapter of Genesis it is stated that God sees as good that which He has created.[1] However, only after the creation of man and woman is it stressed that: 'God saw all that He had made, and indeed it was very good' (Gn 1:31). Creation only becomes 'very good' after man and woman are created as the apex of all God made, creatures endowed with intellect and free will.

In the book of Genesis, the creation of the human person occupies a central place, for the expression *bārā* (to create) is used three times in this context: 'God created man in the image of Himself, in the image of God He created him, male and female He created them' (Gn 1:27). This threefold expression of God's creation of the human being signifies that God is responsible for the creation of man's body and man's soul and for the differentiation between man and woman. It further signifies that God's image is present in man's body, in man's soul and in the differentiation between male and female. The second book of Genesis goes into more detail regarding the creation of man and woman. God 'fashioned man of dust from the soil' (Gn 2:7); it is significant that the Hebrew name of the first man *adam* is derived from the Hebrew word for 'of the soil' (*adamah*). However, God also 'breathed into his nostrils a breath of life, and thus man became a living being' (Gn 2:7); only with the breath of life (*pneuma*) does this creature truly become human. The twofold aspect of the creation of man points to his material nature drawn from the dust of earth and his spiritual nature caused by the breath of God. God is responsible for *both* the material and the spiritual aspects of man, even if the processes of evolution contribute towards the composition of the human body. The creation of woman is also described in the book of Genesis, when God caused Adam to fall into a deep sleep and 'while he slept, He took one of his ribs and enclosed it in flesh' (Gn 2:21). From the rib He had taken from the first man, God made woman and brought her to Adam, who exclaimed: 'This at last is bone from my bones, and flesh from my flesh! This is to be called woman, for this was taken from man' (Gn 2:23).

The creation of the human person is also mentioned at many other places in the Scriptures. The constant *leitmotiv* is one of strength and yet frailty, of a combination of spiritual and material aspects. The psalms affirm man's created excellence: 'Yet You have made him little less than a god, You have crowned him with glory and splendour' (Ps 8:5). For the book of Wisdom, man's creation took place when God 'breathed an active soul into him and inspired a living spirit' (Ws 15:11). However, elsewhere man's frailty is highlighted: 'The Lord fashioned man from the earth, to consign him back to it' (Si 17:1). Man's utter dependence on God is stressed in Job's words: 'You modelled me, remember, as clay is modelled' (Jb 10:9). Job also affirms the strength deriving from God's care of man: 'And then you endowed me with life, watched each breath of mine with tender care' (Jb 10:12).

St Paul refers to the 'first man, being from the earth' (1 Co 15:47) who was also endowed with a living soul (1 Co 15:45). The Apostle nuances his position concerning the creation of woman. While he states that 'Adam was made first and Eve afterwards' (1 Tm 2:13) and that 'woman came from man' (1 Co 11:8), he also points out that 'man is born of woman' and both come from God (1 Co 11:12). The imagery of the Song of Songs and of St Paul's letter to the Ephesians (Eph 5:31–33), leads to man and woman being regarded as symbols for Christ and His Church respectively. The Scriptures therefore imply that the human person is created in the image of Christ, but the picture needs to be coloured in by Christian tradition.

4.2 The manner of creation

4.2.1 The body

Biblical anthropology speaks of the human person as a whole. Among the basic Hebrew terms for man used in the Old Testament, *nèfèš* means the life of a concrete person who is alive (Gn 9:4; Lev 24:17-18, Pr 8:35). However man does not have a *nèfèš*; he is a *nèfèš* (Gn 2:7; Lev 17:10). *Basar* refers to the flesh of animals and of men, and sometimes the body as a whole (Lev 4:11; 26:29). Again, the human being does not have a *basar*, but is a *basar*. The New Testament term *sarx* (flesh) can denote the material corporality of man (2 Co 12:7), but on the other hand also the whole person (Rom 8:6). Another Greek term, *soma* (body) refers to the whole man with emphasis on his outward manifestation. Here again man does not *have* his body, but *is* his body. Biblical anthropology clearly presupposes the unity of man, and understands bodiliness to be essential to personal identity.[2]

The essential teaching of the Scriptures is that the human person in his or her totality was created by God. More will be said later concerning the possible contribution of evolution to the formation of the human body.[3] As regards the creation of the first man and the first woman, the Scriptures do not aim to teach precise details about *how* the couple was created, but rather about the *fact* that they were created by God and depend on Him. Thus the use of mud in the formation of man and the rib of man in the creation of woman are not necessarily to be taken literally. Origen regarded the use of the rib as purely allegorical, but this is not in accord with Christian tradition.[4] Rather, the use of man's rib in the making of woman teaches us that the creation of woman is dependent on that of man. Thus, in the creation of Eve, there is a physical relation between the body of Eve and that of Adam. The Pontifical Biblical Commission stated in 1909 that the historical sense of the first woman's formation from the first man could not be called into doubt.[5] Pope Pius XII later remarked that 'the helpmate given by God to the first man came from man himself and is flesh from his flesh, made into a woman and called such because she came from man.'[6] The historical formation of the original woman from the first man is also to be affirmed in view of the prefiguration of the Church. St Thomas Aquinas, in line with St Ambrose, St John Chrysostom and other Fathers, proposed that just as Eve was formed from the rib of Adam as he slept, so the Church was born from the pierced heart of Christ asleep in death on the Cross.[7]

The author of Genesis portrays the creation of woman as taking place while the man *slept* (Gn 2:21), and some commentators would say that this signifies a phase in the evolution of the sub-human world. 'Deep sleep is without conscious thought… So it was during that period which was without conscious thought but full of life that God divided the sexes, which would in time result in man and woman.'[8] Others would link the drawing forth of Eve while Adam slept as a reference to sexuality and procreation.

The Hebrew word for *woman* indicates her essential link with man, something which the counterparts in modern languages in general, apart from English, are unable to express: 'She shall be called woman (*'issah*) because she was taken out of man (*'is*)' (Gn 2:23).[9] This text provides the basis for affirming the equality of man and woman from the point of view of their humanity and Origen, Clement of Alexandria and Saint Augustine were among the Fathers who taught this truth.[10] Indeed it was only with the advent of Christianity that woman was seen as an equal partner with man. Elsewhere, such as in ancient Greece as well as in Moslem culture to this day, the woman has been regarded as a lesser being. In the Christian Middle Ages on the other hand, there was a current of thought which held that woman was a higher being than man, since while the first man's body was created from the dust of earth, the first woman's body was created from a higher principle than dust, namely man himself.[11] In German Romantic literature, Goethe and Schiller perceived woman as the more perfect being:

> But they, contented with quieter honour,
> Pluck now the women the moment's fine flower,
> Nourish it loving and diligently,
> They have in their bounded work greater freedom,
> Richer than man, too, in districts of wisdom
> And in the unending sphere, poetry.[12]

Furthermore, since the six days of creation give a hierarchical account of creation, beginning with the inanimate beings, proceeding through the creation of plants and animals and finishing with the human person, it could be argued that the last creature, woman, is the highest.

The book of Genesis indicates that all the human race comes from one couple. Elsewhere in the Old Testament, it is affirmed that from Adam and Eve 'the human race was born' (Tb 8:6). St Paul mentions in his speech to the Council of the Areopagus that the whole of the human race is descended from a single couple: 'From one single stock... He created the whole human race' (Ac 17:26). He also parallels the way in which just as the Fall came through one man, Adam, so also the Redemption came through Christ, the New Adam: 'Death came through one man and in the same way the resurrection of the dead has come through one man. Just as all men die in Adam, so all men will be brought to life in Christ' (1 Co 15:21–22; cfr. Rm 5:12–21). St Athanasius further developed the Christological foundation of the doctrine known as *monogenism*, namely that the whole human race is descended from Adam and Eve: 'What was born of Mary, according to Scripture, was by nature human; the Lord's Body was a real one—real, because it was the same as ours. This was so because Mary was our sister, since we are all descended from Adam.'[13] The fact that Cain's wife (Gn 4:17) is not explicitly mentioned among the children of Adam and Eve does not prove that she is not descended from them. Our first parents had many sons and daughters (Gn 5:4). The objection that monogenism is not possible because it involved the sons of Adam marrying their sisters is not valid either: under the special circumstances of the beginning of the human race, generation between close relatives was permitted, as can be seen on at least one other occasion in the Old

Testament (Gn 19:31–38), for the perpetuation of the race.[14] Monogenism is necessarily connected with Christian teaching in regard to original sin. As will be seen in more detail later, original sin as a state of enmity from God was caused by a sin committed at the dawn of human history. This state of sin is found in all human beings, with the exception of Our Blessed Lady, since they are linked with Adam via human generation.

On the other hand, *polygenism* is the theory proposing many couples at the origin of the human race, and would lead to one of the following three unacceptable hypotheses:

i. Original sin is not transmitted to all the members of the human race.

ii. Even though original sin is transmitted to all the members of the human race, it is transmitted by a process other than by generation.

iii. Original sin is transmitted to all men by generation, but Adam is not a single individual, but a collection of persons.

Pope Pius XII stated in regard to polygenism that one could not safely hold:

> a theory which involves either the existence on this earth, after Adam, of true men who would not originate from him, as the ancestor of all, by natural generation, or that 'Adam' stands for a plurality of ancestors. For, it is not at all apparent how such views can be reconciled with the data which the sources of revealed truth and the documents of the Church propose concerning original sin, namely, that it originates from a sin truly committed individually and personally by Adam, and it is a quality native to all of us, only because it has been handed down by descent from him.[15]

In 1950, the Sacred Congregation for Seminaries effectively reaffirmed the descent of all human beings from Adam and Eve.[16]

There is a difference between *monophyletic* and *polyphyletic* polygenism. In the former, the human race is descended from several human beings rather than just Adam and Eve, but all of the original human beings belong to one stem or phylum. In this case it is much easier to say that all of these primary human beings committed original sin together which was then transmitted to their descendants. Nevertheless, even monophyletic polygenism would be unsatisfactory in explaining the Pauline letters and the affirmation of all men dying in Adam. With polyphyletic polygenism, the human race is descended from many stems or phyla and so it would be impossible to guarantee the Church's teaching that original sin is inherited through generation. In any case, Pope Paul VI reaffirmed the Church's reservations with regard to polygenism in the context of inadequate explanations of original sin given by some modern theologians. These authors, whose starting point is polygenism 'which has not been proven', practically deny the doctrine of original sin. The Pope also very strongly indicated Adam as the universal first parent.[17] The descent of the whole human race from a single couple underscores the essential unity of the whole of mankind and the equality of all people in a single nature and is thus a powerful shield against racism.

4.2.2 The soul

Whatever may be said about the creation of the body, be it an immediate creation or a programmed creation through evolution, the human soul is directly created out of nothing by God. Any application of the theory of evolution becomes unacceptable whenever it fails to affirm very clearly the immediate and direct creation by God of each and every human soul.[18] The direct creation of each human soul by God is a consequence of its spirituality. Even though the soul does not die when the body does, nevertheless it is created to go together with the body. It does not exist before the body. The notion of the *pre-existence* of the human soul, which was maintained by Origen and some other ecclesiastical authors and derived from Plato, considered that the soul was united to a material body as a punishment for sins committed in an earlier spiritual state. This concept was repeatedly condemned by the Church as incompatible with the Scriptural doctrine concerning the origin of the human person.[19] Similarly excluded is a pre-existence of the human soul through reincarnation. Also unacceptable is the idea of *traducianism,* according to which the soul is transmitted from the parents. Material traducianism maintained that the human being was generated in much the same way as the animals. The soul was regarded as something almost material, for, in the process of generation, the soul of the parents was said to divide, giving rise to the child's soul. This idea, proposed by ancient philosophers, was also held by Tertullian. Spiritual traducianism proposed that the soul was completely spiritual, but still derived from the parents and then gave rise to a totally new subsistent being. This position is rather like the process of lighting one candle from another, without any diminution of the brightness of the former flame. There would thus be a spiritual seed from which the soul is generated and a material one from which the body arises.[20] In the West, St Augustine did not condemn this theory, and in the East some Fathers such as St Gregory of Nyssa and St Maximus the Confessor have been interpreted in a traducianist sense. However, traducianism was on several occasions outlawed by the Church.[21] Christian tradition has constantly supported creationism where the individual human soul is made immediately by God and infused into the body which is 'provided by' the parents in their procreative act.

Both in the case of the first man and woman and for every human being subsequently created, the soul is made by God out of nothing. Although each soul made by God is new and different, after the creation of the first human beings nothing essentially new is added to the nature of creation.[22] God's creation of each human soul is part of the chain of secondary causes, because when the material is sufficiently disposed, God always infuses the soul. The question remains as to when the soul is infused in the case of those created after Adam and Eve. St Thomas held that the rational soul was given to the embryo only after a certain period of time, once the latter was ready to receive it.[23] The opinion according to which the rational soul is only infused at the moment of birth is absurd and has been condemned by the Church.[24] The definition of the dogma of the Immaculate Conception speaks of the fact that 'the most Blessed

Virgin Mary was, from the first moment of her conception, by the singular grace and privilege of Almighty God and in view of the merits of Christ Jesus the Saviour of the human race, preserved immune from all stain of original sin.'[25] This would imply that Our Lady existed as a human being from the moment of her conception, and the same should be said of every human being. The Church has consistently condemned any type of procured abortion, starting from the premise that human life starts at conception. Christian tradition affirms that 'from the moment of conception, the life of every human being is to be respected in an absolute way because man is the only creature on earth that God has wished for himself and the spiritual soul of each man is immediately created by God; his whole being bears the image of the Creator.'[26] The determination of the precise moment of the infusion of the soul during the process of human fertilization does not lie within the competence of the empirical sciences, which only deal with measurements of successive material states. On the other hand, the *effects* of the presence of the soul are detectable by the sciences.[27]

4.3 *The nature of the human person*

Having seen the creation of the human person, we now to turn to discuss the nature of man and woman. The human person cannot be reduced to what can be investigated and measured scientifically. Man and woman cannot be considered simply as carriers of genetic material.[28] Nor can human beings be considered as instruments of biotechnological research or of cloning.

The dignity of the human person is based on the unity between the corporeal and spiritual dimensions, within a perspective of man and woman made in the image and likeness of God.

4.3.1 *The properties of the human soul*

The existence of the human soul is something which is accessible to human reason alone,[29] even though the full understanding of its nature has come through divine revelation. The human soul is substantial, spiritual, immortal, individual and unique. In the book of Genesis, the difference between the body and the soul is described (Gn 2:7). The book of Wisdom speaks of an essential distinction between the body and the soul (Ws 9:15). The soul has its own subsistence since destruction of the body does not bring about the end of the soul (Mt 10:28). Many aspects of Christian doctrine are based on the supposition that the soul is a *substance* in itself. For example, since Christ has assumed a complete human nature, it follows that in His two natures there are three substances: that of the Word which must be referred to the essence of God alone, that of the body and of the soul which belong to the true Man.[30]

As regards its *spirituality*, the soul is a direct creation on the part of God, and cannot in any way be considered as a flowering or evolution of material processes. There is thus a discontinuity between body and soul, for the soul does not derive its origin from the body nor does it die with the body. P. Teilhard de Chardin held a panpsychistic notion of reality, a confusion between matter and spirit, whereby even material entities are endowed with spiritual properties: 'We are logically forced to assume the existence in rudimentary form of some sort of psyche in every corpuscle, even in those whose complexity is of such a low or modest order as to render it imperceptible.'[31] Thus, in his approach, the soul is not sufficiently distinct from matter.

The Old Testament contains many fine expressions of the *immortality* of the soul: 'The souls of the righteous are in the hands of God, no torment shall ever touch them… their hope was rich with immortality' (Ws 3:1,4). In the New Testament, a very precise indication of the immortality of the soul comes from Jesus' words: 'Do not be afraid of those who kill the body but cannot kill the soul; fear him rather who can destroy both body and soul in hell' (Mt 10:28). Jesus' promise to the good thief (Lk 23:43) and His descent into hell are guarantees of the continuity of His human nature between His death and Resurrection and so demonstrate the immortality of the human soul.[32] The Scriptures indicate that the soul is naturally immortal, and it does not seem that God has ever created a mortal spiritual soul; neither is the immortality of the soul a gratuitous gift on the part of God. The immortality of the human soul was defined by the Fifth Lateran Council in the year 1513.[33]

Lateran V also affirmed, against P. Pomponazzi, that the spiritual soul is an individual entity.[34] This *individuality* of the human soul means that it is not part of a universal spirit or the reflection of some type of world soul. Rather, the soul of each and every human being is distinct and different from that of every other human being. The responsibility and freedom of each human person is based upon this truth. In the Scriptures and elsewhere, the distinction between one individual and another, is indicated by the use of the expressions 'mine' and 'yours'. The *Song of Songs* poignantly illustrates this idea, for example in the words of the bridegroom to the bride:

I awakened you under the apple tree,
there where your mother conceived you,
there where she who gave birth to you conceived you.
Set me like a seal upon your heart,
like a seal on your arm (Sg 8:5–6).

If the word 'I' denotes the human ego, this would mean that, according to the Scriptural revelation, not only is one soul distinct from the other, but also as different from the other as the face of one human person differs from another person. This 'otherness' is also very clearly expressed in the passage quoted above from the Song of Songs. Moreover, if human individuality is more conditioned by the soul than by the body, then it would follow that spiritual diversity is more important than the physical aspect which would merely manifest the spiritual variety.

The notion of reincarnation undermines both the vision of the body and of the soul. It proposes that the body is not an essential aspect of the human person, but only a shell, or an instrument of the spiritual soul. At the same time it destroys the uniqueness of the identity of the soul. Reincarnation (also called *metempsychosis*) is the false notion that souls inhabit a series of bodies and can live many lives on this earth before being completely purified and so released from the need to migrate to another body. According to this error, the soul preexists its embodiment, and after death exists in a disembodied state before animating once again a body of the same or a different species. In various forms, reincarnation has been accepted by Buddhists, Hindus, Neoplatonists, New Agers and others. This error was already refuted in the past by many Fathers of the Church like St Gregory of Nyssa:

> If one should search carefully, he will find that their doctrine is of necessity brought down to this. They tell us that one of their sages said that he, being one and the same person, was born a man, and afterward assumed the form of a woman, and flew about with the birds, and grew as a bush, and obtained the life of an aquatic creature—and he who said these things of himself did not, so far as I can judge, go far from the truth, for such doctrines as this—of saying that one should pass through many changes—are really fitting for the chatter of frogs or jackdaws or the stupidity of fishes or the insensibility of trees.[35]

The human soul is *unique*, in a twofold sense. First, the unicity of the soul implies that there are not various animating principles in man, each differing from the other. Second, it means that each man has only one soul. When St Paul prays: 'May you all be kept safe and blameless, spirit, soul and body, for the coming of Our Lord Jesus Christ' (1 Th 5:23), he seems to have a tripartite division of the human being. However, 'spirit' in this context is generally taken to mean the presence of God the Holy Spirit in the human being, giving new life in union with Christ, or else the depth of the human person open to the presence of God, akin to the concept of the 'heart.' The passage is an indication of man's supernatural destiny. Hebrew thought is so concrete that, despite the Greek influence, the Scriptures do not teach directly the metaphysical make-up of the human being in terms of body and soul, but nevertheless the biblical conception accords well with the later metaphysical understanding. The Manichaeans held that man had two souls, one of which was good and was created by God, while the other was bad and was made by the powers of darkness. The good soul was responsible for man's good actions, while the bad one was responsible for his evil actions. In the patristic literature, the expressions spirit, soul and body are often used, referring to the human person. Some Fathers tended towards this trichotomy of the human person following Platonic lines where three distinct realities made up the human being. This idea was excluded after 870, when the Fourth Council of Constantinople defined the unicity of the rational soul in every human person.[36]

4.3.2 *The unity of the human being*

The Church has consistently taught that the soul is of itself the form of the body. A chief occasion for this was provided by the condemnation of P. J. Olivi (Olieu), the leader of the spiritual Franciscans. He held that although the human body was united to the rational soul, this soul was composed of spiritual matter and various forms (vegetative, sensitive, and intellective). The vegetative and sensitive forms were seen as partial forms of the human body. The third form, the intellective soul, was not a partial form of the body, otherwise one could not explain its spirituality. The composite rational soul was seen as the form of the body, but between the intellective form and the body, there was only a mediated relationship: the intellective form was united with the spiritual matter, the spiritual matter with the sensitive and vegetative form, and these two were also forms of the human body. The Council of Vienne (1311–1312) condemned this error of Olivi.[37] The Fifth Lateran Council (1513) reiterated the Church's teaching in the following words: 'The intellectual soul is … truly, of itself and essentially, the form of the human body.'[38] In the nineteenth century, A. Günther held that man was composed of matter and spirit, but the union between the two occurred through a mixing of spiritual and material activities which was not a substantial unity as traditionally understood. Hence, he denied that the rational soul was truly and immediately, of itself, the form of the body.[39] In the same century, A. Rosmini admitted the distinction of body and soul, but seemed to imply that the soul is united with the body only inasmuch as it knows this to be the case; thus he did not maintain the traditional conception of how they were linked.[40]

An extreme dualist conception of the human being, exemplified in the thought of Descartes, in which the body and soul were only accidentally linked as a pilot would be in a ship is excluded by the Church's doctrine. Similarly outlawed is the occasionalist approach of Malebranche in which body and soul are two substances without any real mutual contact; God would cause separately the ideas in the soul and the movements of the body. Christian doctrine teaches that the union of the body and soul is thus not simply a directive operation and also that there is no third element which forms the 'link' between body and soul. Rather, the soul immediately and directly makes the body human. The statement that the soul is the form of the body means that it is the essential principle of determination of the body, and makes the body indeed a human body, so that together body and soul make up human nature.[41] The body is indeed the expression of the soul and by its gestures makes known what lies in the depths of man's heart; this leads to the human capacity for relationship. Man and woman are essentially social beings,[42] but this social character flows from the nature of the individual human being. Above all, the human person has been created for a relationship with God.[43] The essentially unchanging character of human nature 'has its ultimate foundation in Christ, who is the same yesterday, and today and forever.'[44]

4.3.3 *Male and female*

The expression of the human person as man and woman mirrors the phenomenon of sexual differentiation in the animal kingdom. However, there is an essential gulf, for the human being is spiritual, not merely material. Sexual differentiation in the animal kingdom exists in view of the creation of man and woman. The significance of being male and female in the human being is not merely biological but has repercussions at a deeper level. The psychological differences between man and woman are clearer today as a result of modern research and growth in understanding. However, intuition indicates that the difference goes even deeper and resides in the very being of man and woman. While man and woman share the same human nature, they are two complementary aspects of that same nature, so that the unity and difference between them lies at the level of being. Although man and woman are made for each other, this does not mean that God created them incomplete.[45]

According to the Scriptures, the image of God manifests itself, at the outset, in the difference between the sexes. Human beings exist only as masculine or feminine, since the reality of the human condition appears in the difference and plurality of the sexes. Hence, far from being an accidental or secondary aspect of personality, it is constitutive of personal identity. Each of us possesses a way of being in the world, to see, to think, to feel, to engage in mutual exchange with other persons who are also defined by their sexual identity. The roles attributed to one or the other sex may vary according to time and place, but the sexual identity of the person is not a cultural or social construction. It belongs to the specific manner in which the image of God exists.[46] The Incarnation of the Word reinforces this specificity. He assumed the human condition in its totality, taking up one sex, but He became man in both senses of the term: as a member of the human community, and as a male. The relation of each person to Christ is determined in two ways: it depends on one's own proper sexual identity and that of Christ.[47] Moreover, the Incarnation and Resurrection extend the original sexual identity of the image of God into eternity. The risen Lord remains a man when He sits now at the right hand of the Father. We may also note that the sanctified and glorified person of the Mother of God, now assumed bodily into heaven, continues to be a woman. The sexual differences between man and woman, while certainly manifesting physical attributes, in fact transcend the purely physical and touch the very mystery of the person.[48]

This metaphysical complementarity of the male and female accounts well for the importance given to the relation between the sexes throughout the Old and New Testaments, for instance in the Song of Songs. A profound understanding of the relation between man and woman is necessary in order fully to penetrate the mystery of the Church as the bride of Christ, the true nature of the married state and why the ministerial priesthood presupposes a male subject of ordination.[49] Man and woman are created in view of the coming of Christ, born of the Virgin Mary, and this anchors the difference between the sexes in a Christological setting. The relation between man and woman reflects in some way the mystery of the Holy Trinity. The Apostle states that 'there are no more distinctions between Jew and Greek, slave and free, male and female, but all... are one in Christ Jesus' (Ga 3:28). St Paul does not thus abolish the distinction between the sexes, but rather implies that this difference represents no obstacle in the life of grace.

4.3.4 *In the image of God and Christ*

In the Book of Genesis 1:26–27 we read: 'Then God said: "Let us make man in our image, after our likeness. Let them have dominion over the fish of the sea, the birds of the air, and the cattle, and over all the wild animals and all the creatures that crawl on the ground." God created man in his image; in the divine image he created him; male and female he created them.' Here we find the basis for considering the human being as the image of God. As a creature, man is a *living* being (Gn 2:7), a quality apparently shared by all animals. But human createdness is different in a specific and unique dimension that animals do not have: in addition to having the 'breath of life,' which is the light of self–consciousness, men and women are 'images of God.'

Being the 'image of God' means that men and women not only 'exist,' but are capable of a relationship with God, if God wishes. On the one hand, then, man is connected to his world ('out of the clay of the ground'), and on the other hand he is open ('image of God') to relating with God. Being the image of God is the basis for a relationship of intimacy with God. It is important to point out that being the image of God does not only refer to the human soul, but also to the human body.[50]

Human beings in their entirety were created in the image of God. This perspective excludes interpretations which place the *imago Dei* in one aspect or the other of human nature (for example, in righteousness or in the intellect), or in one of their qualities or functions (for example, sexuality or dominion over the earth). Avoiding both monism and dualism, the Bible presents an understanding of the human being in which his spiritual dimension is seen together with his physical, social and historical dimensions.[51] Far from encouraging an unbridled and anthropocentric exploitation of the natural environment, the theology behind the *imago Dei* affirms man's crucial role in the realization of God's eternal abiding in the perfect universe. Human beings, by God's design, are the administrators of this transformation for which all of creation yearns.[52]

The origins of man are to be found in Christ: for he is created 'through Him and in Him' (Col 1:16), through the Word who is the life and the light of every man who comes into the world (cf. Jn 1:3-4, 9). While it is true that man is created *ex nihilo*, it can also be said that he is created from the fullness (*ex plenitudine*) of Christ Himself who is at once the Creator, the Mediator and the final Destiny of man.[53] The Father destined us to be His sons and daughters, and 'to be conformed to the image of his Son, who is the firstborn of many brothers' (Rm 8:29). Therefore, what it means to be created in the *imago Dei* is only fully revealed to us in the *imago Christi*. It is Christ—in His Incarnation, Death and Resurrection—who restores the image of God in man to its proper form.[54]

4.4 *The original state of the human person*

Man and woman, in addition to the gifts of intellect and free will inherent in their nature as delineated above, were also, in the beginning, endowed by God with other preternatural and supernatural gifts. An absolutely supernatural gift elevates into the divine order of being and activity, while a preternatural one (also called relatively supernatural) perfects within the created order. What is supernatural is natural only to God and not to any creature, while what is preternatural to one creature may be natural to another. For instance, the original gift of immortality was preternatural to man, but immortality is natural to the angelic order. God desired the supernatural order in the first place and the natural order was only willed in relation to the supernatural, since God created the entire cosmos in view of the coming of Christ. However, each of the natural, preternatural and supernatural orders are completely gratuitous on God's part.

Our first parents, after being created and before original sin, were endowed with sanctifying grace and so participated in the divine life. This supernatural gift was gratuitous, as the Church affirmed against the Jansenist denial that the original state of grace was a free gift.[55] There are at least two opinions as to when Adam and Eve were endowed with grace after their creation. According to St Thomas, they received supernatural grace in the same moment as their creation. St Bonaventure and much of the Franciscan school of theology place the gracing of Adam and Eve not at the same moment as their creation, but rather later after a suitable period of preparation. The Old Testament indicates this gift, but does not furnish a decisive proof in the passage which states that our first parents enjoyed a good relationship with God (Gn 1:26–31). The book of Ecclesiasticus refers to the fact that after the creation of man and woman, God 'clothed them with strength like His own' (Si 17:3). The New Testament, however, makes it clear that a state of sanctity existed before that of original sin (Rm 5:12–21; 1 Co 15:21–28). Certain passages from the Pauline letters, speaking of 'a new self which will progress towards true knowledge the more it is renewed in the image of its Creator' (Col 3:10) imply with the word 'renew' that a lost grace is being restored through the redemption. St John Damascene is one of many Fathers who affirmed the beauty of the original state of grace:

> Since man is composed of body and soul, I think that this excellent temple, called paradise, should be understood in both material and spiritual terms… As a matter of fact, as regards his body, man lived

> in a place which excelled all other places in beauty. As to the soul, he found himself in a place still more sublime and marvellous, above any comparison, since God dwelt in him as in a temple and he was dressed in splendid vestments, robed as he was with divine grace.[56]

The Council of Trent stated that Adam was constituted in 'holiness and justice',[57] and this grace in the Catholic theological perspective does not destroy nature but presupposes it, elevates it and perfects it.

Adam and Eve were also endowed with a number of gratuitous preternatural gifts of integrity. They enjoyed the gift of bodily immortality. This gift implied a possibility of not dying, rather than an impossibility of dying,[58] and was a sign and effect of intimate contact with God the source of all life. If Adam had remained obedient to God, he would not have died (Gn 2:17). Man was created with the gift of immortality for 'God did make man imperishable, He made him in the image of His own nature' (Ws 2:23; cfr. Ws 1:13-14). The Pauline letters also teach that death 'came into the world' (Rm 5:12; 1 Co 15:22) and so was not there from the beginning. The Pelagians denied the reality of original sin and so they thought that man's mortality was his natural original state. The Council of Carthage condemned this error in the following terms: 'Whoever says that Adam, the first man, was made mortal in the sense that he was to die a bodily death whether he sinned or not, which means that to quit the body would not be a punishment for sin but a necessity of nature, let him be anathema.'[59]

Before the Fall, our first parents also had the gift of freedom from the 'signs of death', namely pain and suffering. Pain came into being after original sin (Gn 3:16ff.), and before this Adam and Eve enjoyed perfect health of body and total peace of soul. However, their bodies were earthly and not heavenly as is the resurrected body described by St Paul (1 Co 15:35–49). They enjoyed a freedom from irregular desire, also known as the freedom from disordered concupiscence, which does not mean that Adam and Eve were free from every desire or passion, but rather that these were controlled and directed by the spirit. There was thus perfect harmony between body and soul, between man and woman, between the human person and creation and and between man and God. Although St Gregory of Nyssa stated that before the Fall the propagation of the human race would have occurred without sexual relations,[60] the more common and acceptable approach would be to regard sexuality as more beautiful and untouched by disorder before the Fall. The passage in Genesis which indicates that Adam and Eve felt no shame in front of each other when they were naked (Gn 2:25) before the Fall, is an example of freedom from disordered concupiscence, but this gift cannot be reduced only to that aspect. Pope John Paul II showed how this absence of shame symbolized also a transparency and innocence in the relations between Adam and Eve:

> The sentence, according to which the first human beings, man and woman, 'were naked' and yet 'were not ashamed,' unquestionably describes their state of consciousness, in fact, their mutual experience of the body. It describes the experience on the part of the man of the femininity that is revealed in

> the nakedness of the body and, reciprocally, the similar experience of masculinity on the part of the woman. By saying that 'they were not ashamed,' the author tries to describe this mutual experience of the body with the greatest precision possible for him. It can be said that this type of precision reflects a basic experience of man in the 'common' and pre-scientific sense. But it also corresponds to the requirements of anthropology and in particular of contemporary anthropology, which likes to refer to so-called fundamental experiences, such as the 'experience of shame.'[61]

Adam and Eve were also privileged with the gift of knowledge of natural and supernatural truths infused by God. This is symbolized by the fact that Adam knows and names the animals (Gn 2:19ff.). The book of Ecclesiasticus indicates that after Adam and Eve were created, God 'filled them with knowledge and understanding, and revealed to them good and evil' (Si 17:7).

The gratuity of these supernatural and preternatural gifts implies that God could have created man and left him in a state of pure nature, with the possibility of arriving at a purely natural happiness. Instead God was so generous as to endow Adam and Eve with many gifts received not only for themselves but also for their descendents. Had Adam and Eve resisted the temptation which led them to their Fall, they might have received further graces and gifts, beyond our imagination.

4.5 *The beautiful cosmos*

Paradise, the garden of Eden, where our first parents dwelt before original sin should not be seen only as a state, even less as a mere symbol, but also as a place. Otherwise the realist vision of space and time, which is part of the very fabric of Catholic theology, would be undermined. The cosmos, despite its vastness and complexity, is indeed a home which God made for man and woman. The universe 'which consists of many parts, each beautiful in itself, is far more beautiful than the individual parts which, properly combined and arranged, compose the whole, even though each part, taken separately, is itself a thing of beauty.'[62] The gift of initial integrity and that of sanctifying grace imply a beauty in the beginning which was like a priceless work of art ready to be damaged by original sin but not to be completely lost. True beauty is an expression of unity, goodness and truth, rather than just the lure of the apparent good.[63] Creatures radiate something of the beauty of God according to their participation in His likeness. However no one creature radiates everything of this divine beauty. The creature who radiates the divine beauty more than any other is the Blessed Virgin Mary.

> O man, run through all creation with your thought, and see if there exists anything comparable to or greater than the holy Virgin, Mother of God. Circle the whole world, explore all the oceans, survey the air, question the skies, consider all the unseen powers, and see if there exists any other similar wonder in the whole creation… Count, then, the portents, and wonder at the superiority of the Virgin: she

> alone, in a way beyond words, received into her bridal chamber Him before whom all creation kneels with fear and trembling.[64]

Among the visible creatures, only human beings can appreciate beauty, which is indeed to be seen and experienced in the visible realm, but a greater beauty is found in the soul. Indeed, as regards the human person, the body expresses the beauty of the soul:

> As a man
> Must shape a cup to drink from, so the mind
> Must use its finite symbols to enclose
> The eternal vintage of the infinite truth ....
> It was for this
> God made His finite creatures, and enclosed
> Our human love in forms of roseate flesh
> That we might slowly learn, with human eyes,
> To spell His infinite meanings.[65]

However, the source of all beauty is God and its perfection is to be found in Him alone. This means that although the human person is said to be the apex or centre of the created cosmos, an absolute anthropocentrism is excluded in the Christian vision, since it is to God that the human person must be referred. Man and woman are the most beautiful beings in the visible realm precisely because they are formed in the image of Christ, and the most noble aspect of human life is the participation in His life. In any approach to the divine beauty the human person is like a blind man looking at the sun.[66] Divine grace is needed to fully appreciate God's beauty, just as the eyes of the body are employed to see natural wonders:

> But what do I love when I love God? Not material beauty or beauty of a temporal order; not the brilliance of earthly light, so welcome to our eyes; not the sweet melody of harmony and song; not the fragrance of flowers, perfumes, and spices; not manna or honey; not limbs such as the body delights to embrace.[67]

The beauty in creation is here for man and woman to enjoy, and this enjoyment should, at least implicitly, be referred to its Creator, and thus be in harmony with the natural and revealed laws which form part of the tapestry of Christian life.

> By contemplating the beauty and use of each thing, one… is filled with love for the Creator. He surveys all visible things: the sky, the sun, moon, stars and clouds, rain, snow and hail… thunder, lightening, the winds and breezes and the way they change, the seasons, the years…; the four-legged animals, the wild beasts and animals and reptiles, all the birds, the springs and rivers, the many varieties of plants and herbs, both wild and cultivated. He sees in all things the order, the equilibrium, the proportion, the beauty, the rhythm, the union, the harmony, the usefulness, the variety, the motion, the colours, the shapes, the reversion of things to their source, permanence in the midst of corruption. Contemplating thus all created realities, he is filled with wonder.[68]

The radiance, order and integrity which are the hallmarks of natural and supernatural beauty are expressions of the most wise and all-caring providence of the Creator which is to form the topic of the next chapter.

Further Reading

Pope John Paul II, *Man and Woman He Created Them: A Theology of the Body* (Boston: St Paul editions, 2006)

P. Evdokimov, *Woman and the Salvation of the World* (Crestwood, NY: St Vladimir's Seminary Press, 1994)

S. L. Jaki, *Angels, Apes and Men* (La Salle, Illinois: Sherwood Sugden and Company, 1983)

A. A. Maurer, *About Beauty. A Thomistic Interpretation* (Houston, Texas: Center for Thomistic Studies, 1983)

Notes

1 See Gen 1: 4, 10, 12, 18, 21, 25.

2 See International Theological Commission, *Communion and Stewardship: Human Persons Created in the Image of God* (2004), 28.

3 See chapter eight, §8.4.3.

4 See Origen, *Contra Celsum* Book 4 n.38 in *PG* 11, 1085–1088.

5 Pontifical Biblical Commission, *Concerning the historical character of the first chapters of Genesis* Q.3 in DS 3514.

6 Pius XII, *Discourse to the Pontifical Academy of Science* (30 November 1941) in *DP*, p. 43.

7 St Thomas Aquinas, *Summa Theologiae* I, q.92, a.3. See also St Ambrose, *Expositio Evangelii Secundam Lucam*, 2, 85–89 in *PL* 15, 1666–1668; St John Chrysostom, *Catechesis to Catechumens* 3, nn.17–19 in *SC* 50, pp. 176–177.

8 A. Holloway, *God's Master Key. The Law of Control and Direction* (Wallington: Faith Keyway, 1988), p. 50.

9 Cf. Pope John Paul II, Apostolic Letter *Mulieris Dignitatem*, 6. See also Idem, *Discourse at General Audience* (9 April 1986) in *ORE* N.15 (14 April 1986) p. 11.

10 See Origen, *In Iesu nave* Homily 9, n.9 in *PG* 12, 878; Clement

of Alexandria, *The Pedagogue* chapter 1, n.4 in *SC* 70, pp.128–131; St Augustine, *Sermon* 51, chapter 2, n.3 in *PL* 38, 334–335.

11 Peter Lombard notes that this tendency exists when he stresses the essential equality of man and woman, explaining why woman was created from man's rib and not from his head or his feet: 'She was formed neither as a dominator nor a slave of man but rather as his companion' (*Sentences* 3, 18, 3).

12 F. Schiller, *Honour to Woman*, 5.
Aber, zufrieden mit stillerem Ruhme,
Brechen die Frauen des Augenblicks Blume,
Nähren sie sorgsam mit liebendem Fleiß,
Freier in ihrem gebundenen Wirken,
Reicher als er in des Wissens Bezirken
Und in der Dichtung unendlichem Kreis.

13 St Athanasius, *Letter to Epictetus*, n.7 in *PG* 26, 1061–1062.

14 In particular, Cain was the first child of Adam and Eve recorded in Scripture (Gn 4:1). His brothers, Abel (Gn 4:2) and Seth (Gn 4:25), were part of the first generation of children ever born on this earth. Even though only these three males are mentioned by name, Adam and Eve had other children. In Genesis 5:4 this statement sums up the life of Adam and Eve: 'And the days of Adam after he had fathered Seth were eight hundred years. And he fathered sons and daughters.' This does not say when they were born. Many could have been born in the 130 years (Gn 5:3) before Seth was born. During their lives, Adam and Eve had a number of male and female children. The Jewish historian Flavius Josephus wrote that, "The number of Adam's children, as says the old tradition, was thirty-three sons and twenty-three daughters." (Flavius Josephus, *Antiquities of the Jews*, Book 1, chapter 2, n.3, note 8). The Bible does not tell us how many children were born to Adam and Eve. However, considering their long life spans (Adam lived for 930 years according to Gn 5:5), it would seem reasonable to suggest there were many, as our first parents were commanded to 'be fruitful, and multiply' (Gn 1:28). From Scripture, with the first generation, brothers would have

had to have married sisters or there would be no more generations. Many people immediately reject the conclusion that Adam and Eve's sons and daughters married each other by appealing to the law against brother-sister intermarriage, or incest. However, the law forbidding marriage between close relatives was not given until the time of Moses (Lv 18-20). Provided marriage was one man to one woman for life (based on Genesis 1 and 2), there was originally no disobedience to God's law when close relatives (even brothers and sisters) married each other. For example, Abraham married his half-sister (Gn 20:12). God blessed this union to produce the Hebrew people through Isaac and Jacob. Today of course, brothers and sisters (and half-brothers and half-sisters) are not permitted by law to marry also because their children have an unacceptably high risk of being deformed. The more closely the parents are related, the more likely it is that any offspring will be deformed. Each person inherits one gene of each pair from each parent. Unfortunately, genes today contain many defects (a collateral effect of original sin), and these show up in a variety of ways. The more distantly related parents are, the more likely it is that they will have different problems in their genes. Children, inheriting one set of genes from each parent, are likely to end up with pairs of genes containing a maximum of one bad gene in each pair. The good gene tends to override the bad so that a serious deformity does not occur. However, the more closely related two people are, the more likely it is that they will have similar errors in their genes, since these have been inherited from the same parents. Therefore, a brother and a sister are more likely to have similar mistakes in their genes. A child of a union between such siblings could inherit the same bad gene on the same gene pair from both, resulting in two bad copies of the gene and serious defects. Adam and Eve did not have accumulated genetic defects. When the first two people were created, they were physically perfect for God's human creation was described as 'very good' (Gn 1:31), so their genes were perfect. The first generation of children ever born (Cain and Abel and their brothers and sisters) would have have received virtually no imperfect genes from Adam or Eve, since the effects of original sin would have been minimal to start with, as it takes time for these copying errors to accumulate. In that situation, brother and sister could have married with God's approval, without any potential to produce deformed offspring. By the time of Moses (several thousand years later), degenerative defects would have built up in the human race to such an extent that it was necessary for God to forbid brother-sister (and close relative) marriage (Lv 18-20). Also, there were plenty of people on the earth by then, and there was no reason for close relations to marry.

15 Pope Pius XII, *Humani generis*, 37. English translation, modified by me, in ND 420.

16 Sacra Congregatio de Seminariis, *Letter to the Cardinals and Bishops of Brasil* in *AAS* 42 (1950), p. 839.

17 See Pope Paul VI, *Discourse at Symposium on Original Sin* (11 June 1966) in *AAS* 58(1966), p. 654.

18 See *ibid*..

19 See the condemnation of the Origenists at the Provincial Council of Constantinople in the year 543 in DS 403; English translation in ND 401/1. Similarly, the Council of Braga in the year 561 condemned the Priscillianists for saying that 'human souls first committed sin in the heavenly abode and for this reason were thrown down on earth in human bodies.' See DS 456 and the English translation in ND 402/6.

20 See St Augustine, *Letter 190*, chapter 4, n.15 in *PL* 33, 861–862.

21 See the condemnation of errors by Pope Anastasius II in the year 498 in DS 360; the condemnation of errors by Pope Benedict XII in the year 1341 in DS 1007, English translation in ND 407. See also the position taken by Pope Leo XIII against certain aspects of Rosmini's writings in the year 1887, DS 3220–3222.

22 See pp. 74–75 (above) and pp. 135, 157 (below).

23 St Thomas Aquinas, *Summa Theologiae* I, q.118, a.2.

24 See the condemnation of the laxist proposition by Pope

Innocent XI in the year 1679, as found in DS 2135.

25 Pope Pius IX, Bull *Ineffabilis Deus* in DS 2803, English translation in ND 709.

26 Congregation for the Doctrine of the Faith, *Instruction on Respect for Human Life in its Origin and on the Dignity of Procreation* (1987), Introduction, §5. See also Vatican II, *Gaudium et Spes*, 24.3, 51.3.

27 See Pope John Paul II, Encyclical Letter *Evangelium Vitae*, 60.

28 Richard Dawkins proposes this idea and in *The Selfish Gene* described how one might extend evolutionary principles to explain the spread of ideas and cultural phenomena. He gave as examples melodies, catch-phrases, beliefs, and fashion. See *The Selfish Gene*, (Oxford: Oxford University Press, 1989[2]), p. 352.

29 See the promises signed by L. E. Bautain in DS 2766 (English translation in ND 102) and the theses against the traditionalism of A. Bonnetty in DS 2812.

30 Eleventh Council of Toledo, *Symbol of Faith* in DS 535, English translation in ND 630.

31 P. Teilhard de Chardin, *The Phenomenon of Man* (New York: Harper & Row, 1961), p. 301.

32 See S. L. Jaki, *The Savior of Science* (Washington, D.C.: Regnery Gateway, 1988), pp. 154–155.

33 Fifth Lateran Council, Bull *Apostolici Regiminis* in DS 1440, and English translation in ND 410.

34 *Ibid.*.

35 St Gregory of Nyssa, *De hominis opificio*, chapter 28, 3.

36 Fourth Council of Constantinople, canon 11 in DS 657.

37 See General Council of Vienne in DS 902, English translation in ND 405.

38 Fifth Lateran Council, Bull *Apostolici regiminis* in DS 1440, English translation in ND 410.

39 See Pope Bl Pius IX, Letter *Eximiam tuam* to the Archbishop of Cologne (15 June 1857) in DS 2828.

40 See the condemnation of one of his propositions by the Decree of the Holy Office *Post obitum*, 14 December 1887 in DS 3224.

41 See Vatican II, *Gaudium et Spes*, 14, where it is affirmed that 'Man, though made up of body and soul, is a unity.'

42 See *ibid.*, 12.4.

43 See *ibid.*, 21.7 and also St Augustine, *Confessions* Book 1, Chapter 1, n.1 in *PL* 32, 661: 'You made us for Yourself, and our hearts find no peace until they rest in You.'

44 See Vatican II, *Gaudium et Spes* 10.2, and also Heb 13:8.

45 See Pope John Paul II, *Women: Teachers of Peace. Message for World Day of Peace 1995* §3. See also Idem, *Letter to Women* 29 June 1995, §7.

46 See International Theological Commission, *Communion and Stewardship*, 33.

47 See *ibid.*, 34.

48 See *ibid.*, 35.

49 See Pope John Paul II, Apostolic Letter *Ordinatio sacerdotalis* (1994). See also A.-M. Pelletier, 'Masculin, féminin: le sens d'une tradition' in *Nouvelle Revue Théologique* 117 (1995) pp. 199–216.

50 Cf. St Irenaeus, *Adversus Haereses*, Book V, chapter 4, 1, where he says that not only the soul but also the body is important. See also International Theological Commission, *Communion and Stewardship*, 27: 'This truth has not always received the attention it deserves. Present–day theology is striving to overcome the influence of dualistic anthropologies that locate the *imago Dei* exclusively with reference to the spiritual aspect of human nature. Partly under the influence first of Platonic and later of Cartesian dualistic anthropologies, Christian theology itself tended to identify the *imago Dei* in human beings with what is the most specific characteristic of human nature, viz., mind or spirit. The recovery both of elements of biblical anthropology and of aspects of the Thomistic synthesis has contributed to the effort in important ways.'

51 Cf. International Theological Commission, *Communion and Stewardship*, 9.

52 *Ibid.*, 76.

53 See Vatican II, *Gaudium et Spes*, 22 and 1 Tm 2:5.

54 See International Theological Commission, *Communion and Stewardship*, 53, 55.

55 Jansenism is the name given to the erroneous system originating from Cornelius Jansen, Bishop of Ypres (died 1638). The system, continued by others, held that man was completely corrupted by the Fall, so that man's freedom was severely comprised, some of God's commandments were impossible and good works by unbelievers were sinful. Jansenists held that Christ did not die for the whole human race, but only for a few privileged souls. See the Bull *Ex omnibus afflictionibus* issued by Pope St Pius V in 1567 condemning certain propositions of Michael de Bay of which the one under DS 1923 is relevant here (English translation in ND [1984/23]). See also the Constitution *Unigenitus Dei Filius* issued by Pope Clement XI in 1713, where the error of Pasquier Quesnel listed in DS 2435 is pertinent. The errors of the pseudo-Synod of Pistoia were also condemned as they denied the gratuity of the original sanctifying grace as seen for example in DS 2616.

56 St John Damascene, *De fide orthodoxa* Book 2, chapter 11 in *PG* 94, 915–916.

57 Council of Trent, Fifth Session *Decree on Original Sin* in DS 1511; English translation in ND 508.

58 This formulation comes from St Augustine, *De Genesi ad litteram* Book 6, chapter 25, n.36 in *PL* 34, 354: 'It is one thing not to be able to die (*non posse mori*), as are some beings whom God has created immortal; it is another thing to be able not to die (*posse non mori*), as in the case of the immortality of the first man, who received this from the use of the tree of life,but it did not flow from his very nature.'

59 Sixteenth Council of Carthage, Canon 1 on original sin in DS 222, English translation in ND 501.

60 St Gregory of Nyssa, *De hominis opificio*, chapter 17 in *PG* 44, 187–190.

61 Pope John Paul II, *Discourse at General Audience* (12 December 1979), 3. See also M. Scheler, *Über Scham und Schamgefühl* (Halle: Niemeyer, 1914).

62 St Augustine, *Confessions* Book 13, chapter 28 in *PL* 32, 864. Translation into English with an Introduction by R. S. Pine-Coffin (Harmondsworth: Penguin, 1961), p. 341.

63 See J. Navone, 'The Power of Beauty' in *Priests and People* 4/8 (September 1990), p. 324.

64 St Proclus of Constantinople, *Homily* 5, 2 in *PG* 65, 717-720.

65 A. Noyes, *The Torch-Bearers* Vol III 'The Last Voyage' (Edinburgh and London: William Blackwood and Sons, 1930), pp. 191–192.

66 See A. A. Maurer, *About Beauty. A Thomistic Interpretation* (Houston, Texas: Center for Thomistic Studies, 1983), p. 122.

67 St Augustine, *Confessions* Book 10, chapter 6 in *PL* 32, 782. Translation into English with an Introduction by R. S. Pine-Coffin (Harmondsworth: Penguin, 1961) p. 211.

68 St Peter of Damascus, in *Philokalia*, Vol. III, 'The Sixth Stage of Contemplation'.

5

Creation and Providence

Because such perfect education
Began where there's no war to wage:
Deep in the substance of creation
Are shield and sword as one equation,
A never-ending pilgrimage.

C. Haffner, *Oh Climbers of the Mountain Morning*

The previous chapters have portrayed God's action in creating the angels, the cosmos and man and woman. Now, it is necessary to affirm that God not only made all things visible and invisible, but also that He maintains His creation in being, governs it and looks after it. The cosmos and all it contains have not only *been* created by God, but *are* His creatures. To state that the foundation of the cosmos and its developments is the provident wisdom of the Creator is not to say that creation has only to do with the beginning of the history of the world and of life. It implies, rather, that the Creator founds these developments and supports them, underpins them and sustains them continuously. Thomas Aquinas observed that creation is neither a movement nor a mutation. It is instead the foundational and continuing relationship that links the creature to the Creator, for He is the cause of every being and all becoming.[1]

5.1 *Conservation of the cosmos*

The Old Testament already furnishes a clear idea of God conserving His creation. In the book of Wisdom, God's love for what He has made is seen as the basis for His conserving action: How, had You not willed it, could a thing persist, how be conserved if not called forth by You? You spare all things because all things are Yours, Lord, lover of life' (Ws 11:25–26). Thus, the conservation of the world has two aspects. The first involves God's positive action upon His creature to maintain it in being. The second aspect is a negative one, consisting in the fact that the world is not destroyed and not abandoned to destructive forces, but is 'spared'. Nevertheless one creature can still be the object of an action for good or ill at the hands of another, since the cosmos is a system of mutual relationships. However, God always remains the first and supreme Cause, since in the final analysis every being remains in existence in virtue of His divine power. St Paul's reflections showed how Christ is the fulfilment of the Old Testament idea of Wisdom: 'All things were created through Him. Before anything was created, He existed, and He holds all things in unity' (Col 1:16–17). To the men of Athens, the Apostle taught that in God 'we live, and move, and exist' (Ac 17:28). The writer of the Letter to the Hebrews affirms that the Son sustains 'the universe by His powerful command' (Heb 1:3).

Although St Augustine maintained that God's conservation was a continuation of His work of creation, he showed that the effects of the two aspects of this one act were different. God rested from His work of creation in the sense that He no longer adds essentially new natures to the cosmos, but now through His conservation He maintains what already exists.[2] It is as a continuation of God's creative activity that St Augustine interpreted Jesus' words in the New Testament, 'My Father goes on working, and so do I' (Jn 5:17). If God ceased to conserve all of creation, it would fall back into nothingness.[3] Conservation presupposes the existence of beings which have already been created. God acts alone and in an immediate way in the act of creation, whereas in conserving His cosmos, He employs the order established in the creation so that some beings depend on others for their conservation.[4] Created beings are dependent on God that they exist at all, they are contingent upon the choice of God that they were brought into being. They are also dependent on God for their continued existence in being, thanks to His conservation, as St Athanasius pointed out:

> After making everything by His own eternal Word and bringing creation into existence, God did not abandon it to be carried away and suffer through its own nature, lest it run the risk of returning to nothing. But being good, He governs the whole world through His Word Who is Himself God, in order that creation, illuminated by the leadership, Providence, and ordering of the Word may be able to remain firm, since it shares in the Word Who is truly from the Father, and lest it suffer what would happen, I mean a relapse into non-existence, if it were not protected by the Word.[5]

Deism is the false notion according to which, having created the world, God leaves it to its own devices, or at best allows it not to be destroyed. This is the less-than-Christian approach proposed by Voltaire and others, where God is envisaged as a type of distant Clock-maker Who, having 'wound up' the cosmos in the act of creation, thereafter left the universe to its own devices. Deism leads to despair for it encourages the idea that God has deserted the work of His own hands. However, it would be equally mistaken to conceive the conservation of the cosmos as a completely new creation. 'The preservation of things in being by God is a continuation of that action whereby He gives existence, which action is without motion or time; so also the preservation of light in the air is by the continual influence of the sun.'[6] This raises the question as to how God's action at the beginning of the world is different qualitatively from His activity at all subsequent moments. Some would say that there is no essential difference, because God is performing one act outside of time which 'maintains the whole temporal sequence from its first moment onwards.'[7] On the other hand, it would seem to be necessary to stress the importance of the beginning of creation as a privileged moment at least from our point of view, lest one fall into the trap of ignoring the reality of the beginning of the cosmos, and then such a focus on the conservation of the cosmos without a due consideration of its beginning could lead to pantheism.

The question of Providence is related therefore to the doctrine that God is immanent or present within His creation, but at the same time transcends it. In the words of the author of the book of Wisdom, 'The Spirit of the

Lord fills the whole world, and that which holds all things together knows every word that is said' (Ws 1:7). St Augustine incisively expressed the same truth: 'O God, You who are so high above us and yet so close, hidden and yet always present, You have not parts, some greater and some smaller. You are everywhere, and everywhere You are entire.'[8] God's transcendence may be expressed by saying that all creation is present to Him and is open to His gaze (cf. Heb 4:13), and His immanence is formulated in the idea that God is present in His creation. If too much stress is put on the initial act of creation at the expense of the continuation of God's action in His Providence, one is not taking sufficient account of His immanence in the cosmos and so one falls victim to deism. If, on the other hand, the initial act of creation is by-passed leaving God's Providence isolated, there is a danger that God's transcendence as Creator is ignored, with the ensuing problem of pantheism.

Deism and pantheism are not the only errors which compromise an adequate picture of the conservation of the world by God; it is also jeopardized by a view in which God is seen to act everywhere in His creation, but in a voluntaristic and arbitrary way, which would deny coherence and rationality to the cosmos. This approach was exemplified in the thought of William of Ockham who so stressed God's sovereign will at the expense of cosmic rationality that he called into doubt the causal interconnection between the stars and the light produced by them. In this way 'reason was powerless to decide whether the light of stars had a real connection with the stars themselves.'[9] The occasionalism of the orthodox theological school of Islam (the Mutakallimun), and that of Malebranche bear a certain resemblance to Ockham's voluntarism. In occasionalism, the activity of particular beings is suppressed and God acts directly everywhere to supply this activity. On the other hand, in the Christian idea of Providence, God is responsible for the activity of particular beings, but through the laws which govern cosmic processes.

5.2 *Every created action depends upon God*

Since the scholastic period it has been commonly taught by theologians that God cooperates immediately in the action of every creature; this cooperation is given to every creature without exception and is given in an intrinsic way through intimate contact with every being. The word cooperation is used in an analogical sense, since it is more precise to say that man cooperates with God. This cooperation (or *concursus* as it is known in technical parlance) involves a working together of the First and secondary causes which unite to form one principle of action. The activity of the creature does not in any way render God's action unnecessary; by the same token God's action does not render unnecessary that of the creature, which is the second cause dependent on the First Cause.

Scripture and Tradition bear witness to the cooperating activity of God linked to His conservation of creation. In the Old Testament, God acts in the history of individuals and peoples. The Psalmist exclaims: 'Come and see what marvels God has done, so much to be feared for His deeds among mankind: He turned the sea into dry land, they crossed the river on foot' (Ps 66:5–6). The action of God in creation and in history is described by the book of Ecclesiasticus: 'By the words of the Lord His works come into being and all creation obeys His will... Let us praise illustrious men, our ancestors in their successive generations. The Lord has created an abundance of glory, and displayed His greatness from earliest times' (Si 42:15; 44:1–2). In the New Testament, St Paul affirms: 'It is God, for His own loving purpose, who puts both the will and action into you' (Ph 2:13). However, the Scriptures present the action of God and His creatures in a concrete way without entering into the philosophical and theological discussion of the relations between them.

Divine action does not take away the freedom of His creatures. Consideration of the interaction between God's action and that of His creature in terms of the liberty of the creature, brought about a controversy which is more fully dealt with in the theology of grace. The Thomist position teaches that God causes the very action of the creature. No potency can pass into act without a particular act on God's part. The action of the creature is not possible without immediate divine cooperation, and so the beginning of this act cannot take place without God's immediate influence, which precedes it, not so much in time, but in being. The divine initiative thus takes precedence over that of the creature. The Thomist approach is a logical development of the primacy of God's causality and the fact that all creatures are dependent on it. However, the difficulty is the reconciliation of human liberty with divine predetermination and also the problem of how to avoid saying that God is responsible in some way for human sin. The

Molinist approach rejects the notion of predetermination and simply proposes that God upholds the creature's action which has been begun already under the creature's own initiative.[10] This theory has the advantage of offering a better guarantee of human freedom but does not seem to safeguard sufficiently the essential dependence of all created actions on God. The dynamic of the interrelation between God's action and the activity of His creatures highlights one of many mysteries in the theology of creation.

5.3 *God's providential sovereignty*

Throughout the Old Testament, God's Providence is expressed in His calling and protection of the Jewish people, as can be seen for example in their liberation from Egypt and their sojourn in the desert as depicted in the book of Exodus. God's Providence forms the link between creation and salvation history, a tie which finds its culmination in the Incarnation of the Word. The book of Wisdom outlines a profound idea of Providence which also shows the influence of Greek philosophy:

> No doubt that ship is the product of a craving for gain,
> its building embodies the wisdom of the shipwright,
> but Your Providence, Father, is what steers it,
> You having opened a pathway even through the sea,
> a safe way over the waves (Ws 14:2–3).

The prophet Isaiah describes a maternal aspect to God's care for His people: 'Does a woman forget her baby at the breast, or fail to cherish the son of her womb? Yet even if these forget, I will never forget you' (Is 49:15). God guides and directs all created things to their proper end, as is illustrated in Judith's prayer: 'What is, what will be, You have planned; what has been, You designed. Your purposes stood forward; "See, here we are!" they said' (Jdt 9:5–6).

In the New Testament, Christ reveals the doctrine of Providence in its full light. With a graphic use of nature, Christ describes how the Father guides the cosmos and especially the human person in His Providence: 'Look at the birds in the sky. They do not sow or reap or gather into barns; yet your heavenly Father feeds them. Are you not worth more than they are? And why worry about clothing? Think of the flowers growing in the fields; they never have to toil or to spin; yet I assure you that not even Solomon in all his regalia was robed like one of these' (Mt 6:26, 28–29). Our Lord also affirms: 'Can you not buy five sparrows for two pennies? And yet not one is forgotten in God's sight. Why every hair on your head has been counted. There is no need to be afraid: you are worth more than hundreds of sparrows' (Lk 12: 6–7). However, the key to God's Providence is His Kingdom: 'Set your hearts on His Kingdom first, and on His righteousness, and all these other things will be yours as well' (Mt 6:33).

The orientation of Providence is not simply towards creation, but towards salvation. God works His purpose out in the Church on earth and His economy of salvation is brought to its completion at the end of the ages. The formulation of St John Damascene exemplifies the Church's concern to see God's act of creation and His provident ruling of the cosmos in the economy of one plan:

> We call Providence that care with which God looks after all existing beings. Or in other words, Providence is that Will of God which grants to all creatures the appropriate direction. He Who created beings and He Who provides for them must be One and the Same God. It would not be appropriate nor permitted that He Who provides should be different from He Who creates. God the Creator is provident: His creative, conserving and provident force is none other than His good Will.[11]

The First Vatican Council linked God's Providence with His presence within what He had made: 'By His Providence, God protects and governs all things which He has made, "reaching mightily from one end of earth to the other, and ordering all things well" (Ws 8:1).'[12] The Second Vatican Council located divine Providence in a pneumatological perspective, speaking of the Holy Spirit of God, Who 'with wondrous Providence, directs the course of time and renews the face of the earth.'[13]

The Christian doctrine of divine Providence is totally opposed to *fatalism* found in pagan religions and in ancient and modern superstition. Generally speaking, fatalism is the view which holds that all events in the history of the world, and, in particular, the actions and incidents which make up the story of each individual life, are determined by fate. Fatalistic systems conceived of a kind of cosmic destiny which arbitrarily determined the outcome of human actions, and so human freedom was limited. Sometimes in the ancient world, fate was conceived as an iron necessity in the nature of things, overruling and controlling the will and power of the gods themselves. There is no room anywhere for chance or contingency. All changes are simply the expression of unchanging law. There is an eternally established providence overruling the world, but it is in every respect immutable. The pagan view of an external, inevitable force coercing and controlling all action, whether human or divine, found itself in conflict with the conception of a free, personal, infinite God. Consequently, several of the early Christian writers were concerned to oppose and refute the theory of fate. The Islamic conception of God and His government of the world, the insistence on His unity and the absoluteness of the method of this rule as well as the Oriental tendency to belittle the individuality of man, were all favourable to the development of a theory of predestination approximating towards fatalism. Consequently, though there have been defenders of free will among Muslim teachers, yet the orthodox view which has prevailed most widely among the followers of the Prophet has been that all good and evil actions and events take place by the eternal decrees of God, which have been prescribed from all eternity. The more radical reformers of the sixteenth century like Calvin taught a doctrine of predestination scarcely less rigid than Muslim fatalism. With the new departure in philosophy and its separation from theology since the time of Descartes, the ancient pagan notion of an external fate, which had grown obsolete, was succeeded by or transformed into the theory of *necessarianism*.

Spinoza's pantheistic necessarianism is, however, perhaps the frankest and most rigid form of fatalism advocated by any leading modern philosopher. Starting from the idea of substance, which he so defines that there can be only one, he deduces in geometrical fashion all forms of being in the universe from this concept. This substance must be infinite and it evolves necessarily through an infinite number of attributes into an infinity of modes. The seemingly individual and independent beings of the world, minds and bodies, are merely these modes of the infinite substance. The whole world-process of actions and events is rigidly necessary in every detail; the concept of contingence, of possible beings other than those which exist, is purely illusory. Nothing is possible except what actually is. There is no free will in either God or man.

The Christian picture of divine Providence cannot be equated with *determinism*. This is a name employed to denote the theory that all man's volitions are invariably determined by pre-existing circumstances. A further distinction can be made between hard determinism where every event is caused and no one is responsible for their actions, and soft determinism which holds that rational creatures can be held responsible for determined actions as long as they are done voluntarily and without force or coercion.[14] Soft determinism can be also seen as *compatibilism*, whereby an act can be entirely determined and yet be free in the sense that it was done voluntarily and without compulsion.[15] Today the determinist philosophy that reigns supreme, almost uncontested, is Darwinism (also called naturalism). It attempts to explain all human behaviour in terms of our evolutionary past. Darwinism draws its power from the great respect people have for science and its representatives. However, current science contains many discoveries which suggest a more complicated picture than flat mechanistic determinism. Nevertheless, that view of the world and man dominates our culture. It is possible to give a response to the determinist whether Marxist, Freudian, Darwinist or some other kind, by asking 'how is possible that you have risen above the irrational forces which blind the rest of us? No doubt, you are smarter than I but how can you be freer if we are all predetermined?' The determinist is like a person sitting on tree limb which he cuts off with his own philosophical saw. If all judgments are the product of irrational forces, why pay any attention to one he just made? All forms of determinism are at odds with the Christian picture of God who is personal and free, and whose freedom is mirrored in man's own freedom.

Man was at the fateful mercy of cosmic forces before being liberated by Christian revelation and hence was often regarded as an insignificant and helpless creature in world pictures outside of the Judaeo-Christian tradition. Indeed the Christian doctrine of Providence reinforces a healthy optimism and confidence concerning the position of man and woman in the cosmos. In this vision, God transcends the cosmos and is not bound by its laws, which nevertheless generally bind man. These cosmic laws are ordained by God for the good of man. Human destiny is guided by God according to His plan or economy of salvation 'the hidden plan He so kindly made in Christ from the beginning to act upon when the times had run their course to the end: that He would bring everything together under Christ, as Head, everything in the heavens and everything on earth' (Ep 1:9–10). Moreover, 'we know that by turning everything to their good God cooperates with all those who love Him, with all those that He has called according to His purpose' (Rm 8:28). However, the Judge of this good is God, and sometimes we are unable to discern what is truly for the best. Thus the ways of God's economy are very often veiled from us so that we have to live in faith and hope. Thus it is necessary to avoid a facile view of Providence which attempts to read infallibly every event according to a private interpretation of God's plan. Only at the end when we live through vision 'face to face' (1 Co 13:12), will it be possible to see clearly the ways, including those of suffering, through which God had guided us in order that we may finally enter His Sabbath rest.[16]

The Christian idea of Providence also radically differs from a *chance* or *chaotic* vision of the cosmos and of human affairs. It is precisely divine Providence as the transcendent wisdom of the Creator which makes the world a cosmos rather than a chaos.[17] Many secular humanists would extend the theory of evolution unwarrantedly from the scientific into the philosophical realm so as to explain away the emergence of the cosmos, of life and of human beings as the product of blind chance. Instead of creation and Providence, these thinkers would propose a mere interplay of statistical laws. They would ignore the common-sense axiom 'Nothing can give what it has not got' (*Nemo dat quod non habet*) and also the law of causality, and so would allow the cosmos to be a sufficient cause and explanation unto itself. As soon as chance is allowed a foothold in the evolution of the universe and of man, it then maintains its stranglehold on human affairs which are then seen as merely fortuitous, rather than providential. The other side of the coin of chance is that of cosmic necessity which limits human freedom and undermines the revealed picture of divine Providence. The concept of God cannot be reduced to that of a type of cosmic computer programmer, in a cybernetic vision of reality. For the Christian, God is not a 'force' which rules the universe as often seen in the world of science fiction, but a loving Father who guides and governs everything through His Son in the power of the Holy Spirit; in this way the cosmos 'is sustained by the love of its Maker'.[18] Therefore Providence as well as creation must always be framed in a Trinitarian context.

A distinction can be made between general Providence for the universe, a special Providence for men and a very special Providence for the supernatural order in grace and revelation, in the Church and among the just (1P 5:7). Providence must always be set in the context of God's plan and purpose for the cosmos and the creatures in it, an economy of salvation which is recapitulated in Christ. There is thus a hierarchy in the ordering of God's providential action, with no obligation that there should be total equality, because God is free in the distribution of His gifts, as can be seen in the parable of the vineyard workers (Mt 20:1–16).

5.4 *Legitimate autonomy in the created order*

God generally directs and governs His creation via secondary causality, through the laws which He has inscribed upon the cosmos. God not only gives His creatures existence, but also allows them to perform their own actions, to be secondary causes and thus to collaborate with God in His loving economy. He is the

First Cause who works in and through second causes. Created beings, especially if they are rational, become 'God's fellow workers' (Cf. 1 Co 3:9). St Thomas Aquinas affirms:

> God created all things immediately, but in the creation itself He established an order among things, so that some depend on others, by which they are preserved in being, though He remains the principal cause of their preservation.[19]

For example, the angels cooperate with God in looking after the human person, as has already been seen.[20] When He allows His human creatures to participate in His Providential governing action, God raises the dignity of those creatures. This is most eminently true in the cooperation of the Blessed Virgin Mary in God's plan, in her rôle of intercession and distribution of all graces. This is another way in which the Christian vision of the human person and creation is optimistic and confident in contrast to all ancient and modern pagan views. In a certain sense, the human person who is rational and free is allowed to complete God's work of creation, bringing out its harmony, for the good of one and all. By failing to cooperate with God's plan concerning creation, man has disfigured the cosmos and brought dishonour upon himself. However through active collaboration with God's economy of salvation, human beings truly become 'fellow workers with God' (1 Co 3:9; cf. Col 1:24).[21]

What God has made enjoys a certain degree of inner coherence: 'By the very nature of creation, material being is endowed with its own stability, truth and excellence, its own order and laws… It is God the conserver of all things, Who made them what they are.'[22] The fact that creation has its own stability implies that the cosmos is coherent; if this stability were missing, and collapse were evident at many points, the creation would have to propped up. The stability of the creation according to its own laws gives it a relative autonomy; the cosmos is always dependent on God, but in a way that still allows it to have its own proper existence. Indeed, this concept of the relative autonomy of creation helps fend off any danger of confusing God with what He has made, and so safeguards the Christian vision against pantheism in its various forms.

From the idea of the autonomy of creation, flows the consideration of the rightful autonomy of earthly affairs, in which man and society should function according to the laws which the Creator has inscribed upon them. However, any false interpretation of this autonomy should be rejected, including the idea that 'material being does not depend on God and that man can use it as if it had no relation to its Creator.' Christian tradition affirms with great clarity that 'without a Creator there can be no creature' and 'once God is forgotten, the creature is lost sight of as well.'[23] The autonomy of creation should not be understood in the Kantian sense either, where man was so cut off from the rest of reality that he could have no access via reason to the universe, the soul and God.[24] The laws which God in His Providence inscribes upon His creation, so endowing it with a stability of its own represent a further expression of His immanence.[25] The idea of the autonomy of creation would be illegitimate and contrary to the truth of revelation if it proclaimed the 'independence of created things from God the Creator'. Whenever autonomy is misunderstood in this way, man separates himself from the Creator and His laws, he perverts creation and is reduced to the unhappy state of being in slavery to creation.[26]

The application of the concept of autonomy can be applied to the question of relations between science and religion.[27] However, it can also deal with relations between Church and State, which are beyond the scope of this present work. Suffice it to say that the full understanding of these relations and their implementation in practice has not so far been completely worked out. A simple rejection of the confessional state seems rather one-sided, especially since the replacement of the same with a pluralist society based on purely secular forces has been seen to reap disastrous results in recent years. It seems evident that a simple return to an ecclesiastical state would not be the solution. However, the tradition of the Church has always maintained that society should be ordered on Christian principles, and the sphere of competence of the same Church cannot be restricted simply to spiritual matters.[28]

5.5 *Miracles*

A miracle is said to occur when God intervenes in a special way so that events do not run according to the laws of causality which He has inscribed in His creation. More precisely, the Thomistic definition of miracles includes 'those things which God does outside those causes which we know'.[29] The act of creation itself is not a miracle in the strict sense, since it does not proceed from any other created cause. It cannot be said to be an exception to the order of nature, because it does not belong to that order.[30] When St Thomas speaks of things done outside of causes that we know, the question arises whether more precisely an action could be miraculous in the full sense if it were done according to causes which were *at present* outside of human knowledge but later may become known or discovered by science. This clarification is required to avoid classifying as miraculous that which is at present beyond science but one day might not be; this eschews the problem of the 'God of the gaps.' Miracles occur according to the good pleasure of God, for the benefit of His people and are thus part of His special providential care of creation.

The Old Testament supplies a wealth of examples of God's miraculous intervention in nature, especially in the context of the liberation of the chosen people from slavery in Egypt. Moses and Aaron were granted miraculous powers in order to try and convince Pharaoh to let the Jewish people go (Ex 7:8–13). The fact that Aaron was able to turn his staff into a serpent did not convince Pharaoh, since his own magicians were able to do the same by their witchcraft. This is already an indication that miracles are not of themselves a proof of divine intervention, so a process of discernment is required to see whether they come from God, from human powers not yet fully understood, or from the evil one. It is however significant that when Pharaoh's magicians turned their staffs into serpents, 'Aaron's staff swallowed up the staffs of the magicians' (Ex 7:12), as if to indicate that God's miraculous power is infinitely greater that of any other force, be it human or diabolical.

The nine plagues inflicted upon the Egyptians were also miraculous (Ex 7:14–10:23). The Crossing of the Red Sea (Ex 13:17–14:31) was a further miracle, in which the Israelites crossed the sea on dry ground with the waters piled up 'to right and left of them' (Ex 14:22). It is significant that the angel of God played a part in this wonder (Ex 14:19). The miracles of the Old Testament are actions of God upon the cosmos, which alter the normal rhythm of its causality, in the context of the economy of salvation. Thus, in a miraculous occurrence, the order of creation is taken up in a special way into the order of grace and salvation:

> For, to keep Your children from all harm,
> the whole creation, obedient to your commands,
> was once more, and newly, fashioned in its nature.
> Overshadowing the camp there was the cloud,
> where water had been, dry land was seen to rise,
> the Red Sea became an unimpeded way,
> the tempestuous flood a green plain;
> sheltered by Your hand, the whole nation passed across,
> gazing at these amazing miracles (Ws 19:6–8).

God acts in such a way to help His chosen people: He helps them directly in their immediate need, in this case, of escaping from the Egyptians. However, the miracles are not merely for a practical purpose, but rather they manifest God's love for His people in such a way as to arouse faith and devotion. Furthermore, these events are also signs which prefigure the fulness of revelation in the New Testament. The miraculous crossing of the Red Sea foreshadows the Redemption wrought by Christ and Christian baptism:

> The Jews saw miracles. You will see greater and more glorious miracles than those which accompanied the exodus of the Jews from Egypt. You did not see Pharaoh and his troops drowning; but you saw the devil and his armies overwhelmed by flood waters. The Jews passed through the sea; you have passed through death. They were snatched from the grasp of the Egyptians; you from the grip of demons. The Jews cast off a foreign yoke; you the much more galling slavery of sin.[31]

In the New Testament, Jesus performed many miracles. Some were signs like the changing of water into wine at Cana in Galilee or the multiplication of the loaves. Others involved the healing of the sick, the casting out of demons and the raising from the dead of Jairus' daughter and Lazarus. Others again invoked power over the elements such as the calming of the storm on Lake Galilee. These signs wrought by Christ bear witness that He is sent by the Father in the power of the Holy Spirit and therefore miracles evoke faith in Jesus Christ as Son of God. The purpose of Jesus' miracles was not to arouse curiosity nor a desire for the magical, as Ronald Knox pointed out: 'We mustn't let people think of Our Lord's miracles as if they were a set of theatre performances, thrown out by a well-known preacher in order to draw attention to himself. They are part of His message; a sign-language between heaven and earth, pictures of eternity cast on to the screen of time.'[32] Christ's miracles did not automatically produce faith, and indeed some people rejected Him despite the evident signs (Cf. Jn 11:47–48). When Our Lord freed some people from such earthly evils as hunger, injustice, sickness and death, He worked signs of the Kingdom of heaven and did not eliminate all earthly evils. Even those who were the subject of Jesus' miracles still had to suffer. For example, Lazarus must have had to die again at a later stage. Thus, Jesus came to free men and women from the greater evil and slavery of sin.[33] The miracles of Jesus had great importance in the preaching of St Peter and the Apostles: 'Jesus the Nazarene was a Man commended to you by God by the miracles and portents and signs that God worked through Him when He was among you' (Ac 2:22). The supreme sign of Christ's divinity is His Redemptive act and in particular His Resurrection from the dead. In the power of Christ's Resurrection, the Apostles also performed miracles in Christ's name, as when St Peter cured a lame man: 'I have neither silver nor gold, but I will give you what I have: in the name of Jesus Christ the Nazarene, walk!' (Ac 3:6).

Our Lord's miracles were not merely symbols,[34] rather they were historical events richly endowed with theological and symbolic meaning. The transformation of the water into wine and the multiplication of the loaves are prefigurations of the Eucharist. Miracles are of considerable importance as a sign of the credibility of divine revelation:

> In order that the obedience of our faith be nevertheless in harmony with reason, God willed that exterior proofs of His revelation,... especially miracles and prophecies, should be joined to the interior helps of the Holy Spirit; as they manifestly display the omnipotence and infinite knowledge of God, they are the most certain signs of the divine revelation, adapted to the intelligence of all men.[35]

Scriptural accounts indicate the possibility of miracles, which are not simply to be dismissed as myths; these wondrous signs can be recognized with certainty.[36] Miracles did not of course end within the Church at the time of the Apostles, but in the lives of holy men and women, God continues to grant extraordinary graces to His Church throughout history. The why, when and wherefore of miraculous intervention lie among the secrets of divine Providence, but these are surely signs of God's intervention among His people at various points in time, consolations which arouse and encourage faith, hope and love.

It is interesting to consider that miracles nearly always involve some natural 'raw material', a natural course of events which is changed for some greater good. In this way the miracle presupposes an already-existing order of creation and Providence. There are two opposite dangers with miracles: one is that of the rationalists who deny that they happen at all. The other is to propose that they happen indiscriminately all the time or that they are a necessary part of the natural cosmos. In the former category fall many modern thinkers after the Enlightenment who are suspicious of anything which smacks of the supernatural, anything which can point from within creation to the existence of its Creator. The second error is common among those who wish to over-spiritualize creation, or those who deny that it has been endowed with a true value of its own, or further those who would say that the creation is so destroyed after the Fall that there is no longer any nature, but only supernature. Among the exponents of the latter error would be Ockham who with his occasionalism so over exaggerated the will of God at the expense of His rationality, that every action of Providence is a separate sovereign command, disconnected from every other sovereign command and which each time amounts to a miraculous intervention of God in His creation. Certain pietistic currents in both Catholic and Protestant spirituality, which derive from a pessimistic view of creation, make it a necessity that God act everywhere in a miraculous way to prop up what has become a very defective system as a result of original sin.

A balanced view of the miraculous was expressed with great beauty by Ronald Knox:

> Our Lord's coming, if it was what we think it was, must be regarded as nothing less than an invasion of the natural by the supernatural world. And when it is confronted with the supernatural, the reaction of the natural world can only express itself in miracle... Richard Crashaw, the poet, was asked to write a copy of Latin verses about the miracle at Cana in Galilee... I have seen it quoted in different forms, but the form I like best is *Vidit et erubuit conscia lympha Deum*—the conscious water saw its Lord and blushed. The conscious water, caught out in being what it was, just natural water, in the presence of something supernatural.[37]

The miraculous is thus the irruption according to divine Providence of the supernatural into the natural order so that the natural order is altered in some fashion. However God's intervention is not arbitrary, and while the reasons for a miracle cannot immediately and always be discerned, it is always a part of the economy of revelation and salvation. Miracles can thus be viewed in terms of the partial penetration of the New Creation into the present order.[38]

Within the perspective of how God conserves, governs and cares for His creation, one important aspect was not squarely faced, namely that Providence guides creation in the face of the evil and imperfection which has entered into the cosmos; evil cannot thwart God's Providence. The origin and nature of this problem will be dealt with in the coming chapter.

Further Reading

S. L. Jaki, *Miracles and Physics* (Front Royal, VA: Christendom Press, 1989)

C. S. Lewis, *Miracles. A Preliminary Study* (London: Collins, 1960)

L. Scheffczyk, *Creation and Providence* (London / New York: Burns and Oates / Herder and Herder, 1970)

Notes

1 See Pope Benedict XVI, *Discourse to the Pontifical Academy of Sciences* (31 October 2008). Cf. St Thomas Aquinas, *Summa Theologiae*, I, q.45, a. 3.

2 The human souls which God creates out of nothing every day (as seen in §4.2.2 above) are new in the sense that each constitutes a different person, but they do not make up a new *nature*.

3 See St Augustine, *De Genesi ad litteram* Book 4, chapter 12, nn.22–23 in *PL* 34, 304–305.

4 See St Thomas Aquinas, *Summa Theologiae* I, q.104, a.2.

5 St Athanasius, *Oratio contra gentes* n.41, in *PG* 25, 83–84.

6 St Thomas Aquinas, *Summa Theologiae* I, q.104, a.1.

7 See E. L. Mascall, *Christian Theology and Natural Science* (London: Longmans, Green and Co, 1957), pp. 148–149.

8 St Augustine, *Confessions* Book 6, chapter 3 in *PL* 32, 721. Translation into English with an Introduction by R. S. Pine-Coffin (Harmondsworth: Penguin, 1961) p. 115. See also *Confessions* Book 3, chapter 6 in *PL* 32, 688: 'You were deeper than my inmost understanding and higher than the topmost height that I could reach.' (*interior intimo meo et superior summo meo*).

9 S. L. Jaki, *The Road of Science and the Ways to God* (Edinburgh: Scottish Academic Press, 1978) pp. 42 and 347 who cites William of Ockham *Quodlibeta septem*, Quodlibet 6, qu.6, 'Whether there can be intuitive knowledge of a non-existent object.'

10 Molinism is the name given to the theological system elaborated by the Jesuit, L. Molina (died 1600). This approach, in contrast to the Thomist approach of D. Bañez (died 1604), sought to defend the liberty of the creature with respect to God's foreknowledge of the free actions of His rational creatures.

11 St John Damascene, *De fide orthodoxa*, Book 2, Chapter 29 in *PG* 94, 963–964.

12 Vatican I, Dogmatic Constitution *Dei Filius*, Chapter I in DS 3003; English translation in ND 413.

13 Vatican II, *Gaudium et Spes* 26.4.

14 See L. P. Pojman, *Philosophy: The Quest for Truth* (New York: Wadsworth Publishing Company, 1996), p. 586.

15 *Ibid.*, p. 596.

16 See *CCC* 314.

17 See Pope John Paul II, *Discourse at General Audience* (14 May 1986), §4 in *IG* 9/1 (1986), p. 1413. The Pope used this formulation on another occasion at his discourse to the Pontifical Academy of Sciences (31 October 1992): 'Those who engage in scientific and technological research admit, as the premise of its progress that the world is not a chaos but a "cosmos", that is to say, that there exist order and natural laws which

can be grasped and examined.' From *OR* 132/254 (1 November 1992), p. 8.

18 Vatican II, *Gaudium et Spes*, 2.2.

19 St Thomas Aquinas, *Summa Theologiae* I, q.104, a.2.

20 See pp. 34–44, 55, 58–59 above.

21 Cf. *CCC* 306–308, 372–373.

22 Vatican II, *Gaudium et Spes* 36.1.

23 *Ibid*, 36.2.

24 See my work *Creation and Scientific Creativity* (Leominster: Gracewing, 2009), pp. 67, 119–120.

25 See Pope John Paul II, *Discourse at General Audience* (2 April 1986), §1.

26 Cf. *ibid.*, 3.

27 This will be seen in chapter eight, pp. 233, 235, 241–245 below.

28 Among the documents of the Church which condemn the principle of the separation of Church and State are Pius IX, Encyclical Letter *Quanta cura* in DS 2893–2896 and the *Syllabus* in DS 2955 and 2977; Pius XII, *Allocution to the Sacred College and to the Bishops* (2 November 1954) in *AAS* 46 (1954) pp. 666–677, especially p. 671 where it is noted that the power of the Church cannot be restricted solely to the religious sphere, but touches on all the matters of the natural law. The Second Vatican Council is nuanced in its position for it affirms on the one hand that 'the political community and the Church are autonomous and independent of each other in their own fields' (*Gaudium et Spes* 76.3). On the other hand it refers to the Catholic who 'ceaselessly and efficaciously seeks for the return of all humanity and all its goods under Christ the Head in the unity of His Spirit' (*Lumen gentium*, 13.2). For further discussion of this topic see also P. Haffner, *Mystery of the Church* (Leominster: Gracewing, 2007), pp. 229-261.

29 St Thomas Aquinas, *Summa Theologiae* I, q.105, a.7.

30 Cf. *ibid.*

31 St John Chrysostom, *Catechesis to catechumens* 3, 24 in *SC* 50, p. 165.

[32] R. A. Knox, *The Hidden Stream* (London: Burns Oates, 1952), p. 104.

[33] See *CCC* 548–549.

[34] See the *Syllabus* of condemned errors of the modernists, and in particular the error which regards miracles as 'poetic fictions' in DS 2907, English translation in ND [112/7].

[35] Vatican I, Dogmatic Constitution *Dei Filius* on the Catholic Faith, Chapter III, in DS 3009. English translation in ND 119. See also canon 4 on chapter III in DS 3033, English translation in ND 127.

[36] Cf. *Ibid*, canon 5 on chapter III in DS 3034, English translation in ND 128.

[37] Knox, *The Hidden Stream*, pp. 99–100.

[38] For more on the New Creation, see chapter ten below.

6

Creation and Evil

He lay a grovelling babe upon the ground,
Polluted in the blood of his first sire,
With his whole essence shatter'd and unsound,
And coil'd around his heart a demon dire,
Which was not of his nature, but had skill
To bind and form his op'ning mind to ill.

John Henry Newman, *The Dream of Gerontius*

Until this point in the unfolding of the mystery of creation, evil has hardly made its presence felt. The reason for a delayed treatment of this problem was to stress the basic goodness of what God had made, and only then against this background could a discussion begin concerning the darker side of the cosmos. So only now will the Fall of the some of the angels and the original sin of Adam and Eve be treated, as well as some of the consequences of these sins.

6.1 *The sin of the angels*

The angels were created good, and now it remains to see how some of them fell from their state of friendship with God. Traditionally, the sin of some of the angels is linked to a 'period' of probation that the angels had to undergo before being admitted to the beatific vision; however we know nothing from divine revelation concerning the nature and length of this period. Newman describes the trial period of the angels in poetic fashion:

The Angels, as beseemingly
  To spirit-kind was given,
At once were tried and perfected,
  And took their seats in heaven.

For them no twilight or eclipse;
  No growth and no decay:
'Twas hopeless, all-engulfing night,
  Or beatific day.[1]

In the Middle Ages, it was disputed whether or not the angels received grace in the moment of their creation, or in some later 'stage'.[2] There was also a discussion as to whether the fallen angels had ever possessed grace for a while, since being in a state of grace does not prevent an angel from sinning. While God is by His very nature absolutely impeccable, a created rational being participates by gift in God's impeccability only once it has attained the beatific vision and thus can no longer fall from this state of glory. St Thomas maintained that the angels were given grace in the moment of their creation; this grace was the seed of glory, and divine providence progressively guided the angels to their perfection.[3]

There was thus a stage at which the angels had to make a choice for God or against Him. St Anselm explains that this free will is necessary so that the good angels can really be considered good. If the good angels had been incapable of sinning, then they kept goodness not by their own ability but by necessity. Therefore, they would no more have merited grace from God because they remained standing while the others fell, than because they preserved rationality, which they were unable to lose. Thus they would not rightly be called just.[4] The good angels, before entering into glory, thus made a single act of supernatural love for God, with which they merited that state; with a second act, they actually entered into possession of it.[5] The evil angels also made a meritorious act immediately after their creation, like the good angels; however, their sin immediately blocked their entry into glory.[6]

The good angels chose God as the supreme and definitive Good, known to the intellect enlightened by Revelation. To have chosen God means that they turned to Him with all the interior force of their freedom, which means they loved Him totally. God became the total and definitive scope of their spiritual existence. The others instead turned their backs on God contrary to the truth of the knowledge which indicated Him as the total and definitive good. Their choice ran counter to the revelation of the mystery of God, to His grace which made them partakers of the Trinity and of the eternal friendship with God in communion with Him through love. On the basis of their created freedom they made a radical and irreversible choice on a parity with that of the good angels, but diametrically opposed to it. Instead of accepting a God full of love they rejected Him, inspired by a false sense of self-sufficiency, of aversion and even of hatred which becomes rebellion.[7]

However, what kind of sin did the angels commit? In a Jewish apocryphal work known as the first book of

Enoch (which finds certain echoes in Genesis 6:1–4 and in the letter of Jude 14–15), the legend runs that two hundred angels seeing the beauty of the daughters of men decided, along with their head, to unite themselves sexually with these women, and from this union a race of giants was born to whom the fallen angels taught magic arts. As a result of this, suffering increased among men, and God decide to punish mankind by means of the flood. The giants then fought among themselves, while the fallen angels were locked away under the earth by the faithful archangels Raphael and Michael. Some Fathers, including St Irenaeus, St Justin, St Cyprian, and Tertullian maintained that the sin of the fallen angels was of a sexual nature. These writers were not always clear about this explanation and sometimes thought that the sin of sexual misconduct had been preceded by another spiritual sin like envy or pride. In any case, by the fourth century after Christ, there evolved a clearer idea of the nature of the angels, who were increasingly envisaged to be without a body and thus different from the human being, so that a carnal angelic sin was gradually excluded. According to St John Chrysostom, it would be blasphemous and stupid to interpret Genesis 6:4 (which referred to the fact that 'the sons of God resorted to the daughters of man, and had children by them') in the sense of a sexual sin committed by the angels. After all, the angels sinned *before* Adam and Eve, and their incorporeal nature is not capable of such sins.[8]

A second opinion among the Fathers concerning the devil's sin was that some angels were envious of man or refused to see in him the image of God. This idea is to be found in St Irenaeus, St Gregory of Nyssa, St Augustine and others. For St Irenaeus, the devil's apostasy had its root in envy of man, and Satan sought to make man rebel against his Creator.[9] According to Suarez, after having endowed the angels with grace, God revealed to them the image of Christ, God made Man, and commanded that they should recognize Him as their Head, their Lawgiver and the Author of their salvation. Lucifer refused to adore the sacred humanity of Christ, and thus failed to worship the Second Person of the Blessed Trinity, and also drew other angels into his rebellion, a most grave sin of pride and disobedience.[10] The fallen angels adored themselves instead of God. The advantage of this formulation of spirit sin is that it brings to life the idea of a period of angelic probation, and also highlights the relation between Christ and the angels. The basic concept is that pride is at the root of envy, and it is indeed pride which is the third approach to the devil's sin as perceived by the Fathers. Origen, St Gregory Nazianzen, St Athanasius, St Ambrose, St Augustine, St Leo the Great, St Gregory the Great and others see spirit sin lying in the fact that the devil wished to become equal to God. This approach seems probable also in the light of the Fall of Adam and Eve which mirrored the sin of Satan, who tempted our first parents along the lines of his own sin: 'God knows in fact that on the day you eat it your eyes will be opened and you will be like gods, knowing good and evil' (Gn 3:5). St Paul also seems to have regarded the devil's sin as one of pride (1 Tm 3:6). This sin can be conceived in various ways, either in terms of a desire for domination or as the devil's disordered appraisal of his own self. The differences in explaining the sin of pride are not however of great importance; the essential point is rather that it is a most grave offence against God, which merited the most serious of punishments.

Christian tradition has commonly used a text from the prophet Isaiah to indicate the fall of the prince of the demons who was symbolized by a pagan tyrant:

How did you come to fall from the heavens,
Daystar, son of dawn?
How did you come to be thrown to the ground,
you who enslaved the nations?
You who used to think to yourself,
'I will climb up to the heavens;
and higher than the stars of God
I will set my throne…
I will rival the Most High.'
What! Now you have fallen to Sheol
to the very bottom of the abyss! (Is 14:12–15)

It is significant that the word 'Daystar, son of Dawn' is rendered in the Vulgate by Lucifer, the name commonly given to the devil. It is not possible, however, to give a complete idea of the Fall of the angels from this text alone. An allusion to the sin of the devil is also found in the book of the Apocalypse:

> And now war broke out in heaven, when Michael with his angels attacked the dragon. The dragon fought back with his angels, but they were defeated and driven out of heaven. The great dragon, the primeval serpent, known as the devil or Satan, who had deceived all the world, was hurled down to the earth and his angels were hurled down with him (Rv 12:7–9).

However, this passage does not deal with the sin by which some angels became devils, since the time sequence already involves the fact that the devil 'had deceived all the world'; rather the passage describes the triumph of Christ in the Church against Satan. Christ refers to the sin of the devil in the following terms: 'He was a murderer from the start; he was never grounded in the truth; there is no truth in him at all: when he lies he is drawing on his own store, because he is a liar, and the father of lies' (Jn 8:44). For this reason, he lives in radical and irreversible denial of God, and seeks to impose on creation—on the other beings created in the image of God, and in particular on people—his own tragic lie about the good that is God.[11] In this condition of existential falsehood, Satan—according to St. John—also becomes a 'murderer' (Jn 8:44), that is one who destroys the supernatural life which God had made to dwell from the beginning in him and in the creatures made in the likeness of God: the other pure spirits and men. Satan wishes to destroy life lived in accordance with the truth, life in the fullness of good, the supernatural life of grace and love. The author of the Book of Wisdom writes: 'death has entered the world through the envy of the devil, and those who belong to him experience it' (Ws 2:24).[12]

A further description of diabolical sin is to be found in the letter of Jude: 'Next let me remind you of the angels who had supreme authority but did not keep to it and left their appointed sphere; He has kept them down in the dark, in spiritual chains, to be judged on the great day' (Jude 6). This text seems to imply the element of disobedience in the diabolic sin, since the fallen spirits 'left their appointed sphere'. The Second Letter of St Peter is very similar to that of Jude: 'When angels sinned, God did not spare them: He sent them down to the underworld and consigned them to the dark underground caves to be held there till the day of Judgement' (2 P 2:4).

The inspired Scriptures are very circumspect about the sin and nature of the devil and his fallen angels, only teaching the essentials necessary for salvation. In this way they discourage any unhealthy fascination with the powers of evil. Nevertheless, from the New Testament it is clear that there are many fallen angels. When Christ asked the man possessed by demons for the name of the fallen spirit, he answered: 'My name is legion, for there are many of us' (Mk 5:9). When the unclean spirits were then expelled from the Gerasene demoniac, they entered a herd of about two thousand pigs. The names or characters of the individual devils are not important in the history of salvation. However, there is a certain unity in diabolic action, at least for a time: Satan can continue because he is not divided in himself (Mt 12:24). Among the demons, one stands out, Satan, the prince of demons (Mt 9:34; Mk 3:22). Jesus makes such a distinction when he refers to 'the devil and his angels' (Mt 25:41) and St Paul refers to 'an angel of Satan' (2 Co 12:7). Satan had a prime rôle in the original rebellion of the angels, seducing other angels into sinning. This idea is reinforced by the description of the dragon in the Apocalypse whose tail dragged 'a third of the stars from the sky and dropped them to the earth' (Rv 12:4). The passage has been interpreted as the seduction of one third of the angelic host by Satan, since stars in the Scripture are symbolic for angels. In any case, it would seem inconsistent with God's goodness that there should exist more demons than good angels. Differences in the diabolic hosts can be explained on the basis of the natural perfections which remained in the demons after their Fall or in terms of the various degrees of punishment inflicted on them. St Gregory the Great and St Thomas Aquinas inclined to the view that Lucifer was previously the very highest spirit of all, since the devil's sin was that of pride and the motive for pride is excellence, which was greater in the higher spirits.[13]

The demons were punished with the loss of grace and the eternal loss of the beatific vision as well as a further eternal punishment as is clear from Our Lord's words: 'Go away from me, with your curse upon you, to the eternal fire prepared for the devil and his angels' (Mt 25:41). This fire was not, however, 'prepared since the foundation of the world' (Mt 25:34) like the kingdom of heaven. In the book of the Apocalypse it is stated that at the end of time the devil and his armies 'will be thrown into the lake of fire and sulphur, where the beast and the false prophet are, and their torture will not stop, day or night, for ever and ever' (Rv 20:10). Origen's theory of final restoration (known as *apokatastasis*) allowed fallen angels and damned human beings to be returned to a state of purity, but this was based on a mistaken notion that the goodness of God could not permit any other end than the final happiness of all beings: this theory undermines free will. The idea was effectively condemned under Pope Vigilius in the year 543,[14] as well as by the Fourth Lateran Council in 1215, which stated that the wicked would suffer 'perpetual punishment with the devil'.[15]

The gravity of the angelic sin lies in the fact that a pure spirit, with so high an intellectual perfection and so powerful a will, should have sought its own happiness without reference to God. The angelic sin was committed with full knowledge, either refusing the beatific vision or desiring it as a right rather than a grace. The fundamental option of an angel is immutable, and this flows from the doctrine that a pure spirit knows and wills intuitively and is absolutely free from any action of the senses.[16] The fallen angels are thus damned eternally, and the change of the place of damnation alluded to in the Book of Revelation ('thrown into the lake of fire and sulphur'—Rv 20:10) signifies that before the final judgement, the demons are permitted to fight against the Kingdom of God, but once the Kingdom comes to final fruition they will no longer be allowed to do so. According to the New Testament, before the universal judgement, the time has not yet come (Mt 8:29) in which Satan must be thrown into the abyss (Lk 8:32) but he lives in the air (Ep 2:2; 6:12). The devil is the enemy, 'prowling round like a roaring lion, looking for someone to eat' (1 P 5:8).

Already in the Old Testament, the devil opposed the just as can be seen in the case of Job. God allows such a temptation within certain limits, for, in regard to Job He orders Satan: 'But keep your hands off his person' (Jb 1:12) and 'spare his life' (Jb 2:6). The permission of evil by God is based on the premise that somehow a greater good will come of it; in the case of Job, God's Providence can eventually be seen in a clearer light and proclaimed to others; moreover all Job's fortunes are in some way eventually restored. The devil tries to struggle against Christ and His Kingdom, but is already defeated by His very coming (Jn 16:11); the demons know that Christ has come to destroy them (Mk 1:24). When Jesus goes into the desert to prepare His public ministry, the devil tries to tempt Him away from His true mission (see Mt 4:1–11). Since in Jesus there was no concupiscence, the temptations all consist in using His power in ways which would contrast with His mission which was not of this world. The disciples of Christ are also given power to overcome the assaults of the evil one, and Jesus tells them on their return from a mission:

> I watched Satan fall like lightning from heaven. Yes, I have given you power to tread underfoot serpents and scorpions and the whole strength of the enemy; nothing shall ever hurt you. Yet do not rejoice that the spirits submit to you; rejoice rather that your names are written in heaven (Lk 10:18–20).

With this last rejoinder, Our Lord reminds the disciples not to focus their attention on the powers of evil, but rather on God's goodness. The Church has also always had this attitude, discouraging any unhealthy interest in the fallen angels.

As the result of the sin of our first parents, the devil has acquired a certain dominion over man. This is the doctrine that finds a dramatic expression in the liturgy of baptism, when the catechumen is asked to renounce the devil and all his empty promises. In Sacred Scripture we find various indications of this influence on man and on the dispositions of his spirit (and of his body). In the Bible, Satan is called 'the prince of this world' (cf. Jn

12:31; 14:30; 16:11), and even 'the god of this world' (2 Co 4:4). We find many other names that describe his nefarious relationship with man: 'Beelzebul' or 'Belial, 'unclean spirit': 'tempter', 'evil one' and even 'Antichrist' (1 Jn 4:3). He is compared to a 'lion' (1 P 5:8), to a 'dragon' (in Revelation) and to a 'serpent'(Gn 3). Very frequently, he is designated by the name 'devil': from the Greek *diaballein* (hence *diabolos*), which means: to 'cause destruction, to divide, to calumniate, to deceive'. All this takes place through the working of the evil spirit who is presented by Sacred Scripture as a person, while it is declared that he is not alone: 'there are many of us' as the devils cry out to Jesus in the region of the Gerasenes (Mk 5:9); and Jesus, speaking of the future judgment, speaks of 'the devil and his angels' (cf. Mt 25:41).[17]

According to Sacred Scripture, and especially the New Testament, the dominion and the influence of Satan and of the other evil spirits embraces all the world. The words of the Apostle John, 'The whole world lies under the power of the evil one' (1 Jn 5:19), allude also to the presence of Satan in the history of humanity, a presence which becomes all the more acute when man and society depart from God. The influence of the evil spirit can conceal itself in a more profound and effective way: it is in his interests to make himself unknown. Satan has the skill in the world to induce people to deny his existence in the name of rationalism and of every other system of thought which seeks all possible means to avoid recognizing his activity. It is possible that in certain cases the evil spirit goes so far as to exercise his influence not only on material things, but even on man's body and soul, so that one can speak of diabolical possession (cf. Mk 5:2-9). It is not always easy to discern the preternatural factor operative in these cases, and the Church does not lightly support the tendency to attribute every evil to the direct action of the devil; but in principle it cannot be denied that Satan can go to this extreme manifestation of his strength, in his will to harm and lead to evil.[18]

The devil also tries to fight against the Church, both from the outside, by causing troubles so that she cannot reach her aim easily (Rv 2:10), and also from within by tempting her to be unfaithful to her mission and by inducing division and discontent among her members (Ep 4:27). However, Christ has promised St Peter that the gates of hell cannot hold out against the Church (Mt 16:18), and prayed that His followers be protected from the evil one (Jn 17:15). The Church has to struggle against 'the spiritual army of evil in the heavens' (Ep 6:12). Satan's power is finite, and while his action out of hatred for God and His Kingdom causes damage to people and to society, this action is permitted by divine Providence, who guides man's history with strength and love.[19] Christ's faithful are protected by the good angels against the wiles and assaults of evil spirits.[20] Diabolic action against the Church may well be envy, since tradition holds that the places in heaven lost by the fallen angels will be filled up by the saints, as Newman illustrated:

> Thy tale complete of saints Thou dost provide
> To fill the throne which angels lost through pride![21]

It should be always borne in mind that evil, even in the spirit world, is 'a certain lack, limitation or distortion of good'[22] and not a positive quality or nature. Just as cold is a lack of warmth, evil may be regarded as a lack of goodness. If one were to admit a positive entity in evil, there would arise either the problem of a radical dualism of equal and opposite good and evil principles, or else the proposal of evil as a reflection of the one ultimate Reality. Both these notions are totally unacceptable to the Christian. Nevertheless, Satan and his devils are not, as some modern thinkers propose, simply symbols for human evil or projections of the darker side of man's psyche.[23] Thus, evil cannot just be reduced to the totality of human faults or the imperfections in socio-political structures. Rather, Christian faith and liturgical experience teach as revealed truth the real existence of the world of demons.[24]

Christ has already won the victory over the world of unclean spirits. In a parable Jesus exclaimed: 'When a strong man, well armed, guards his palace, all his goods are secure. But if one stronger than he comes and overpowers him, he takes away the armour in which he trusted, and divides his spoils'(Lk 11:21-22). The words which Christ speaks about the tempter find their historical fulfilment in the Cross and Resurrection of the Redeemer. As we read in the Letter to the Hebrews, Christ became a sharer in human nature even to the Cross 'in order to reduce to powerlessness, by means of death, the one who has the power over death, that is, the devil… and thus to free those who… were held in slavery' (Heb 2:14-15). This is the great certainty of the Christian faith: 'the prince of this world has been judged' (Jn 16:11); 'the Son of God has appeared, in order to destroy the works of the devil' (1 Jn 3:8), as St. John bears witness. It is therefore the crucified and risen Christ who has revealed himself as that 'stronger one' who has overpowered 'the strong man', the devil, and has cast him down from his throne. The Church shares in Christ's victory over the devil, for Christ has given to his disciples the power to cast out demons (cf. Mt 10:1 and parallels; Mk 16:17). The Church uses this victorious power through faith in Christ and prayer (cf. Mk 9:29; Mt 17:19ff.), which in particular cases can take the form of exorcism.[25]

6.2 *Original sin*

Human existence was also marked with the tragedy of sin at its beginnings. To be precise, the Fall is the name given to the sin of Adam and Eve, while the sin which all human beings have inherited from them is termed original sin. Sometimes, this distinction is expressed in terms of *original sin at the origins* which gives rise to the inherited sin called *original sin which has originated* in the Fall.[26]

6.2.1 *The Fall of man and woman*

Adam and Eve were created in a state of original integrity and received certain preternatural and supernatural gifts.[27] Like the angels, however, they were subjected to a kind of trial period, in which they were invited to obey God's command reminding them that they were creatures. In the words of the book of Genesis, the injunction ran as follows: 'You may eat indeed of all the trees in the garden. Nevertheless of the tree of the knowledge of good and evil you are not to eat, for on the day you eat of it you shall most surely die' (Gn 2:16–17). Adam and Eve were, at this point, living by faith and not by vision, and so they were still in a position to commit sin. Thus the state of the first man and the first woman, living as they were by faith and grace, was not dissimilar from that of the angels before their Fall. Traditionally, the sources of temptation for fallen man are the world, the flesh and the devil. In their pristine state, Adam and Eve could not have fallen victim to the first two forms of temptation; the only way that they could be diverted from their union with God was through a direct seduction by the devil, which is in fact what happened. Some may ask why God allowed this to occur. A possible solution is that in order to be perfected in their love of God, our first parents needed free-will, a double-edged sword which could also be turned to ill. Moreover, God in His infinite wisdom and love saw that a greater good could emerge from the crisis of the Fall in terms of the Redemption wrought by Christ.

The Fall of our first parents is vividly described in the third chapter of the book of Genesis. The serpent, here a biblical symbol for the devil, tempted the woman to eat of the fruit of the tree of the knowledge of good and evil with the following persuasive words: 'No! You will not die! God knows in fact that on the day you eat it your eyes will be opened and you will be like gods, knowing good and evil' (Gn 3:4–5). Eve then took some of the fruit of the tree and ate it. 'She gave some also to her husband who was with her, and he ate it. The eyes of both of them were opened and they realised that they were naked' (Gn 3:6–7). Passages of other Old Testament books also speak of the Fall of our first parents: 'Yet God did make man imperishable, He made him in the image of His own nature; it was the devil's envy that brought death into the world as those who are his partners will discover' (Ws 2:23–24).

There are various interpretations concerning the exact nature of the original sin, in some ways parallel to the various approaches to the offence of the angels as seen above. Clement of Alexandria and St Ambrose regarded original sin as having a sexual nature, consisting in the premature use of marriage against the will of the Creator. They based their opinion on the punishment inflicted upon Eve condemned to pain in childbirth and also in the shame felt immediately after the Fall by Adam and Eve because of their nakedness. Most theologians would reject this position, since already before the Fall it is stated that 'a man leaves his father and mother and joins himself to his wife, and they become one body' (Gn 2:24).[28]

Generally, the most common and acceptable interpretation of original sin is that of disobedience based on pride, a desire to be like God, but in a disordered way, rather than through a participation in His divine life. This type of grave sin accounts for the severity of the punishment occasioned by the Fall. Also, if the sin of our first parents was one of disobedience and pride, it would reflect once more the sin of the fallen angels. The devil tempted our first parents to commit a sin similar to his own. In the theology of some of the Eastern Churches, the first sin, rather than being only pride and disobedience, consists more in the lowering of man from the divine and the eternal to the human and the temporal spheres. The divine plan was that man should know the earthly realities only after having known the heavenly and divine mysteries. However man gave way to the devil's temptation and preferred first to know the things of earth represented by eating of the tree of the knowledge of good and evil:

> Partaking of the fruit, he was entirely deprived of all those good and heavenly things and was lowered to the impassioned sensations of earthly and visible creatures… He became deaf, blind, insensible in relation to that from which he had fallen. At once become mortal, corruptible and irrational, he became like the beasts which are without intelligence.[29]

Theologians through the ages have investigated the respective parts played by Adam and by Eve in the Fall. Eve's sin was committed first: 'Sin began with a woman, and thanks to her we all must die' (Si 25:24). St Paul states on the one hand that 'sin entered the world through one man' (Rm 5:12; see 1 Co 15:22), and on the other 'it was not Adam who was led astray but the woman who was led astray and fell into sin' (1 Tm 2:14). Despite the position of a few theologians that the sin of Eve was greater because Adam gave way to sin out of love for her,[30] it is clear that original sin in the strict sense as the cause of the ruin of the human race is the sin of Adam.[31] It is also evident that Adam compounded his sin by blaming Eve (Gn 3:12). The serpent addressed his temptation to Eve not because she was the weaker partner, but rather because woman has a greater capacity of self-giving and sharing than man. The serpent played upon Eve's good quality of sharing, and in that way arrived at Adam, in order to seduce him. It would seem that the specific ways in which our first parents participated in original sin reflect the difference between male and female, which the devil cunningly used and so 'succeeded in attacking life itself, the creation itself at its highest point, in the assault on the bond between man and woman'.[32]

6.2.2 *The effects of the Fall*

What happened to our parents as a result of their Fall can be summarized by the adage attributed to St Bede the Venerable: they were 'stripped of their gifts, wounded in their nature'.[33] This expression is consonant with the idea that among the Fathers, including Origen, St Ambrose and St Augustine, the parable of the Good Samaritan (Lk 10:30–36) is given an allegorical interpretation which has a bearing on original sin. The man who fell among robbers represents Adam and his descendants. Jerusalem is the place of peace and original integrity, which man leaves by going down to Jericho which is the state of trouble and sin. The robbers symbolize the devil and his fallen angels who stripped man of his supernatural gifts and left him wounded in his natural faculties. The priest and the Levite represent the Old Law which was incapable of really helping man. The Samaritan represents Christ, and the beast of burden, His Sacred Humanity. The wine which the Samaritan uses to heal man is the sacrament of the Eucharist, and the oil His mercy. The inn symbolizes the Church, the innkeeper signifies St Peter and his successors, and the bishops and priests of the Church. The coins represent the Gospel and the Sacraments.

Through his sin, Adam lost the supernatural and preternatural gifts with which he had previously been endowed, as the Council of Trent indicated:

> If anyone does not profess that Adam, the first man, by transgressing God's commandment in paradise, at once lost the holiness and justice in which he had been constituted; and that, offending God by his sin, he drew upon himself the wrath and indignation of God and consequently death with which God had threatened him, and together with death, captivity in the power of him who henceforth 'has the power of death' (Hb 2:14) i.e. the devil; and that the whole Adam, body and soul, was changed for the worse through the offence of his sin, let him be anathema.[34]

Hence as a result of the Fall, Adam and Eve lost the following gifts: Sanctifying grace, freedom from concupiscence, bodily immortality, freedom from suffering, the infused knowledge of certain natural and supernatural truths.

The loss of sanctifying grace is the result of every grave sin and must especially be the consequence in this case. The punishment fits the crime, for in the loss of grace, our first parents are deprived of sharing God's inner life, of being like Him by gift, after they had in a disordered way wished to become like God by disobedience. After the Fall, Adam felt unworthy of being in the presence of God: 'I was afraid because I was naked and so I hid' (Gn 3:10). The expulsion of Adam and Eve from the garden of Eden also symbolizes their interior separation from God. The realisation of their nakedness (Gn

3:7) is a reminder of the awakening within Adam and Eve of concupiscence after the Fall. Concupiscence consists of three aspects, slavery to the pleasure of the senses, inordinate desire for earthly goods and the disordered affirmation of self against the dictates of reason (1 Jn 2:16).[35]

> For since Adam's transgression we are all subject to the passions because of our constant association with them. We do not gladly pursue goodness, nor do we long for the knowledge of God, nor do we do good our of love, as the dispassionate do; instead we cling to our passions and our vices and do not aspire at all to do what is good unless constrained by fear of punishment. And this is the case with those who receive God's word with faith and purpose. The rest of us do not even aspire to this extent, but we regard the afflictions of this life and the punishments to come as of no account and are wholeheartedly enslaved to our passions.[36]

The punishment consisting in the loss of the gift of immortality is alluded to in the words: 'From dust you are and to dust you shall return' (Gn 3:19). Man and woman would have been immune from bodily death had they not sinned.[37] Bodily death is also linked to spiritual death, and both are related to man's separation from God:

> As the separation of the soul from the body is the death of the body, so the separation of God from the soul is the death of the soul. This is made clear by the commandment given in paradise, when God said to Adam: 'On whatever day you eat from the forbidden tree you will certainly die' (cf. Gn 2:17). And it was indeed Adam's soul that died by becoming separated from God through his transgression;

> for bodily he continued to live after that time, even for nine hundred and thirty years (cf. Gn 5:5). The death, however, that befell the soul because of the transgression not only crippled the soul and made man accursed; it also rendered the body itself subject to fatigue, suffering and corruptibility, and finally handed it over to death. For it was after the dying of his inner self brought about by the transgression that the earthly Adam heard the words, 'Earth will be cursed because of what you do, it will produce thorns and thistles for you.' Thus the violation of God's commandment is the cause of all types of death, both of soul and body, whether in the present life or in that endless chastisement.[38]

The general suffering resulting from the Fall consisted among other things in 'pains in childbearing' for Eve and difficulties in daily work for Adam (Gn 3:16–19). Part of the suffering in daily life was caused by the confiscation of those gifts of knowledge which man had prior to the Fall.

Adam and Eve lost the infused knowledge of certain natural and supernatural truths. This loss is intimately connected with their loss of communion with God as St Macarius points out:

> When, using the woman as his accomplice, the devil deceived Adam, he divested him of the glory that enveloped him. Thus Adam found himself naked and perceived his disfigurement, of which he had been unaware until that moment since he had delighted his mind with celestial beauty. After his transgression, on the other hand, his thoughts became base and material, and the simplicity and goodness of his mind were intertwined with evil worldly concerns. The closing of paradise, and the placing of the cherubim with the burning sword to

> prevent his entrance, must be regarded as actual events; but they are also realities encountered inwardly by each soul. A veil of darkness—the fire of the worldly spirit—surrounds the heart, preventing the intellect from communing with God, and the soul from praying, believing and loving the Lord as it desires to do.[39]

The image of God within our first parents was also tarnished by their Fall:

> Adam, when he transgressed the commandment, lost two things. First he lost the pure possession of his nature, so lovely, created according to the image and likeness of God. Second, he lost the very image itself in which was laid up for him, according to God's promise, the full heavenly inheritance. Take the example of a coin bearing the image of the king. If it were mixed with a false alloy and lost its gold content, the image also would lose its value. Such, indeed, happened to Adam. A very great richness and inheritance was prepared for him. It was as though there were a large estate and it possessed many sources of income. It had a fruitful vineyard; there were fertile fields, flocks, gold and silver. Such was the vessel of Adam before his disobedience like a very valuable estate. When, however, he entertained evil intentions and thoughts, he lost God. We nevertheless do not say that he was totally lost and was blotted out of existence and died. He died as far as his relationship with God was concerned, but in his nature, however, he still lives. For look, the whole world still walks on the earth and carries on its business. But God's eyes see their very minds and thoughts and, as it were, He disregards them and has no communion with them, because nothing that they think is pleasing to God.[40]

Adam and Eve retained their human nature, intellect and free will. St Thomas indicates that, as a result of the Fall, the will suffered a greater wound than the intellect.[41] This clouding of the intellect and weakening of the will represent only a *relative* and not an *absolute* deterioration of human nature, and one which is *extrinsic* to the human faculties.[42] Man can still know natural truths (including religious ones) through reason, and can perform morally good actions. Human nature was wounded by the Fall, but not totally corrupted (as the Reformers and Jansenists maintained). In particular, while the Catholic position affirmed that free will was not lost by the Fall, the Protestant notion held that free will was damaged to the extent that only a certain civil liberty remains in the fallen human being. The Jansenists admitted that some exterior human freedom remained after the Fall, but denied an interior freedom from necessity and affirmed like the Protestants that there was a complete predominance of concupiscence against which human nature was totally impotent.

An obscure passage in the book of Wisdom seems to imply that our first parent was still capable of receiving redemption: 'The father of the world, the first being to be fashioned, created alone, he had her (i.e. Wisdom) for his protector and she delivered him from his fault' (Ws 10:1). St Paul points explicitly to the natural law written on the heart of fallen man through which he would have the will and desire for good (Rm 2:14–15). St Augustine and St Gregory Nazianzen held that Adam and Eve were saved by the Passion of Christ.[43] The tradition of some of the Eastern Churches permits Adam and Eve to be honoured with a public cult, and they are mentioned as redeemed in an Alexandrine Eucharistic prayer.[44] An ancient tradition also maintains that Adam was buried on the spot where Christ was later to be crucified; in any case Adam and Eve could have only experienced the fruits of the Redemption after Holy Saturday, when Christ descended into the underworld to free them and other Old Testament figures. Among the descendants of Adam and Eve, a further effect of original sin would be that, in the absence of the grace of justification, after death they would be deprived of the beatific vision of God. However, this would not be the same as the positive punishment of hell suffered by those dying in mortal sin.

6.2.3 *The transmission of original sin*

If Adam and Eve had not fallen, the gifts which they had received in their state of innocence would have been transmitted to all their descendants. Instead, original sin and its effects are transmitted from our first parents to all human beings with the exception of Our Lady, as the Council of Trent affirmed:

> If anyone asserts that Adam's sin harmed only him and not his descendants and that the holiness and justice received from God which he lost was only for him and not for us also; or that, stained by the sin of disobedience, he transmitted to all mankind only death and the sufferings of the body but not sin as well which is the death of the soul, let him be anathema.[45]

The Greek Fathers saw the essence of original sin in terms of the loss of sanctifying grace and the power of Satan over man, while the Latin Fathers and especially

Saint Augustine focussed more upon concupiscence. Alexander of Hales and St Thomas Aquinas regarded the material element of original sin as concupiscence, while the formal element was the deprivation of sanctifying grace. The Protestants of the Reformation and the Jansenists exaggerated the Augustinian tendency and put the stress on concupiscence as the essence of original sin. The Council of Trent taught that the Catholic Church has never understood that concupiscence is 'called sin because it would be sin in the true and proper sense in those who have been reborn',[46] but rather in the sense that it derives from sin and inclines to sin.

The fact that all men have been from earliest times infected with an original sin is one of those truths which we can see partially from reason. It is indeed the most empirical of all Christian dogmas as G. K. Chesterton implied.[47] Looking inside ourselves we see the effects of original sin encapsulated in the graphic words of St Paul: 'I cannot understand my own behaviour. I fail to carry out the things I want to do, and I find myself doing the very things I hate' (Rm 7:15). However we can really only fully understand this mystery from divine Revelation.

The truth that all Adam's descendants suffer from original sin and its effects is evident from the Scriptures. The Old Testament presents the idea that all men are infected with the guilt of a primordial fault, but it is not called original sin. After the occupants of Noah's ark had disembarked, following the Flood, God made this promise: 'Never again will I curse the earth because of man, because his heart contrives evil from his infancy' (Gn 8:21). The Wisdom Literature hints at the evil in man, but the human person is not totally corrupted: 'What is man, what purpose does he serve? What is the good in him, and what the bad?' (Si 18:8). The Psalmist describes man as 'a sinner from the moment of conception' (Ps 51:5). In the New Testament, in the light of Christ, the doctrine of original sin becomes much clearer: 'sin entered the world through one man, and through sin death, and thus death has spread through the whole human race because everyone has sinned' (Rm 5:12; see 1 Co 15:21–22). Original sin is a true sin, passed down from Adam to all his descendants with the exception of Our Lady. However, this sin differs from actual sin by the absence of personal consent, as Pope Innocent III indicated in a letter to the Archbishop of Arles in the year 1201: 'We say that two kinds of sin must be distinguished, original and actual: original which is contracted without consent and actual which is committed with consent.'[48]

If there is no physical consent involved in the case of Adam's descendents, how is original sin then contracted? Early on in her history, the Church rejected the solution of the Pelagians who undervalued this sin to the extent that it was only transmitted by imitation of the bad example of Adam. This opinion was condemned by the Council of Carthage in the year 418 where it was asserted that the sin was transmitted by generation.[49] An unacceptable modern approach goes even farther than Pelagius and asserts that original sin is a kind of 'sin of the world', a sinful environment which oppresses us, and also affirms that original sin takes concrete form only in the personal sins of each of us. Other insufficient recent attempts to understand the primordial tragedy and its transmission speak merely of a solidarity in sin, of the compulsion of unjust social and political structures, of a fault of male oppression and sexism, of a basic psychological fear or of evil as an essential component of the cosmos.[50] The Council of Trent used the traditional formulation saying that the sin is 'transmitted by propagation, not by imitation'.[51] The Church has not gone into precise details about the mechanics of this transmission, though evidently natural generation is involved in some way. Some of the Fathers thought that all of humanity was somehow included at the moment of Adam's sinful choice. Others, following St Augustine, stressed concupiscence to the extent that, for them, the transmission of original sin lay in the disordered nature inherent in every sexual act.[52] This view would not square easily with the teaching of Vatican II which stated that 'acts in marriage by which the intimate and chaste union of the spouses takes place are noble and honourable.'[53] It would be incorrect to maintain that the soul infused by God is in some way sinful. Nor would it be appropriate to regard the sperm or the egg as somehow 'containing sin' for Our Lady's parents, St Joachim and St Anne, conceived her Immaculate, without stain of original sin, in a normal but blessed conjugal act.[54] One possibility is that original sin is contracted in the *process* of generation as the *link* with our first parents.

In the Scholastic period, the idea of the unity between Adam and the human race was understood to be in terms of hereditary transmission. The ultra-realists, such as St Anselm, affirmed that the whole human race made up one single specific reality so that when Adam fell, the whole human race fell with him. So Adam received and lost for himself and all his descendants the gifts of his original state.[55] Alexander of Hales and St Thomas Aquinas looked to a moral unity of the human race as well as a physical unity. St Thomas likened humanity to a community in which each person is responsible for the other or to an organism in which the members do not act of their own volition but at the will of the head. Adam is the head of the human race. Then alongside this moral unity, there is the physical unity based on generation, from which results an infection of each person: 'The semen by its own power transmits the human nature from parent to child, and with that nature, the stain which infects it: for he that is born is associated with his first parent in his guilt, through the fact that he inherits his nature from him by a kind of movement which is that of generation.'[56]

More recent theology would simply state that Adam by virtue of being the first man was constituted head of the human race, and alone bore the responsibility for all his progeny, with which he forms a moral and physical unity. Through his gifts of knowledge and commonsense, Adam must have also realized the importance of his position, according to St Anselm's poetic expression:

> Why did he not keep for us that which he possessed so easily,
> and we lack despite our labour?
> Why did he shut out our light
> and surround us with darkness?
> Why did he take away our life
> and give us the hurt of death?[57]

The propagation of the sin then takes place by means of generation, not because of some disorderedness in the sexual act which soils and infects the one who is generated, but rather because this process is the ontological link through which each man is connected with the first parent in whom we have all sinned. The transmission of original sin by means of natural heredity should be understood in terms of the unity of the entire human nature, and of the coessentiality of all men, who, connected by nature, constitute one mystic whole. Inasmuch as human nature is indeed unique and unbreakable, the imparting of sin from Adam to the entire human race descended from him, is rendered explicable in these terms. As from the root, the sickness proceeded to the rest of the tree, Adam being the root who had suffered corruption.

6.2.4 The problem of evil

The problem of evil is often framed in the following terms: 'If God the Father almighty, the Creator of the ordered and good world, cares for all His creatures, why does evil exist?' This question is urgent, as many ask it, and is thus unavoidable. It is painful as it challenges both faith and reason. Finally it is mysterious, and no quick answer will suffice to answer the problem of evil.[58] A further formulation could be: 'Why did God not create a world so perfect that no evil could exist in it?' One answer is that with infinite power God could always create something better.[59] Among erroneous answers to the problem of evil is monism, or the notion that good and evil are simply twin aspects of the same ultimate reality. Other false views would be Zoroastrianism and Manichaeism, which on the other hand, explicitly posit an ultimate dualism in the universe. Here, good and evil have existed both co-eternally and independently, in the form of finite deities. Neither has so far destroyed the other. This accounts for the mixture of good and evil in our world. Another insufficient approach is that of Leibniz who contended that God was morally bound to create the best of all possible worlds.[60]

The Christian picture proposes instead that, with infinite wisdom and goodness, God freely willed to create a world in pilgrimage towards its ultimate perfection.[61] In God's plan, this process of becoming involves the appearance of certain beings and the disappearance of others, the existence of the more perfect alongside the less perfect, both constructive and destructive forces of nature. This allows the possibility that alongside physical good there exists also physical evil insofar as creation has not reached perfection.[62] Even worse than physical evil is the moral evil which arises from the sins of rational creatures. God is in no way, directly or indirectly, the cause of moral evil.[63] God permits it, however, because He respects the freedom of his creatures and, mysteriously, knows how to derive good from it. Almighty God, because He is supremely good, would never allow any evil whatsoever to exist in His works if He were not so all-powerful and good as to cause good to emerge from evil itself.[64]

It is possible that physical evil, such as earthquakes and other natural disasters, could be a secondary consequence of original sin. Diabolical action against God's creation is also not to be excluded. Thus even the irrationality of sin may even lie behind apparent physical evil. Now evil is a privation of good: 'there is no such thing as a nature of evil, because all nature, as nature is good.'[65] St Augustine was one of the first Christian thinkers to stress this fundamental point, that evil is the privation of good:

> In this universe, even what is called evil, when it is rightly ordered and kept in its place, commends the good more eminently, since good things yield greater pleasure and praise when compared to the bad things. For the Omnipotent God, whom even the heathen acknowledge as the Supreme Power over all, would not allow any evil in his works, unless in his omnipotence and goodness, as the Supreme Good, he is able to bring forth good out of evil. What, after all, is anything we call evil except the privation of good? In animal bodies, for instance, sickness and wounds are nothing but the privation of health. When a cure is effected, the evils which were present (namely the sickness and the wounds) do not retreat and go elsewhere. Rather, they simply do not exist any more. For such evil is not a substance; the wound or the disease is a defect of the bodily substance which, as a substance, is good. Evil, then, is an accident, namely a privation of that good which is called health. Thus, whatever defects there are in a soul are privations of a natural good.[66]

Evil therefore has its origin, not in nature, but in the will. Sin is an action which is against the right use of reason. The existence of evil therefore is sometimes used against proofs of God's existence. Nevertheless, evil is connected with free choices of rational creatures, and without freedom it is impossible to love. Sometimes, to counter the argument of those who maintain that evil represents an obstacle to the affirmation of God, the reply could be that what we see is only part of the mosaic, and that within the whole picture God can bring a final good out of evil, the supreme example being the crucifixion of His Son as the source of human salvation. From the greatest moral evil ever committed, the rejection and murder of God's only Son, caused by the sins of all men, God, by his grace that 'abounded all the more' (Rm 5:20), brought the greatest of goods: the glorification of Christ and our redemption. Nevertheless, evil is not simply imaginary nor does it ever become a good.[67] The very human capacity of being able rationally to identify evil for what it is, to reject it, and to perceive its incongruity in a good world created by God, is in itself a pointer towards God. As Josef Pieper pointed out: 'The incomprehensibility of evil in the world becomes fully apparent only against the background of the indestructible happiness of God.'[68] Thus the very fact that all evil is to some degree shocking and remarkable triggers an argument for God's real existence.[69] Or, in other words, if the universe were chaotic and absurd, we would not be able to identify evil as evil.

A world in which earthquakes, tsunamis and hurricanes occur is not the world that God originally made. We see a world filled with natural disasters and death, but that is not the original order of things. Originally, God created a very good world. Originally, man lived in perfect communion with God. Originally, all creation was unified with its components functioning in symbiotic balance. There was no death, no violent natural upheavals by a world out of balance, a world convulsing harmfully against itself. For God saw all that He had made, and behold, it was very good (Gn 1:31). The earth itself was also affected as a consequence of Adam's sin.

Death enveloped creation. The components of the perfectly balanced creation became separated, disjointed, and imbalanced. The earth was cursed and man's body would return to the dust in physical death (Gn 3:17-19). The world that previously sustained life would continue to do so, but as a cursed earth. Fallen man is consigned to live in a cursed earth in which both he and the world are visited by death. The state of the earth continues to be integrally bound up with the state of man's relationship to God. This is a good world that has been brought by man's sin, into a bad state. When we experience death and the tragedies of things like tsunamis, we are experiencing the repercussions of the Fall. We are experiencing life in a world enveloped by death, a world essentially separated from God, a world in need of deliverance – for we are a people in need of deliverance. Once we view suffering and death in the context of Creation and the Fall, we are then able to perceive how it is that God is at work redemptively in the world. Suffering, for the Christian, is not meaningless, but is to be viewed in the context of God's redemptive purpose for this fallen world.

The Fall thus seems to have caused a deleterious effect on the cosmos as a whole, an effect which is more than just the result of bad human choices which are themselves the fruit of concupiscence. Rather, an echo or repercussion of original sin has hit the cosmos. If a young person dies in a road accident, it is usually clear that someone is to blame, it is a result of human carelessness at the very least. However, if a young person of the same age dies as a result of cancer, it is more difficult to see where the responsibility lies. Perhaps the person has been exposed to certain factors which cause cancer such as smoking. However, it is not easy to trace a precise biological cause. It is clear nonetheless that there is some genetic predisposition, some disorder at the micro-biological level. The same may be said of the violence which viruses wreak upon the human body. Some writers propose that 'the result of angelic sin may well have been to introduce into the material realm a disorder which has manifested itself in a distortion of the evolutionary plan.'[70] Then what is the ultimate cause of such natural disasters as earthquakes? It would seem that after the Fall, the cosmos is left for the worse, but it is difficult to see precisely how the cosmic laws have been altered as a result. Opinions vary as to the difference between the cosmos before and after the Fall. For instance, St Thomas held that there would have been some violence in nature even before the Fall:

> In the opinion of some, those animals which are now fierce and kill others, would, in that state, have been tame, not only in regard to man, but also in regard to other animals. But this is quite unreasonable. For the nature of animals was not changed by man's sin, as if those whose nature now it is to devour the flesh of others, would have lived on herbs, as the lion and the falcon… Thus there would have been a natural antipathy between some animals.[71]

Nevertheless, St Paul speaks of the entire creation 'groaning in one great act of giving birth' (Rm 8:22), which implies a cosmic dimension of original sin and also of Redemption. Despite the fact that the cosmos has been left worse off after the Fall, its beauty has not been completely obscured, and man continues to exercise his stewardship within creation. Through the Redemption the universe is repaired in some way.

Thus, the problem of evil also has an eschatological sense. History is linear according to Scripture and Christian tradition: it has a beginning and an end and moves like a straight line. History is not a revolving circle, an endless repetition whose beginning and ultimate purpose is unknown. History began at Creation and is moving to Final Judgment. As the line of history progresses, the world will experience more frequent and more intense eschatological 'birth pains'. In teaching about the end of the world, Jesus employs the metaphor of a woman in childbirth:

> And you will be hearing of wars and rumours of wars; see that you are not frightened, for those things must take place, but that is not yet the end. For nation will rise against nation, and kingdom against kingdom, and in various places there will be famines and earthquakes. But all these things are merely the beginning of birth pangs (Mt 24:6-8).

The human person in his redeemed, justified state as a baptised Christian is freed from original sin, regains sanctifying grace, and receives knowledge of revealed truths. However, until the resurrection of the just, he or she must still struggle with concupiscence, suffering and death. It would not be fully accurate to say that evil helps us to see the good more clearly, in a similar way that a shadow makes the light seem brighter. Rather, the fact that God's providential economy works *despite* the imperfection of His creatures, in a certain sense manifests His greatness more forcefully than if He were operating only through sinless creatures. The whole of the Christian faith is, in various ways an answer to the problem of evil,[72] but most especially the Paschal Mystery:

> Even though the victory over sin and death achieved by Christ in His Cross and Resurrection does not abolish temporal suffering from human life, nor free from suffering the whole historical dimension of human existence, it nevertheless *throws a new light* upon this dimension and upon every suffering: the light of salvation.[73]

It is precisely this particular light which the Redemptive Incarnation of Christ sheds upon the mystery of creation that will be examined in the next chapter.

Further Reading

P. Kreeft, *Making Sense Out of Suffering* (Cincinnati: St Anthony Messenger Press, 1986)

C. S. Lewis, *The Problem of Pain* (New York: MacMillan, 1962)

Notes

1 J. H. Newman, *The Dream of Gerontius* §5.

2 See pp. 56–57 above.

3 See St Thomas Aquinas, *Summa Theologiae* I, q.62, a.3.

4 See St Anselm, *De casu diaboli*, c.5.

5 Cf. *Ibid*, I, q.62, a.4–5.

6 Cf. *Ibid*, I, q.63, a.5–6.

7 See Pope John Paul II, *Discourse at General Audience* (23 July 1986), §4.

8 See St John Chrysostom, *Homily* 22 on Genesis, n.2, *PG* 53, 187–188.

9 See St Irenaeus, *Adversus Haereses* Book 5, Chapter 24, n.4 in *PG* 7, 1188.

10 See F. Suarez, *De angelis* Book 5, Chapter 12, n.13 in *Summa, seu Compendium* First Part, Tome II, volume 1 (Paris: J. B. Migne, 1861).

11 See Pope John Paul II, *Discourse at General Audience* (13 August 1986), §5.

12 See *ibid*., 6.

13 See St Thomas Aquinas, *Summa Theologiae* I, q.63, a.7.

14 See the condemnation of Origen's errors, issued in the Edict of Justinian in DS 411.

15 Fourth Lateran Council, Chapter I : On the Catholic Faith, in DS 801, English translation in ND 20.

16 See St Thomas Aquinas, *Summa Theologiae* I, q.64, aa.1–2.

17 See Pope John Paul II, *Discourse at General Audience* (13 August 1986), §7.

18 See Pope John Paul II, *Discourse at General Audience* (13 August 1986), §8, 9.

19 See *CCC* 395 and St Thomas Aquinas, *Summa Theologiae* I, q.109, a.4 where it is stated that God allows 'some evil to be done by bad angels or men, for the sake of the good that follows'.

20 See St Thomas Aquinas, *Summa Theologiae* I, q.113, aa.4–5.

21 J. H. Newman, *The Dream of Gerontius*, §2. See St Thomas Aquinas, *Summa Theologiae* I, q.63, a.9. Earlier, St Anselm had proposed that the celestial state was not complete in its original number, but must be completed from among men. At the same time he made it clear that, even had no angel fallen, men would yet have had their place in the celestial kingdom. See St Anselm, *Cur Deus homo*, Book I, chapter 18.

22 Pope John Paul II, Apostolic Letter *Salvifici doloris* 7.4. See also St Thomas Aquinas, *Summa Theologiae* I, q.48, a.1 who talks about evil as a lack or privation of good.

23 See M. Godwin, *Angels. An Endangered Species* (New York: Simon and Schuster, 1990), p. 250, where it is suggested that

'just as angels can be seen as a stage in the development of awareness, so can devils.'

24 See Pope Paul VI, *Discourse at General Audience* (15 November 1972) in *IP* 10(1972) pp. 1168–1173; Pope John Paul II, *Discourses at General Audience*, 23 July, 13 and 20 August 1986 in *IG* 9/2 (1986) pp.282–285, 362–366, 395–398; Congregation for the Doctrine of the Faith, *Les multiples formes de superstition* (26 June 1975), VII. English translation from A. Flannery, *Vatican II. More Postconciliar Documents* (Leominster: Fowler Wright, 1982), pp. 475–476.

25 See Pope John Paul II, *Discourse at General Audience* (20 August 1986), §2.

26 In Latin, the expressions are *peccatum originale originans* and *peccatum originale originatum*.

27 This was seen in chapter 4, section 4.4 above.

28 Hence also the difficulty in the position of St Gregory of Nyssa who stated that, for man and woman before the Fall, the propagation of the human race would have occurred without sexual relations. See chapter four, pp. 82, 87 above.

29 St Symeon the New Theologian, *On the Mystical Life, Ethical Discourses* 13.

30 See St Thomas Aquinas, *Summa Theologiae* II–II°, q.163, a.4.

31 *Ibid.*, I–II°, q.81, a.5. St Anselm in his *De conceptu Virginali et originali peccati*, chapter 9 (*PL* 158, 442–443) states that original sin is to be imputed more to Adam than to Eve.

32 P. J. Elliott, *What God Has Joined…* (Homebush: St Paul Publications, 1990), p. 10.

33 See M. Flick and Z. Alszeghy, *Il Creatore* (Florence: Libreria Editrice Fiorentina, 1964) p.493f.. The Latin expression is *spoliatus in gratuitis, vulneratus in naturalibus*.

34 Council of Trent, Fifth Session. Decree on Original sin. Canon 1 in DS 1511. English translation from ND 508.

35 See *CCC* 377.

36 St Peter of Damascus, *A Treasury of Divine Knowledge*, Book 1.

37 Vatican II, *Gaudium et Spes* 18.2. See also Ws 1:13; 2:23-24; Rm 5:21; 6:23; Jm 1:15.

38 St Gregory Palamas, *Topics on Natural and Theological Science*, Chapters 9-14.

39 St Macarius the Great, *Patient Endurance and Discrimination*, 37.

40 St Macarius the Great, *The Fifty Spiritual Homilies*, Homily 12.

41 See St Thomas Aquinas, *Summa Theologiae* I–II°, q.83, aa.3–4.

42 See Pope John Paul II, *Discourse at General Audience* (8 October 1986), §7 in *IG* 9/2 (1986), p. 972. There is discussion as to whether the wound to human nature consists simply of the loss of preternatural gifts or of an intrinsic but accidental weakening. The Thomist approach considers that a person born in original sin compares to the human being in the state of pure nature as a person stripped of his clothes is to a naked person. Those who admit some intrinsic weakening use the analogy between the healthy man (before the Fall) and the sick person (in original sin).

43 See St Augustine, *De peccatorum meritis et remissione* Book 2, Chapter 34, n.55 in *PL* 44, 183; St Gregory Nazianzen, *Oratio* 37 n.7 in *PG* 36, 289–290.

44 See the anaphora of St Athanasius in the Ethiopian Liturgy in *Prex Eucharistica* (Fribourg: Editions Universitaires, 1978), p. 177: 'O Adam and Eve, you have certainly been redeemed and enter into your ancient inheritance without any obstacle, by the Blood of Him Who has redeemed you.'

45 Council of Trent, Fifth Session, *Decree on Original Sin*, Canon 2 in DS 1512. English translation from ND 509.

46 Council of Trent, Fifth Session, *Decree on Original Sin*, Canon 5 in DS 1515. English translation from ND 512.

47 See G. K. Chesterton, *Orthodoxy* (Garden City, New York: Image, 1959) p. 15: 'Certain new theologians dispute original sin, which is the only part of Christian theology which can really be proved.'

48 Pope Innocent III, Letter *Maiores Ecclesiae causas* to Humbert, Archbishop of Arles in DS 780. English translation in ND 506.

49 See Sixteenth Council of Carthage in DS 223. See also the Letter of Pope Zosimus (DS 231) in the same year which used the expression 'propagation' as the means of transmission of original sin.

50 See S. Wiedenhofer, 'The main forms of contemporary theology of original sin' in *Communio* 18/4 (Winter 1991), pp. 514–529.

51 Council of Trent, Fifth Session, Decree on Original Sin, Canon 3 in DS 1513. English translation from ND 510.

52 Some medieval writers also followed this line, such as Peter Lombard who wrote: 'praecipue pollutio quaedam, quam ex fervore coitus parentum et concupiscentia libidinosa contrahit caro, dum concipitur, causa est originalis peccati.' (Principally, a certain pollution which the flesh contracts from the heat of the sexual act and from pleasurable longing while the flesh is being conceived, is the cause of original sin.) *Book II of the Sentences* d.31, c.6, in *PL* 192, 725.

53 Vatican II, *Gaudium et Spes*, 49.2.

54 See St Anselm, *De conceptu Virginali et originali peccato*, chapter 7 in *PL* 158, 441 where he states that there is no sin inherent in the semen: 'non quod in semine sit immunditia peccati, aut peccatum sive iniquitas.'

55 See St Anselm, *De fide Trinitatis et de Incarnatione Verbi* chapter 2, *PL* 158, 265.

56 St Thomas Aquinas, *Summa Theologiae* I–II°, q.81, a.1.

57 St Anselm, *Proslogion*, Chapter 1, in *PL* 158, 226. English translation by Sister Benedicta Ward from *The Prayers and Meditations of St Anselm* (Middlesex: Penguin, 1973), p. 241.

58 See *CCC* 309.

59 Cf St Thomas Aquinas, *Summa Theologiae* I, q.25, a.6.

60 See chapter three, pp. 81-82 above.

61 See *CCC* 310.

62 Cf. St Thomas Aquinas, *Summa Contra Gentiles* III, 71.

63 Cf. St Augustine, *De libero arbitrio*, Book 1, chapter 1, n.1 in *PL* 32, 1221-1223; St Thomas Aquinas, *Summa Theologiae* I-II, q.79, a.1.

64 See St Augustine, *Enchiridion*, chapter 11 in *PL* 40, 236.

65 Council of Florence, *Decree for the Copts* in DS 1333. See also St Thomas Aquinas, *Summa Theologiae* I, q.48, a.1.

66 St Augustine, *Enchiridion*, chapter 11 in *PL* 40, 236.

67 See *CCC* 312.

68 J. Pieper, *Happiness and Contemplation* (New York: Pantheon Books, 1958), p. 31.

69 See St Thomas Aquinas, *Summa Contra Gentiles*, Book 3, chapter 71: 'A certain philosopher… asks: "If God exists, whence comes evil?" But it could be argued to the contrary: "If evil exists, God exists." For, there would be no evil if the order of good were taken away, since its privation is evil. But this order would not exist if there were no God.'

70 E. L. Mascall, *Christian Theology and Natural Science* (London: Longmans Green and Co, 1957), p. 301. See also *CCC* 395.

71 St Thomas Aquinas, *Summa Theologiae* I, q.96, a.1.

72 See *CCC* 309.

73 Pope John Paul II, Apostolic Letter *Salvifici doloris*, 15.3.

7

Christ and Creation

Christ came to make a new world. He came into the world to regenerate it in Himself, to make a new beginning, to be the beginning of the creation of God, to gather together in one, and recapitulate all things in Himself. The rays of His glory were scattered through the world… The world was like some fair mirror, broken in pieces, and giving back no one uniform image of its Maker. But He came to combine what was dissipated, to recast what was shattered in Himself.

John Henry Newman, *Sermons bearing on Subjects of the Day*

The ground covered so far has dealt with the work of God the Creator, the nature of His creatures, the Fall of some of the angels and that of man. Now it is opportune to examine the specifically Christian flavour of the doctrine of creation in terms of Christ who has taken part of the creation to Himself in the mystery of the Incarnation and has redeemed man and creation. The gift of creation is a preparation for man and woman to accept from God's hands the infinitely greater grace of His Word Incarnate and His Holy Spirit.

7.1 Creation and Incarnation

The doctrine of the Incarnation, of Christ God made Man, sets the Christian concept of creation apart from that of all other religions. The cosmos was created through the eternal Word, Who left a mark or a seal upon His creation, and this stamp is an image of His own rationality. Since the Son of God has taken part of His creation to Himself, the intelligibility of creation is compatible with His own divine rationality and moreover His coming as man adds to the rationality of creation, it changes the created reality for the better by making it more rational, more intelligible. Thus the realist vision which permeates these pages really only finds its ultimate basis, guarantee and anchor in Christ. St Paul says that in God's secret, the mystery of Christ, are found 'all the jewels of wisdom and knowledge' (Col 2:3). New Testament revelation furnishes a Trinitarian context to any Christological discussion of creation with its use of the Pauline expression: 'there is one God, the Father, from Whom all things come and for Whom we exist; and there is one Lord, Jesus Christ, through Whom all things come and through Whom we exist' (1 Co 8:6).

The fact that the cosmos was created through Christ already means that it must be good. The doctrine of the Incarnation not only reinforces the affirmation of the goodness of creation but also enhances this wholesomeness, for matter is created in view of the future coming of the Son of God as man. God the Word assumed human nature, which is a microcosm of the whole universe, and can hardly be anything but good in order to be hypostatically united to His Godhead. The creation of all things through Christ gives the entire universe a oneness in Him. The further event of the Incarnation in which He took some of the creation to Himself in His human nature makes a permanent relation between all the creation and Himself which strengthens both the reality and the idea of the unity of the cosmos. In St Paul's words: 'Before anything was created, He existed, and He holds all things in unity' (Col 1:17). God 'would bring everything together under Christ, as Head, everything in the heavens and everything on earth' (Ep 1:10).

From the rationality, goodness and oneness of the universe, flows the idea of beauty of the cosmos.[1] St Paul remarks concerning the human creation: 'We are God's work of art, created in Christ Jesus' (Ep 2:10). In a certain sense, the beauty of creation takes its cue from the beauty of Christ. One famous passage from the psalms affirms:

> You are the fairest of the children of men
> and graciousness is poured upon your lips:
> because God has blessed you for evermore. (Ps 45:2)

While this passage is part of a royal wedding song, St Thomas Aquinas and other commentators have no difficulty in applying it to Christ in a prefigurative sense. The voice of the bride in the Song of Songs can also be seen to refer to Christ: 'Let me hear your voice; for your voice is sweet and your face beautiful' (Sg 2:14). Christ's beauty is based on the truth that 'In His body lives the fullness of the divinity' (Col 2:9), and that He is 'full of grace and truth' (Jn 1:14). At the same time, the Fourth Song of the Suffering Servant is a powerful reminder that Christ underwent the disfigurement of suffering to renew the beauty of the human person and that of all of the creation:

> Without beauty, without majesty (we saw him),
> no looks to attract our eyes;
> a thing despised and rejected by men,
> a man of sorrows and familiar with suffering,
> a man to make people screen their faces;
> he was despised and we took no account of him. (Is 53:2–3)

The Christian vision of creation stands out in sharp relief against most ancient religious systems where the cosmos was considered to be eternal and also cyclic with regard to its time sequence. In China of old, despite the differences between them, the Taoist, Confucian and Buddhist approaches all held in common a view of an eternal cosmos and a certain cyclicity with respect to time.[2] Similarly, the Hindu religions of India regarded the cosmos as eternal and punctuated with inexorable cycles.[3] Within the world view of pre-Columbian America, similar features are observable. The Aztec gods were personifications of various periodically changing forces and phenomena in nature. The cosmos was cyclic, and the concepts of space, time and causality were notable for their absence. The Incas could not break out of a cyclic picture of time. The Maya also held a cyclic notion of time, in which the cosmos had no beginning.[4] For the Egyptians of old, the cosmos was considered as an enormous animal, giving rise to an organismic, animistic rhythmic cosmogony.[5] The Babylonians, Sumerians and Assyrians were trapped in a cyclic and animistic world picture markedly different from that of the Old Testament.[6] In the Aristotelian, the Stoic and Epicurean cosmologies of ancient Greece the universe was cyclic and matter and processes were eternal.[7] In the neo-pagan philosophies of the Renaissance, in German idealism as well as in attempts of modern scientists to exclude God from His cosmos, there is renewed cavorting with an eternal cyclic cosmos.[8]

The Judaeo-Christian vision of creation is diametrically opposed to that series of eternal returns which is to be found in most ancient and modern pagan systems. The fact that the eternal Word became incarnate of the Virgin Mary at a specific moment within history guarantees the uniqueness of Christ's redemptive act:

> Another contribution of orthodox, dogmatic Christianity is… a strong appreciation of time as actually experienced. That the Incarnation took place at a fixed point of time, marked by the invariable reference to Pontius Pilate in all credal formulas, could but enhance the perception of the uniqueness of each moment and therefore of history. Since such uniqueness is inconceivable within the recurrence of cyclic ages, the Incarnation added further emphasis to a linear perception of time, which had been an integral part of Old Testament salvation history.[9]

The Christian idea of a linear progressive cosmos is further guaranteed by the truth that at another specific point in time, Christ will come again in glory to bring all history to its completion; of this eschatological dimension, more will be said later.

Christ took human nature to Himself, which also demonstrates His absolute supremacy over the material realm. While the Word exists from all eternity, His human nature began in time with the Incarnation, meaning that matter is not eternal. Hence the dogma of the

Incarnation closes the door to pantheism which is almost always present in eternal cyclic cosmic visions. The doctrine of Christ the only-begotten Son of the Father excludes the possibility that any other entity is also begotten by the Father. Hence the cosmos does not have the status of a begotten entity, but is in a very real sense put in its place: 'In the Christian perspective the exaltedness of the universe remained intact as it is lowered through that infinite distance which is between Creator and Creature'.[10] The expression that Christ and the Holy Spirit are one in substance with the Father also excludes the idea that the cosmos could enjoy this privilege. St Paul transfers to Christ and His Church the concepts of *body* and *fulness* (Col 1:15–20) as a bolster against pantheism.[11] The doctrine that the work of creation is carried out *through* Christ is a shield against the Gnostic error that the cosmos emanated from God.

The doctrine of Christ, true God and true Man, safeguards those truths concerning the nature of the human person. St Ambrose, St Jerome, and St Gregory Nazianzen affirmed against Apollinaris of Laodicea that Christ's human nature included a human soul using the well-known axiom 'what is not assumed is not saved'.[12] Christ must have had a human soul as this guaranteed the continuity of His human nature between Good Friday and Easter Sunday and in particular for the descent into hell, which the Creed affirms. The completeness of Christ's human nature is thus also an affirmation that the nature of all human beings consists of body and soul. The doctrine that Christ assumed a human nature like ours in all things but sin, strongly reinforces the goodness and dignity of the human being: 'Human nature, by the very fact that it was assumed, not absorbed, in Him, has been raised in us also to a dignity beyond compare. For, by His Incarnation, He, the Son of God, has in a certain way united Himself with each man.' Christ thus reveals the fullness of truth concern the human person: He 'reveals man to himself'.[13]

The Incarnation of the Word is also a guarantee of purpose and Providence within the cosmos. The Christian approach excludes an idea of Providence which is merely fate as in pagan systems, or the impersonal cosmic force featured in science fiction. Instead, purpose is rooted in the economy of salvation of the Father who has revealed Himself in the Son and guides us in the power of His Holy Spirit. Cosmic meaning is rooted in the Providence of God's plan as it has specifically been revealed to us in Christ: 'He has let us know the mystery of His purpose, the hidden plan He so kindly made in Christ from the beginning to act upon when the times had run their course to the end' (Ep 1:9–10). Thus there is no longer a possibility of a fatalistic, chaotic or chance vision of cosmic events. 'Thanks to the Word, the world of creatures appears as a "cosmos", an ordered universe. And it is the same Word who, by taking flesh, renews the cosmic order of creation'.[14]

Cosmic Christology has theological roots in the Scriptures and the Fathers though its development has taken place during the past century.[15] Pope John Paul II has also articulated this dimension of the mystery of creation:

> The Incarnation, then, also has a cosmic significance, a cosmic dimension. The 'First-Born of all creation', becoming incarnate in the individual humanity of Christ, unites Himself in some way with the entire

> reality of man, which is also 'flesh'—and in this reality with all 'flesh', with the whole of creation.[16]

For the foundation of a sound cosmic Christology it is necessary to have a clear idea of the transcendence and immanence of Christ in relation to everything which was created through Him. In particular, the intimate bond between Christ and the cosmos should not be exaggerated at the expense of His sovereignty over all creation. Otherwise there is a danger of implying that Christ emerges or evolves from the cosmos. It would be equally false to regard Christ as part of the very fabric of nature itself, and that therefore He is a necessary part of the cosmos in the sense that God is somehow bound to send His Word cloaked in human flesh. This would destroy the gratuity of the Incarnation and the gratuity of grace. It must always be borne in mind that Christ is Son of God by nature, while we become children of God only by the adoption of grace.

Indeed the best way to present a cosmic rôle for Christ is in terms of a development of the Pauline statement that the Father 'would bring everything together under Christ, as Head, everything in the heavens and everything on earth' (Ep 1:10). This is what St. Thomas Aquinas, following the Pseudo-Dionysius, called the *exitus* and *redditus* of God. Creation itself had come forth from God in a free choice of love and finds its goal in God, whose Holy Spirit vivifies and orders it. When it fell from that plan through the fall of Lucifer and the human race he seduced, God Himself recapitulated the movement by descending into the depths of creation so that He could elevate it by His victory and ascension. The Word of God was made man, 'recapitulating in

Himself His own handiwork'.[17] This recapitulation of all things in Christ means that the Father leads all things back to Himself through His Son in the power of the Holy Spirit. In Christ all humanity and the whole of creation speaks of itself to God.[18] Christ sums up everything in the cosmos because all was created through Him and He has taken on human nature. He is the Head of all created reality, the angels, human beings, the material cosmos. He is also the Head of the cosmos, the Centre of all created reality, He is the Pivot upon which all creation turns. However, Christ is also Universal King through the victory which He has won on Calvary.

7.2 *Creation and Redemption*

Christianity is the only religion where God has taken creation to Himself, in the Incarnation. It is also the only religion where through the human nature assumed by His Son, God also enters into the mystery of evil and suffering so as to change it. Redemption is dependent on the existence of a created universe with rational creatures forming part of it: 'salvation history makes no sense if there is no creation properly so called, that is, a creation of all, or the Universe, out of nothing'.[19] An old theological question asks whether the Incarnation took place purely as result of the Fall. St Thomas' approach to the problem ran along these lines:

> Hence, since everywhere in the Sacred Scripture the sin of the first man is assigned as the reason of the Incarnation, it is more in accordance with this to say that the work of the Incarnation was ordained by God as a remedy for sin; so that, had sin not existed,

> the Incarnation would not have been. And yet the power of God is not limited to this;—even had sin not existed, God could have become incarnate.[20]

Thus although St Thomas inclined to the position that the Incarnation would not have taken place unless it were with a view to a Redemption from sin, he left the possibility open that even without sin God could have become incarnate. Blessed Duns Scotus took a different line: that in the absence of the Fall, God not merely could, but *would* have become man. The Scotist approach stresses that the Incarnation is so great an action of divine love, and the primacy of Christ so central that the Fall could not have been the occasion for this primacy. If man had not fallen, Christ would have come no longer as man's Redeemer, but as He Who would take man to glory.

It would seem that the Scotist position accords more clearly with certain passages of Scripture like St Paul's Letter to the Ephesians: 'Before the world was made, He chose us in Christ' (Ep 1:4). The text implies that we are chosen in Christ before original sin took place, namely the Incarnation is predestined from all eternity. However, it could still be argued that this was because God knew from all eternity that man was to sin. The Scotist approach gives a greater sense of unity to all theology and is especially appropriate in the illustration of the Immaculate Conception of Our Lady. It is more consonant with the omnipotence of God to suppose that Christ's coming is predestined in any case from all eternity, and that the Saviour would have acted, in a wholly gratuitous way, in whatever circumstance man was to be found. In the Scotist approach creation must always be seen in the light of Christ. An exaggeration of either position leads to problems. In the Thomist position, it would seem that the Incarnation is motivated by the Fall, or in the words of the *Exsultet* from the Easter Vigil, 'O happy fault, O necessary sin of Adam, which gained for us so great a Redeemer!' Yet if the Scotist position were to be exaggerated it could tend to by-pass the Fall and underestimate the Redemptive act. In a balanced view, both positions must be taken into account. Perhaps the approach 'If man had not sinned', is a less helpful formulation of the question than the consideration of the primacy of Christ.

The fallen angels are beyond Redemption,[21] and men and women are redeemed by Christ. However, what can be said about the sub-human creation? After the Fall of Adam, God said 'Accursed be the soil because of you' (Gn 3:17). This seems to imply that the cosmos is left worse off after the Fall.[22] Moreover, St Paul implies that creation as a whole needs to be set free: 'It was not for any fault on the part of creation that it was made unable to attain its purpose, it was made so by God; but creation still retains the hope of being freed, like us, from its slavery to decadence, to enjoy the same freedom and glory as the children of God' (Rm 8:20–21). Material creation was left worse off after the Fall, not as a result of its own fault, since it cannot sin, but rather as a consequence of man's sin. Christ's redemption heals and restores creation. In the Fall, part of creation was directly involved, namely man and woman, as well as the tree of knowledge of good and evil, and the fruit of that tree. Even if the tree and its fruit are to be understood symbolically, that symbol also teaches an essential truth concerning the involvement of the material creation in man's temptation and Fall. Many of the Fathers make much of the parallel between the involvement of the created reality in original sin and in the Redemption.[23] The whole cosmos regains its freedom through Christ's work of Atonement.[24]

The concrete mechanism or modality of the Redemption of the sub-human cosmos is also significant. Since creation became 'decadent' as a result of man's Fall, it should also be healed through the cooperation of the human person. In the first place, Christ applies his redemption primarily to man and woman:

> Look at the spittle on my face, which I received because of you, in order to restore you to that first divine inbreathing at creation. See the blows on my cheeks, which I accepted in order to refashion your distorted form to my own image.[25]

Redeemed humanity then in its turn mediates Christ's Redemption to the rest of creation. In this way man and woman become stewards of the new creation, a doctrine which can be also applied to the problem of ecology. In Christ, God the Word uses His human nature to redeem His creation, so that man is always involved in some way in the redemption of creation:

> He was the Elder Brother of all created things, and it was suitable that when God determined to reconcile His rebel world to Himself, Christ should be the focus in which all creation should be at once resumed and renewed.[26]

The healing-process of the entire cosmos is one which takes place slowly and silently. It finds its origin in Christ's redemptive act and began on the morning of

Easter Sunday, as G. K. Chesterton powerfully illustrated:

> On the third day the friends of Christ coming at daybreak to the place found the grave empty and the stone rolled away. In varying ways they realised the new wonder; but even they hardly realised that the world had died in the night. What they were looking at was the first day of a new creation, with a new heaven and a new earth; and in a semblance of the gardener God walked again in a garden, in the cool not of the evening but the dawn.[27]

While the seventh day brought the first creation to a close, the eighth day marked the beginning of the new creation. Thus the act of creation finds its culmination in the greater act of the Redemption.[28] After the Resurrection, Christ's Ascension also has a significance for the restoration of creation. When Christ ascended into heaven, He brought His risen humanity to present to His Father:

> Human nature was exalted above the dignity of all the creatures of heaven, passing beyond the ranks of the angels, being raised above the high seat of the archangels, to receive an elevation that would have no limit until it was admitted into the eternal Father's dwelling, to share the glorious throne of Him with Whose nature it had been united in the Person of the Son.[29]

The sending of the Holy Spirit from the Father through the Son at Pentecost is the seal which is set upon the mystery of Easter. Just as the Holy Spirit hovered over the waters in the first creation (Gn 1:2), so also it is He in Whom the new creation receives life. The Old Testament furnishes prophecies and prefigurations of the pneumatological aspect of the re-creation of the cosmos: 'You send forth Your spirit, they are created and You renew the face of the earth' (Ps 104:30). On the evening of Easter Sunday, the Risen Lord appeared to His disciples and renewed the same action which God had performed upon Adam. God breathed life into the first man; Jesus breathed on the disciples and said 'Receive the Holy Spirit'(Jn 20:22).[30] Within the picture of the human person created in the image and likeness of God and renewed by the Holy Spirit in the likeness of Christ there lies the basis for natural and revealed laws for Christian living. In particular, it is only through this perspective of man and woman created and redeemed in Christ that there can be obtained a true understanding of human dignity in its individual and social dimensions. Apart from the angels the human person is the only creature that God has desired for its own sake, and who has the capacity of knowing and loving his Creator.[31] Moreover, man and woman only find their full significance in relation to God in Christ. This is beautifully expressed in the poetry of Gerard Manley Hopkins:

> I am all at once what Christ is,
> since He was what I am, and
> This jack, joke, poor potsherd, patch,
> matchwood, immortal diamond
> Is immortal diamond.[32]

Often in contemporary thought, the relation of man and woman is distorted. In certain forms of feminism, which do not hide their Marxist inspiration, woman is depicted in a continual ongoing struggle with man, until she is finally freed by force and against her true nature. While it is true that women have been oppressed in many non-Christian cultures, a genuine liberation has been brought about by the advent of Christianity.[33] Sometimes a superficial desire for equality with man leads to confusion in terms of identity of gender, leading to the errors of the so-called 'unisex' culture. These notions are far from the Christian vision in which woman and man are equal co-heirs with Christ but different in their biological and psychological constitution. The differences between man and woman enrich the creation and the full theological consequences of this complementary nature need to be further explored, so that the true rôle of woman in society and in the Church may reach full development.[34] However, the authentic liberation of woman is that of freedom in Christ, rather than a mere socio-political liberty. Without this vision we are left with merely subjectivist and relativist trends which do not respect the human person in their richness and finish by imprisoning him or her in the vortex of anarchy or the trap of totalitarianism.

The restoration of the cosmos will continue without interruption until the end of the ages when Christ will come again. This process of transformation gives the Christian a measured sense of optimism; however the process is not smooth and problem-free, for man by his sins still wounds and hurts what God has made. Sometimes, poetic visions of the Redemption in relation to creation try to show that the Atonement is indeed an integral part of the cosmos:

> Did His creation, then, involve descent,
> Renunciation, Sacrifice in Heaven,
> A Calvary at the very heart of things,
> Wherein the Eternal Passion still enacts

In an eternal world what mortal eyes
Saw dimly on one shadowy hill of Time?[35]

This idea shows to its advantage that the Calvary mystery is not extrinsic to the creation. However the danger lies once more in jeopardizing the gratuity of God's action, this time in the Redemption. God's free gift is nowhere clearer than in the one who is already an example of the new creation in Christ, namely His Blessed Mother Mary. Through her, Christ has been able to redeem the cosmos.

7.3 *Creation and the Mother of God*

In Mary, the Mother of God, who was preserved from the stain of Original Sin, it is revealed that the new creation is even more marvellous than the old:

> It is an error to think that the day of the redemption can be compared with the day of the creation. In the beginning the earth was created, today it has been renewed; at the beginning, its produce was cursed through Adam's sin, but today peace and security are restored to it. In the beginning, death passed to all men because of the sin of our first parents; but today, through Mary, we have passed from death to life.[36]

In Mary the Mother of the Creator the mystery of grace and nature reaches its apex. She is the flower of all creation, the thornless rose who bore her Creator. In her is focussed all the goodness of creation, all the perfection of nature. At the same time, she is the one filled with grace and in her response to God, grace and nature find a perfect partnership, a true marriage. She is the Seat of

Wisdom and held in her womb Him who the world cannot hold within its bounds. She gave birth to Him Who bestows truth, goodness, oneness and beauty to all created things. Mary is the new Eve, the Mother of the New Creation, and the hope of creation on its earthly pilgrimage. Through her glorious Assumption, she is also the hope of the new heavens and the new earth where Christ will 'be all in all' (Col 3:11). She helps all humanity to be constantly renewed in the image of Him Who is the Creator of man (cf. Col 3:10).

Mary was predestined from all eternity to be Mother of God, and this predestination was associated with the Incarnation of the Divine Word.[37] Theological tradition has seen the divine choice of Mary as somehow connected with the act of creation; liturgical tradition has illustrated this idea in its choice of the following passage from the Old Testament Wisdom literature for Masses in honour of Our Lady:

> The Lord created me when His purpose first unfolded,
> before the oldest of His works.
> From everlasting I was firmly set,
> from the beginning, before earth came into being.
> I was by His side, a master craftsman,
> delighting in day after day, ever at play in His presence,
> at play everywhere in His world,
> delighting to be with the sons of men. (Pr 8:22–23, 30–31)

The key to interpreting this passage is to realize that it refers both to the eternal predestination of Christ and of Our Lady in such a way that the Our Lady's rôle is clearly subordinate to that of Christ. Thus, within the mystery of Christ, Mary is present even before the creation of the world, as the one whom the Father has chosen as Mother of His Son in the Incarnation.[38]

The bridegroom in the Song of Songs calls his bride an 'enclosed garden' and a 'sealed fountain' (Sg 4:12). Tradition has applied these expressions to Mary, the Mother of God. Our Lady is an 'enclosed garden' and 'sealed fountain' because of her perpetual virginity and at the same time her fruitful maternity. Mary welcomed into her womb the God who created her and thus, in a sense, she became a new garden of paradise, in which was planted Christ, the true Tree of Life: 'O blessed and more than blessed Virgin, through your blessing all creation is blessed... God Himself, who made all things, made Himself from Mary. In this way, He remade all that He had made'.[39] Not only is Our Lady truly the Model of the New Creation, but she also exercises an *active* and *dynamic* rôle in the restoration of creation. She is the Apex of all creation as St. Proclus of Constantinople remarks:

> O man, run through all creation with your thought, and see if there exists anything comparable to or greater than the holy Virgin, Mother of God. Circle the whole world, explore all the oceans, survey the air, question the skies, consider all the unseen powers, and see if there exists any other similar wonder in the whole creation... Count, then, the portents, and wonder at the superiority of the Virgin: she alone, in a way beyond words, received into her bridal chamber Him before whom all creation kneels with fear and trembling.[40]

The Mother of God was associated in a special way with her Son's life and ministry, for example in the Wedding Feast at Cana (Jn 2:1–12), where Christ's miraculous powers over the Creation were expressed when He changed water into wine. This miracle prefigures the still greater wonder of the Holy Eucharist. The intimate link between Christ and His Mother perdured until the moment of the Crucifixion and continued thereafter (Jn 19:26–27). Mary is, in a manner totally subordinate to Christ and completely dependent on Him, the Mediatrix of all graces. Thus all graces which the Spirit bestows to restore and recreate the cosmos come to us through the hands of the Blessed Virgin Mary. This manifold work of Mary is well-expressed by the Acathist hymn of the Byzantine tradition:

> Hail, O Tendril whose Bud shall not wilt;
> hail, O Soil whose fruit shall not perish!
> hail, O Gardener of the Gardener of Life!
> Hail, O Earth who yielded abundant mercies;
> hail, O Table full-laden with appeasement.
> Hail, for you have greened anew the pastures of delight;
> hail, for you have prepared a haven for souls.
> Hail, acceptable Incense of prayer;
> hail, expiation of the whole universe!
> Hail, o you favour of God to mortal men;
> hail, O you trust of mortals before God!.[41]

It is significant how this hymn uses images from created reality to illustrate Our Lady's part in the restoration of creation by her Son. Mary is a member of the Church *par excellence,* whose part in cosmic redemption will now be examined.

7.4 *Creation and the Church*

The doctrine of the Church as bride of Christ 'is rooted in the biblical reality of the creation of the human being as male and female'.[42] This is highlighted in the Song of Songs, which uses human love between a man and a woman as an image of God's love for His people or Christ's love for His Church. In a certain sense, the kiss imparted by the bridegroom to the bride in the Song of Songs (Sg 1:2) is symbolic of the new Creation. It is highly significant that the kiss is given right at the beginning of the Song in a type of analogy with the start of the book of Genesis (see Gn 2:7) and thus represents a new inbreathing of life into redeemed humanity. St Gregory of Nyssa observed the similarity between the kiss exchanged between the man and his spouse in the Song of Songs and the gratuitous and life-giving action of the Word and the Holy Spirit upon the soul.[43]

The Scriptural basis for the relation between the Church and the cosmos is outlined principally in the Letters to the Ephesians and to the Colossians. St Paul illustrates a double Lordship of Christ, that over the cosmos (Ep 1:10; 4:10; Ph 2:9–11) and that over the Church (Col 1:18). While the Church is presented as the Body of Christ (Col 1:18), the cosmos is never proposed as such and this contrasts sharply with the ancient Greek idea in which the universe is conceived as an enormous body. The glorified Christ acts in the cosmos through the mediation of the Church, the organ through which Christ gradually brings the universe into unity. Among the Greek Fathers it is especially Origen who highlights the idea that Christ is the cosmos of the Church and then the Church is the 'cosmos' of the cosmos.[44] This is, in fact, a play on the Greek expression 'cosmos' which can mean either adornment, order or world, so that 'Christ is the initiator of order in the world and the Church its mediator'.[45] The Church is sent to the world 'to gather together all people and all things into Christ'.[46] Not simply 'all people' but also 'all things' which therefore implies a cosmic rôle for the Church. The power of Christ through His Church does not bring human beings inexorably into an automatic unity with God: the free cooperation of rational creatures is required. However, as regards the non-rational creation, Christ is dependent in a certain sense and up to a certain point on the cooperation of human beings for bringing about His plan, as expressed in the command to His apostles which seems to imply a cosmic dimension: 'Go out to the whole world; proclaim the Good News to all creation' (Mk 16:15).

The *cosmic universality* of the Church's mission raises the question of rational extra-terrestrial beings. The possibility of other intelligent life in the cosmos is not incompatible with Christian tradition. However, infatuation with extra-terrestrial intelligence 'has always sought support in the materialist ideology of Darwinism which presents man as a chance product of purely material forces'.[47] The presence of other rational beings in the cosmos would raise many theological questions. Not least among these would be whether these creatures also fell from friendship with God, or whether they have simply been adversely affected by the cosmic repercussions of man's Fall. If they have not fallen, are they in a state of nature or of grace? If they have fallen, has the Word taken their nature and redeemed them as well as ourselves? Some theologians would see 'no fundamental reason why, in addition to human nature being hypostatically united to the Person of the divine Word, other finite rational creatures should not be united to that Person too. If finite and infinite natures are compatible in the Person of the Word, there seems no reason why several finite natures should not be equally compatible'.[48] However, this must be conceived in such a way that the uniqueness of Christ is not jeopardized. The idea of a multiple Incarnation smacks of the error that Jesus would simply be one of the many faces which the Logos has assumed in the course of time to communicate in a salvific way.[49] Instead, 'the doctrine of faith must be *firmly believed* which proclaims that Jesus of Nazareth, Son of Mary, and He alone, is the Son and the Word of the Father.'[50] Moreover, according to both the Letter of St Paul to the Ephesians (Ep 1:20–21) and the Letter to the Hebrews (Heb 2:7–8), through the redemptive Incarnation, Christ has supremacy over the cosmos not only as God, but also as man. The problem arises whether this teaching would allow an Incarnation of the Son in a rational species apart from human beings. The argument of 'both Ephesians and Hebrews rests upon the unquestioned, but also unformulated, assumption that there are no corporeal rational beings in the universe other than man'.[51] In any case, the question still remains whether the cosmic dimension of the mission of the Church would also include these hypothetical extraterrestrials within its purview.

The Sacraments of the Church involve the use of material elements such as water, oil, bread and wine. This means that creation is taken up into the new reality of God's economy of salvation. Nowhere is this more true than the most Holy Eucharist. At the Offertory of the Mass, the bread is presented as that 'which earth has given and human hands have made' and the wine is presented as 'fruit of the vine and work of human hands'. In each case we are reminded of the origin of the bread and wine in God's first creation and then of how the bread and wine are the result of man's work upon the raw materials of grain and grape. The transformation which man effects through his own efforts upon the grain and the grape in making the bread and wine, are however to be completely overshadowed by another transformation, effected by God. Transubstantiation, the complete change of the bread and wine into the Body and Blood of Christ so as to render present the Sacrifice of Calvary then leads to a further transformation. Christ's faithful themselves participate in this Sacrifice and Communion and are themselves changed into more perfect images of Christ. They can then be Christ's instruments in re-shaping creation according to His will. Thus it should never be forgotten that the offering of every Mass leaves the cosmos better off and in a more redeemed state. In this way the priest refashions creation, restoring it to God's image.[52]

The irruption of grace into the cosmos via its human stewards raises an important issue regarding the relationship between the sacred and the secular.[53] Some theologians would maintain that after the redemptive Incarnation, all creation has in a way become sacred, and that the old division between the sacred and the profane falls away. We would not go so far. First, the effects of Christ's Incarnation and Redemption are applied *through* the Church and her Sacraments which implies a zone of greater efficacious sacredness. Also, the cosmos has not yet been completely set free in

Christ, who is not yet 'all in all' (Col 3:11). Furthermore, there is a question of hierarchy, for some creatures are more sacred by reason of a higher position in the order of being (e.g. human life is more sacred than that of a dog) or of a greater participation in the life of grace.

If it is true that the Church is the cosmos which redeems the universe, then men and women need the Church even to live as decent human beings. As a result of the Fall, the human intellect is darkened and the human will confused, though man is not totally wounded. The human person therefore cannot see clearly all those truths of the natural law which would enable him to live in a truly civilized manner. Normally, from the natural law it would be clear that stealing is wrong. However, because of the disorder of concupiscence, man feels assaulted by irregular desire for that which belongs to someone else. Without those supernatural means which are to be found in the Church, humanity is unable to achieve fully even its own natural goals, such as harmony, peace and justice. Therefore, human society has need of the Church, a need which is more than ever evidenced by the problems facing society at the end of the twentieth century. The idea of a pluralist society in which a philosophical law of the jungle and of minority pressure groups rules the day is unacceptable. The further the nations distance themselves from the Church, the more they fall away into degradation, even at a material level; to be far from the Church is to be separated from Christ who alone can give the grace for human beings to live in harmony with each other and with the whole of creation. Grace flows from the Church and heals the cosmos, just as the water issuing from the

Temple brought health and life wherever it went (Ez 47:1–12). One area where this whole question is particularly highlighted is in the scientific aspect of modern society and some of its technological consequences, which form the material of the next two chapters.

Further Reading

Pope Benedict XVI, *Jesus of Nazareth: from the Baptism in the Jordan to the Transfiguration* (London : Bloomsbury, 2007)

J.-F. Bonnefoy, *Christ and the Cosmos* (Paterson, N. J.: St Anthony Guild Press, 1965)

S. L. Jaki, *The Savior of Science* (Washington, D.C.: Regnery Gateway, 1988)

Notes

1 The rationality, goodness and unity of the cosmos has already been discussed on pp. 13, 19–20, 83–88 above. The beauty of creation has been mentioned on pp. 13, 122–124 above.

2 See S. L. Jaki, *Science and Creation* (Edinburgh: Scottish Academic Press, 1986), Chapter Two 'The Lull of Yin and Yang', pp. 25–48.

3 See *ibid.*, Chapter One 'The Treadmill of Yugas', pp. 1–24.

4 See *ibid.*, Chapter Three 'The Wheels of Defeat', pp. 49–67.

5 See *ibid.*, Chapter Four 'The Shadow of Pyramids', pp. 68–83.

6 See pp. 19–20 above and Jaki, *Science and Creation*, Chapter Five 'The Omen of Ziggurats', pp. 84–101.

7 See Jaki, *Science and Creation*, Chapter Six 'The Labyrinths of the Lonely Logos', pp. 102–137.

8 See *ibid.*, Chapters Eleven 'The Interlude of "Re-naissance"',

pp. 248–275, Thirteen 'On Murky Backwaters', pp. 306–335, and Fourteen 'Oscillating Worlds and Wavering Minds', pp. 336–360 respectively.

9 P. Haffner, *Creation and Scientific Creativity: A Study in the Thought of S. L. Jaki* (Leominster: Gracewing, 2009), p. 189.

10 S. L. Jaki, *The Savior of Science* (Washington, D.C.: Regnery Gateway, 1988), p. 73.

11 See *ibid.*, p. 74.

12 See St Gregory Nazianzen, *Letter 101 to Cledonius* in *PG* 37, 181–184.

13 Vatican II, *Gaudium et Spes*, 22.

14 Pope John Paul II, Apostolic Letter *Tertio Millenio Adveniente*, 3.2.

15 For a development of cosmic Christology terminology see J. A. Lyons, *The Cosmic Christ in Origen and Teilhard de Chardin* (New York: Oxford University Press, 1982), pp. 1–73.

16 Pope John Paul II, Encyclical Letter *Dominum et Vivificantem*, 50.3.

17 St Irenaeus, *Against the heresies* Book 3, chapter 22, n.1.

18 See Pope John Paul II, *Tertio Millenio Adveniente*, 6.2. See also J.-F. Bonnefoy, *Christ and the Cosmos* (Paterson, N.J.: St Anthony Guild Press, 1965), p. 245.

19 S. L. Jaki, *Is There a universe?* (New York: Wethersfield Institute, 1993), p. 89.

20 St Thomas Aquinas, *Summa Theologiae* III, q.1, a.3.

21 See pp. 51, 167–170 above.

22 See pp. 191–197 above and p. 297 below.

23 See St John Chrysostom, *On the burial place and the Cross* 2 in *PG* 49, 396: 'At the foot of the tree the devil overcame Adam; at the foot of the tree Christ vanquished the devil. And that first tree sent men to Hades; this second one calls back even those who had already gone down there.'

24 See Vatican II, *Gaudium et Spes*, 2.2: 'It is the world… which in the Christian vision has been created and is sustained by the

love of its Maker, which has been freed from the slavery of sin by Christ, Who was crucified and rose again in order to break the stranglehold of the evil one, so that it might be fashioned anew according to God's design and brought to its fulfilment.'

25 See the *Reading from an ancient homily for Holy Saturday* which is the Second Reading in the Roman Breviary for Holy Saturday. Original text in *PG* 43, 461–462.

26 R. A. Knox, *The Hidden Stream* (London: Burns Oates, 1952), pp. 90–91.

27 G. K. Chesterton, *The Everlasting Man* (Garden City, New York: Image Books, 1955), pp. 216–217.

28 See *CCC* 349. See also St Augustine *Sermon 8 in the Octave of Easter* in *PL* 46, 841: 'This is the octave day of your new birth. Today is fulfilled in you the sign of faith that was prefigured in the Old Testament by the circumcision of the flesh on the eighth day after birth. When the Lord rose from the dead, He put off the mortality of the flesh; His risen body was still the same body, but it was no longer subject to death. By His resurrection He consecrated Sunday, or the Lord's Day. Though the third after His passion, this day is the eighth after the Sabbath, and thus also the first day of the week.'

29 St Leo the Great, *Sermon 1 on the Ascension* 4 in *PL* 54, 396.

30 See Pope John Paul II, *Discourse at General Audience* 10 January 1990 in *IG* 13/1 (1990), p.49.

31 See Vatican II, *Gaudium et Spes*, 24.2.

32 G. M. Hopkins, 'That Nature is a Heraclitean Fire and of the comfort of the Resurrection.'

33 See *Message of the Second Vatican Council to Women*, 8th December 1965, in *Enchiridion Vaticanum 1* (Bologna: EDB, 1981), 501, which points out that the Church is proud of having exalted and liberated woman, and having highlighted, over the centuries, her fundamental equality with man, within a diversity of characters. See also pp. 113–115 above.

34 See V. Hartley von Knieriem, unpublished thesis *Towards a Theology of Woman according to Paul Evdokimov* (Rome: Pontifical Institute Regina Mundi, 1995).

35 A. Noyes, *The Torch-Bearers* Part III (Edinburgh and London: William Blackwood and Sons, 1930) p. 201.

36 St Ephraem the Syrian, deacon, *Sermo III de diversis* in *Enchiridion Marianum* (Rome: Cor Unum, 1974), N° 325, p. 211.

37 See Vatican II, *Lumen Gentium*, 61.

38 See Pope John Paul II, Encyclical Letter *Redemptoris Mater* 8.5.

39 St Anselm, *Oration 52*, *PL* 158, 955–956.

40 St Proclus of Constantinople, *Homily* 5, 2 in *PG* 65, 717-720.

41 *The Acathist Hymn*, Fifth Chant.

42 Pope John Paul II, Apostolic Letter *Mulieris Dignitatem* 23.2.

43 See St Gregory of Nyssa, *Sermon 1 on the Song of Songs* in *PG* 44, 785–786.

44 See Origen, *Commentary on St John's Gospel* Book 6, n.38 in *PG* 14, 301–302: 'Mundus autem et ornamenti est Ecclesia, Christo exsistente mundo et ornamento Ecclesiae, quippe qui sit prima lux mundi.'

45 Lyons, *The Cosmic Christ in Origen and Teilhard de Chardin*, p. 142.

46 Congregation for the Doctrine of the Faith, *Letter to the Bishops of the Catholic Church on Some Aspects of the Church Understood as Communion*, 28 May 1992, 4.2 in *ORE* N.24 (17 June 1992), p. 8.

47 Haffner, *Creation and Scientific Creativity*, p. 130.

48 E. L. Mascall, *Christian Theology and Natural Science* (London: Longmans Green and Co, 1957), p. 41.

49 See Congregation for the Doctrine of the Faith, Declaration *Dominus Iesus* (2000), 9.

50 *Ibid.*, 10.

51 Mascall, *Christian Theology and Natural Science*, p. 45.

52 See St Gregory Nazianzen, *Oratio* 2, 71-74 in 35, 480-481.

53 See our discussion on legitimate autonomy in the created order in chapter five, section 5.4 above.

8

Christian Revelation and Scientific Revolution

With such a mind,
We might achieve, not that armed truce of thought
Between the Faith and Science, reconciled
Only to pass, and shun each other's gaze,
But that great golden symphony of thought
Which, long ago, the Angelic Doctor heard
Throbbing from hell to heaven, organic truth,
Wherein each note, in its own grade, rings clear,
As in a single orchestra, whose chords
Were chaos, till each filled its own true place
In the one golden cosmos of the song.

Alfred Noyes, *The Torch-Bearers*

Over the past century, society has changed more profoundly and more rapidly than during any other period in history. Transport by land, sea and air, space travel, computer technology, telecommunications, the information superhighway, antibiotics, are only some examples of the scientific revolution which has taken place. Mankind has advanced greatly in its understanding of the universe from atoms to galaxies; the Human Genome

Project which seeks to map all human genes should herald a new era in medical understanding of the human body and in treating disease. These rapid developments have given rise to a variety of questions which have a bearing upon the theology of creation.

8.1 A Linguistic Perspective

An introduction to the vast area of relations between faith in God the Creator and modern science may be obtained by considering various meanings of faith and of science:

Faith

1. The act of believing.
2. The consequences of faith, religious practice as a way of life.
3. Statements of faith (creeds, theologies).
4. Faith organized institutionally and communities of faith.

Science

1. The method of knowing in science.
2. The scientific enterprise; its technological application and practice.
3. The cumulative and growing corpus of tested and acknowledged propositions and hypotheses in science.
4. Science organized institutionally and the scientific communities.[1]

Any approach to relating faith in God the Creator with science must take into account the multi-faceted meanings of both faith and science. Science consists of many branches, and often physics is taken to be the prime model of the exact sciences, because of its phenomenology which can be clearly traced, its mathematical structure, its power of describing reality and its precision. The question then arises as to how the multifarious dimensions of faith relate to the various aspects of science. It is soon perceived that science and religion make up, even from a linguistic point of view, two different systems. Corresponding to the differences between scientific and religious language, there is also a difference in *method*. Essentially, while science deals with human investigation of creation, Christian faith treats of the initiative taken by God in revealing that which is beyond the reach of the human mind, and also that which, as a result of the Fall, the human mind would have great difficulty in deducing.[2]

However, it is insufficient to consider the issue of relations between faith and science merely from a linguistic viewpoint; rather the question must be faced of what lies beneath language and gives it meaning and its foundation:

> Belief in the Word (Logos), eternally uttered by the Father, has become the salvation of human words as well. Only in that perspective have these words remained immune to being degraded into mere tools of facile intellectual games, all aimed at undermining the intellect itself.[3]

Thus, language cannot simply be defined in terms of its use, nor solely with regard to the individuals or community who express themselves with it, nor simply considering the interrelation between the various words which make it up. Rather, language must be referred to what lies beneath, namely *being* which it seeks to describe; language must be seen in terms of its metaphysical basis. In this sense, religious language and scientific language will have points of contact to the extent that they both deal with created reality. However, scientific language cannot approach God the Creator, for He is beyond its sphere of competence. Nevertheless, scientific language requires a grounding in metaphysics so as to be able to answer such questions as (a) the relationships between science and other disciplines, (b) the implicit assumptions of science and (c) the limits of science.

8.2 A Historical Perspective

While, at first sight, the centuries-long history of theology and science seems to have been plagued with problems, such as the Galileo affair, at a deeper level there is a better relationship than might be imagined. First, the idea of estrangement between the Church and science has been exaggerated by the enemies of both the Church and science. It is beyond the scope of this work to enter into the details of the Galileo case but even there 'the agreements between religion and science are more numerous and above all more important than the incomprehension which led to the bitter and painful conflict that continued in the course of the following centuries'.[4] It is true that in the Galileo affair, as in other misunderstandings, a healing of memories is needed.

What can be learned from the Galileo case is that is necessary to delineate with increasing clarity the respective fields of competence, methods and value of the conclusions of science and theology, according to their respective nature. In particular, the Holy Scriptures do not teach us scientific details about the physical world but rather the fact that it was created.[5] However, it is also true that the Galileo affair has been so highlighted as to obscure the many examples of harmonious and fruitful collaboration between the Church and science. Indeed there have been many cases where devout Christians have made a prodigious contribution to science, including Nicolaus Copernicus, the astronomer (+1543), Gregor Mendel (+1884), the author of Mendel's law of heredity, and Bishop Niels Stensen (+1686), the great geologist and anatomist who discovered the duct (*Ductus Stenonianus*) which carries saliva from the parotid gland to the mouth.

One fundamental historical question stands out in bold relief, namely why science only came to its viable birth during the high Middle Ages. Modern experimental science was rendered possible as a result of the Christian philosophical atmosphere of the Middle Ages. Although a *talent* for science was certainly present in the ancient world (for example in the design and construction of the Egyptian pyramids), nevertheless the philosophical and psychological climate was hostile to a self-sustaining scientific process. Thus science suffered stillbirths in the cultures of ancient China, India, Egypt, Babylonia. It also failed to come to fruition among the Maya, Incas, and Aztecs of the Americas. Even though ancient Greece came closer to achieving a continuous scientific enterprise than any other ancient culture, science was not born there either. Science did not come to birth among the medieval Muslim heirs to Aristotle. Jaki links these stillbirths in science with the doctrine concerning original sin.[6] It is the weakening of the intellect which was the cause of false visions of the cosmos, involving eternal cycles and a necessary universe. The psychological climate of such ancient cultures was often either hopelessness or complacency,[7] and in either case there was a failure to arrive at a belief in the existence of God the Creator, and an inability to produce a self-sustaining scientific enterprise.

If science suffered only stillbirths in ancient cultures, how did it come to its unique viable birth? The beginning of science as a fully fledged enterprise took place in relation to two important definitions of the Magisterium of the Church. The first was the definition at the Fourth Lateran Council that the universe was created out of nothing at the beginning of time.[8] The second magisterial statement was at local level, enunciated by Bishop Stephen Tempier of Paris who, on 7th March 1277 condemned 219 Aristotelian propositions, so outlawing the deterministic and necessitarian views of the creation. These statements of the teaching authority of the Church expressed an atmosphere in which faith in God the Creator had penetrated the medieval culture and given rise to philosophical consequences. The cosmos was seen as contingent in its *existence* and thus dependent on a divine choice which called it into being; the universe is also contingent in its *nature* and so God was free to create this particular form of world among an infinity of other possibilities. Thus the cosmos cannot be a necessary form of existence, and so has to be approached by *a posteriori* investigation. The universe is also rational, and therefore a coherent discourse can be made about it. Indeed the contingency and rationality of the cosmos are like two pillars supporting the Christian vision of the cosmos.

> The contingency of the universe obviates an *a priori* discourse about it, while its rationality makes it accessible to the mind though only in an *a posteriori* manner…; the rise of science needed the broad and persistent sharing by the whole population, that is, an entire culture, of a very specific body of doctrines relating the universe to a universal and absolute intelligibility embodied in the tenet about a personal God, the Creator of all.[9]

Therefore it was not chance that the first physicist was John Buridan, professor at the Sorbonne in Paris around the year 1330, just after the time of the two above-mentioned statements of the Church's teaching office. Buridan's vision of the universe was steeped in the Christian doctrine of the creation; in particular, he rejected the Aristotelian idea of a cosmos existing from all eternity. He developed the idea of impetus, in which God was seen as responsible for the initial setting in motion of heavenly bodies, which then remained in motion without the necessity of a direct action on the part of God. This was different from Aristotle's approach, in which the motion of heavenly bodies had no beginning and would also have no end. Buridan's work was continued by his disciple, Nicholas Oresme, around the year 1370; impetus theory anticipated Newton's first law of motion.[10]

As already indicated in the preceding chapter, the redemptive Incarnation guarantees the Christian vision of Creation and has effected a process of conversion not only in individuals, but in culture as a whole. This conversion to Christianity has had material as well as spiritual effects for, 'even in the secular history of mankind the Gospel has acted as a leaven in the interests of liberty and progress'.[11] Thus Christian faith, although primarily connected with eternal life, has a real effect on the here and now. This idea has its basis in the scriptures where Christ says to his followers that setting their hearts first on God's Kingdom will have beneficial effects not only in heaven, but also here upon earth: 'Set your hearts on his Kingdom first, and on his righteousness and all these other things will be yours as well.' (Mt 6:33) The followers of Christ are promised something of a recompense in this life (despite persecutions) as well as the reward in the life to come: 'And everyone who has left houses, brothers, sisters, father, mother, children or land for the sake of my name will be repaid a hundred times over and also inherit eternal life' (Mt 19:29).[12] One specific 'reward' which Christian faith in God the Creator has brought about is a reinforcement of the realist vision of the universe which was germane to the unique rise of science. The healing power of Christ has changed human society for the better, and scientific progress is but one example of the advance in human culture, as a fruit of divine Providence.

Nevertheless, there are those who would claim that the scientific progress stimulated by Christianity has in fact brought in its wake many problems and much evil.[13] If Christianity is responsible for the unique birth of science, is it not also to be blamed for the technological ills which beset the world of today? A distinction needs to be made here between scientific discovery and its technological application. Now the reason why there is a moral crisis concerning technological application of various products of science (for example, discoveries in nuclear physics and in bio-engineering) is that while the philosophical framework conducive to scientific discovery has been handed on as an implicit (and often subconscious) body of principles, nevertheless because Western society is no longer (in many parts) explicitly Christian, it lacks the courage and the apparatus to tackle such moral questions. The application of science therefore rests upon purely political or economic criteria which can only be described as utilitarian, without proper regard for the good of the human person and his environment, about which more will be said in the following chapter.

A few vaguely Christian ideals have therefore been inherited by a secularized and secularizing society where there is a lack of radical Christian culture and vision to back up the vague ideals. Agnostics feel frustrated because they are unable to link up the implicit cultural principles with a synthetic Christian vision, and some Christians feel inadequate because they do not see the way forward very clearly. Progress lies in seeing that since science grew up in a Christian milieu, its applications were, at first, put to use according to a Christian ethic arising from Christian faith in God the Creator who had left these moral laws imprinted upon creation. It is of course true that man has the power to read the natural law written upon his heart, even aside from

Revelation, but because of the Fall, the will of man is adversely affected in making moral decisions. Furthermore, Revelation does not merely reinforce the natural law, but shows a more perfect way. Christ reveals to mankind perfect Man as well as true God; through the Incarnation and Redemption, grace is given to guide man towards this ideal revealed by and in Christ.[14] Hence the need for a specifically Christian morality to provide criteria which guide mankind away from purely greedy or destructive applications of science. Since they do not contain their own explanation within their own fields, science, language and history all need to be referred to metaphysics, before any dialogue between faith and science can be made or before any consistent ethical discourse can be pursued.

8.3 A Philosophical Perspective

The philosophical vision of the Christian Middle Ages perceived the cosmos as demythologized, free from the capricious whims of pantheistic voluntarism reified in pagan deities. The universe was seen as a unity, therefore offering a challenge to investigators to search for the connections in nature and make them explicit. It was regarded as intelligible and consistent, and therefore encouraging a reliable investigation which would hold in all experiments; it was seen as good and therefore attracting man to take an interest in it. Finally the cosmos was seen as beautiful, and therefore investigation of it gave a participation in such beauty which elevated the mind and heart of the believing scientist to the Creator.

Often without being aware of it, scientists make some basic, implicit assumptions about their work, which are inherited from the medieval realist vision. Four implicit properties of the cosmos make scientific endeavour possible. First, the cosmos has an objective existence and reality independent of the observer, which of course does not negate a real interaction between the scientist and the universe. Second, the material entities in the universe must have a coherent intelligibility, the basic condition for rendering possible their investigation. Third, for science the universe has to be one, a true cosmos. This guarantees the consistent interaction of things (with order, stability and predictability) which is the basis for physical laws. Fourth, the very specific form in which the coherent whole or universe exists cannot be considered as a necessary form of existence.[15] Scientists also assume that scientific knowledge is worth having and sharing, and also believe in scientific progress. In other words they would hold that as science goes forward it acquires a body of knowledge which is, despite the ebb and flow of human fortunes, an increasingly accurate account and description of the created world.

The inherent limits of science and also its relations to other disciplines is a many-faceted question. Its intrinsic limitation is connected with the method of investigating the reality which is its object. For instance, in the study of the human person, physics, chemistry, biology and psychology all enjoy their respective limited spheres of competence. One question is whether, given time, a particular science can arrive at a *complete* description of the reality which is its object. An answer to this problem should avoid both agnosticism or excessive confidence. Despite setbacks, science proceeds to give an increasingly complete picture of reality. However, will this progress ever yield a final complete theory? The journey inside the atomic microstructure of matter illustrates this process.

> About a century ago, atoms were considered to be the ultimate, indivisible components of matter. At that time, the quality of indivisibility was attributed to electrons, protons and neutrons. Today, the physicist 'prefers to compare the structure of matter to a succession of layers that, like the layers of an onion, reveal themselves only one at a time.' The physicist is faced with the question: 'Will there be an end to these layers in terms of the ultimate in matter or will the process of peeling away these layers continue ad infinitum?'[16]

The adventure of investigation cannot continue indefinitely since a finite entity cannot have 'an infinite number of constituents'.[17] However the journey cannot be easily or quickly concluded. First, more and more precise and high energy instruments are needed to arrive at ever smaller constituents of matter. Then how can one know that the smallest particle of matter has been reached? Further, what restrictions does Heisenberg's Uncertainty Principle impose on the search for the bases of matter?[18]

A related question is whether it is possible, given a complete physical theory of the microstructure of matter, to obtain an entire overview of the macrostructure or of the material universe as a whole. Pope John Paul II inclines to the view that this should be possible: 'A person who believes in the essential goodness of all creation is capable of discovering all the secrets of creation, in order to perfect continually the work assigned to him by God'.[19] In the Pope's approach however, there is none of the arrogance of Stephen Hawking who claimed that the complete vision of the universe would enable us 'to know the mind of God'.[20] In any case, a complete vision of the cosmos cannot be arrived at soon, simply because of the highly sophisticated scientific instruments required in this area of investigation. Even if and when a complete description of the cosmos is realised 'that theory or understanding will not be *necessarily* true. In other words, its truth will not be demonstrated on a priori grounds'.[21] On the other hand, the limits within any current scientific vision cannot be regarded as a proof of the existence of God, because once this gap in our knowledge is closed, our belief in God may be compromised. This error is known as that of the 'God of the gaps', and is a reduction of the doctrine concerning God. Why should He be placed only at the point of human ignorance, rather than in the universe as a whole and also beyond it in His transcendence?

Science is not only limited by the ever-advancing frontier of its own knowledge at a given time, but also in relation to other disciplines. To reduce other spheres of human knowledge and experience such as philosophy, art, poetry to a purely scientific discourse would be to commit the error of scientism. Science has its own sphere of competence with its own legitimate autonomy:

> By the very circumstance of their having been created, all things are endowed with their own stability, truth, goodness, proper laws and order. Man must respect these and recognize the appropriate methods of the individual sciences or arts.[22]

However, the autonomy of science is not absolute, because no discipline can furnish a complete view of the whole gamut of human experience. Thus each science needs to be complemented by other spheres of knowledge. This is true even within the sciences themselves. For example, to construct a scientific picture of the human person it is necessary to put together the results of the various branches of medicine, as well as psychology and anthropology. However, even this would only give a partial view, for the history of man is also needed to colour in the picture further. The sciences themselves need to be complemented by philosophy to give a deeper and broader understanding of their own material. On many occasions, science uncovers evidence of a purpose or design within the universe, of which it is incapable of giving a complete explanation. In this sense the scientific enterprise points beyond its own sphere to philosophy. Indeed, in the relationship of faith and science, realist philosophy is a kind of 'bridge' linking the two in a way which respects the proper nature, method and content of each of these disciplines:

> Man is created *one* in his different capabilities to know the real, whether they be analytical or synthetical, inductive or deductive, observational or intuitive... It is our conviction that in realizing our own unity as persons we may be able to deepen ever more the inner connection between the science of the divine origin and aim of all things and the science of their functions and mutual interactions.[23]

8.4 Theology and Science

Pope Pius XI enunciated what must be the first principle concerning relations between science and religion, when he stated that 'science as a true understanding of reality can never contradict the truths of the Christian faith'.[24] Pope Pius XII further delineated this relationship:

> Science, which has encountered the Creator in its path, philosophy, and, much more, revelation, in harmonious collaboration because all three are instruments of truth, like rays of the same sun, contemplate the substance, reveal the outlines, and portray the lineaments of the same Creator.[25]

The Second Vatican Council reaffirmed the fundamental link between faith and science in terms of the legitimate autonomy of earthly affairs:

> Methodical research in all branches of knowledge, provided it is carried out in a truly scientific manner and does not override moral laws, can never conflict with the faith, because the things of the world and the things of faith derive from the same God.[26]

The respect for the proper sphere of competence of each of science and theology is reflected in three particular concrete problems.

8.4.1 Modern cosmology and creation out of nothing

Recent history illustrates various attempts of scientists leaving their own proper sphere of competence to steal for themselves the rôle of Creator through a series of increasingly greater thefts: 'The story is the cheater's progress from infinitesimally petty thefts to a robbery which has for its target the empirically ultimate robbery or the universe itself'.[27] The first theft in the chain was very small. It occurred in 1927, when Heisenberg formulated and interpreted his Uncertainty Principle, which expresses the minimum possible degree of inexactitude in the measurement of certain complementary variables. For example, the more accurately we measure the position of an electron, the greater is the uncertainty in the determination of its velocity. However, Heisenberg interpreted the uncertainty principle as uncertainty at the level of being, rather than within the purely operational sphere of measurement. In this way, considering radioactive decay, the proponents of inexactitude in ontological causality allowed a small amount of matter to be 'unaccounted for in the sense of being an uncaused entity that can come and go for no reason whatever'.[28]

The next step in this cosmic robbery occurred when the so-called Steady State Theory was proposed in 1948 by Bondi, Gold and Hoyle. The idea was that, as galaxies receded from each other, new galaxies would be continuously formed from fresh matter which emerged spontaneously. The steady state theorists wished to assure that the universe was not created out of nothing but effectively generated itself. According to this theory, the universe should appear uniform from whatever point in space or time it was observed from. There should also be an excess of radiation given out by the hydrogen atoms which are produced according to the theory. However, the artificial satellites of the 1970's failed to show up the radiation postulated by the Steady State Theory. A clearer calculation of the number of galaxies carried out with radiotelescopes discredited this theory, and its final death knell was sounded by the discovery in 1964 by Penzias and Wilson of a cosmic background radiation which indicated that the cosmos must have been much denser in the past.

Even around the 1960's, some cosmologists tried to prevent the cosmos from inevitable aging by proposing an oscillating universe, in which expansion would be followed by a contraction and then expansion and contraction would go on for ever. Naturally, they could not ignore the law of entropy.[29] Successive cycles would be progressively less energetic. Therefore they supposed that at the end of every cycle the universe would suck 'new' matter from 'nothing' outside of the universe, rather like a cosmic petrol pump. However how could matter appear on its own from nothing?

Finally, the ultimate theft was proposed by Hawking, who seems to give an ontological status to the Uncertainty Principle, which he says 'is a fundamental, inescapable property of the world'.[30] At first, he thought that there was an initial singularity of the cosmos, and then in 1981 he used quantum gravity considerations to propose the idea that time and space together form a surface of finite dimensions, but without any edge or boundary. In Hawking's words:

> There would be no singularities at which the laws of science would break down and no edge of space-time at which one would have to appeal to God or some new law to set the boundary conditions for space-time. One could say: 'The boundary condition of the universe is that it has no boundary.' The universe would be completely self-contained and not affected by anything outside itself. It would be neither created or destroyed. It would just BE.[31]

Significantly, Hawking admits that 'this idea that space and time could be finite without boundary is just a *proposal*: it cannot be deduced from any other principle. Like any other scientific theory, it may initially be put forward for aesthetic or metaphysical reasons, but the real test is whether it makes predictions that agree with observation. This, however, is difficult to determine in the case of quantum gravity'.[32] It would seem that Hawking departs from the sphere of competence of science, saying that a theory may be put forward for aesthetic or metaphysical reasons. We would say that a hypothesis should be proposed on the basis of an already existing hypothesis and some empirical data, however remote. It seems that Hawking eliminates God with an *a priori* hypothesis, which makes his argument circular. His conclusion is: 'So long as the universe had a beginning, we could suppose it had a creator. But if the universe is really self-contained, having no boundary or edge, it would have neither beginning or end: it would simply be. What place, then, for a creator?'[33] Hawking seems to limit God's action to an initial singularity in a deistic approach, resulting in a 'God of the gaps'. The proposition that the universe gave birth to itself in a type of quantum fluctuation is but one example of an illegitimate extrapolation of science outside its own sphere. Physical science has to be related to real or possible experiments, and this cannot be the case in the consideration of the absolute origin of the whole universe from nothing. Science is radically incapable of measuring the boundary of the *whole* universe in space or time, because a scientist cannot get outside of the cosmos.

The world, far from originating out of chaos, resembles an ordered book; it is a cosmos. Notwithstanding elements of the irrational, chaotic and the destructive in the long processes of change in the cosmos, matter as such is legible and as such has an inbuilt mathematics. The human mind therefore can engage not only in a cosmography studying measurable phenomena but also in a cosmology discerning the visible inner logic of the cosmos. We may not at first be able to see the harmony both of the whole and of the relations of the individual parts, or their relationship to the whole. Yet, there always remains a broad range of intelligible events, and the process is rational in that it reveals an order of evident correspondences and undeniable finalities: in the inorganic world, between microstructure and macrostructure; in the organic and animal world, between structure and function; and in the spiritual world, between knowledge of the truth and the aspiration to freedom.[34]

8.4.2 *Modern cosmology and creation with time*

The second concrete example of relations between spheres of competence of theology and of science concerns the link (if any) existing between the Big Bang theory and the doctrine of creation with time. In brief, the Big Bang theory traces its origins back to the beginning of this century when, between 1915 and 1917, A. Einstein proposed the first coherent theory of the cosmos as a whole. In 1922, the Russian mathematician A. Friedmann adapted Einstein's model for a universe in expansion. In 1927, the Belgian priest and astronomer Mgr. G. E. Lemaître suggested the idea of a primitive atom and an initial explosion. In 1929, the American E. Hubble showed, from spectroscopic considerations, that the elements making up the universe were receding from each other in the manner of an expanding sphere. Then, the cosmic background radiation discovered in the mid-sixties by A. Penzias and R. Wilson was seen to represent the final cooling-down phase after an enormous initial explosion of the cosmos. To these scientific data it is necessary to add considerations of the relative proportions of common elements in the cosmos today, as well as the latest understanding of sub-atomic physics: these are the basic ingredients of the Big Bang theory which consists of several variants with various corrections.

The theory shows how the physical cosmos has evolved in various stages from the first tiny fraction of a second of its existence until today. However, is the Christian justified in saying that the Big Bang theory really indicates the beginning of time? The answer is in the negative, again because it is beyond the field of competence of science to affirm this. Whether philosophy can arrive at the truth of creation with time is already a disputed question,[35] but the beginning of time is certainly outside the competence of science:

> Physics in no way contains a proof of a temporal beginning of the universe. The method of physics always means an inference from one observable state to another... There is no observable state, however primordial, about which physics could establish that it had to be preceded by that very nothing... which has really nothing to it.[36]

Even philosophy, when it examines the Big Bang theory, is faced with a difficulty in trying to demonstrate the beginning of the cosmos. The cosmos is like a safe with a combination-lock and the combination is locked inside the safe.[37] We cannot be sure that the initial state indicated by science was not preceded by some other more primitive state:

> Any scientific hypothesis on the origin of the world, such as the hypothesis of a primitive atom from which derived the whole of the physical universe, leaves open the problem concerning the universe's beginning. Science cannot of itself solve this question: there is needed that human knowledge that rises above physics and astrophysics and which is called metaphysics.[38]

Philosophically, it may be possible to argue that all physical cosmic processes are temporal and have a beginning. Therefore it seems reasonable that the cosmos taken as a whole should also have a beginning in time.

8.4.3 Evolution and creation

A third potential minefield of relations between science and theology deals with the contribution of evolution to the understanding of creation. In a manner analogous to the study of the development of the material cosmos, the study of evolution seeks to uncover the secrets of the world of living creatures from its earliest phases. Evolutionary analysis seeks to examine the development of more complex living organisms from simpler ones. The scientific theories of evolution are based on various pieces of empirical data. From palaeontology, which studies the fossils and other remains of ancient organisms buried in earth and ice, is obtained the only direct evidence of evolution. There are, however, many theories regarding the passage from one animal to another, to attempt an explanation of how the various transitions took place. Comparative anatomy and physiology indicated relations between living beings and also uncovered evidence of evolutionary adaptation. Comparisons between the genetic make-up of different species of living organisms have demonstrated a link between various living beings, even between plants and animals. The geographical distribution of various species yields evidence concerning evolution, if continental drift is taken into account. From all the data, it has been possible to draw up evolutionary trees, to show how some living organisms have developed from others. The various strands of evidence corroborate each other, pointing to the theory that evolution played a part in the development of life upon this planet.

Nevertheless, in the scientific domain, several empirical links are missing in the chain of evidence needed to prove evolution at every stage in the biological process. Moreover while *micro-evolution* (the study of transitions between very similar organisms) can in some cases be clearly documented, *macro-evolution* (which studies a larger picture of relations between very different living organisms) is a much more difficult proposition. However attractive it may be to extrapolate, it does not necessarily follow that, because a certain degree of evolution has been shown to occur, therefore *any* degree of evolution is possible: "There is obviously an enormous difference between the evolution of a colour change in a moth's wing and the evolution of an organ like the human brain, and the fruit flies of Hawaii, for example, are utterly trivial compared with the differences between a mouse and an elephant, or an octopus and a bee."[39]

The theory of evolution is not a complete, scientifically proven theory. The immense time span that evolution covers makes it impossible to conduct experiments in a controlled environment to finally verify or disprove the theory. As Pope Benedict XVI remarked: 'We cannot haul 10,000 generations into the laboratory.'[40]

The empirical data cannot justify the proposition of some evolutionists that genetic mutations came about by pure chance. Care must be taken to distinguish between hard scientific fact (obtained in an *a posteriori* manner) in the theory of evolution and an unjustified *a priori* extrapolation of this theory to form an atheist ideology. A complete understanding of the evolution of living beings should take into account not only the effects of the environment or genetic modifications, but above all should be open to considering the power of Providence guiding created beings through the laws inscribed upon them. Blind chance cannot be responsible for coordinated developments which gave rise to complex biological structures like the eye or the ear:

> It is the affair of the natural sciences to explain how the tree of life in particular continues to grow and how new branches shoot out from it. This is not a matter for faith. But we must have the audacity to say that the great projects of the living creation are not the products of chance and error. Nor are they the products of a selective process to which divine predicates can be attributed in illogical, unscientific, and even mythic fashion.[41]

Evolution cannot be seen as a means to exclude the Creator but rather presupposes creation. Indeed creation can be seen in the light of evolution as an event which is extended in time—like a continuous creation—in which God is clearly seen as the Creator of heaven and earth.[42] The theory of natural evolution, understood in a sense that does not exclude divine causality, does not necessarily contradict the truth which the Book of Genesis presents concerning the creation of the visible world.[43] Evolution may be envisaged as a kind of programmed creation, in which God has written into creation the laws for its evolution; in this way a clear link can be seen between God's action at the beginning and His constant Providence.

Currently, there seems to be a somewhat fierce debate raging between so-called 'creationism' and evolutionism, presented as though they were mutually exclusive alternatives: those who believe in the Creator would not be able to conceive of evolution, and those who instead support evolution would have to exclude God. This antithesis is unhelpful because, on the one hand, there is scientific proof of evolution which enriches our knowledge of life and being as such. However on the other, the doctrine of evolution does not answer every query, especially the great philosophical question: Where does everything come from? Moreover, how did everything start which ultimately led to man?[44]

In this context, *Intelligent Design* refers to a scientific research program as well as a community of scientists, philosophers and other scholars who seek evidence of design in nature.[45] The theory of intelligent design holds that certain features of the universe and of living things are best explained by an intelligent cause, not an undirected process such as natural selection.[46] Through the study and analysis of a system's components, a design theorist is able to determine whether various natural structures are the product of chance, natural law, intelligent design, or some combination thereof. This research is carried out by observing the types of information (specificity, interacting parts and irreducible complexity) produced when intelligent agents act. Scientists then seek to find objects which have those same types of informational properties which we commonly know come from intelligence. Intelligent design has applied these scientific methods to detect design in irreducibly complex biological structures, the complex and specified information content in DNA, the life-sustaining physical architecture of the universe, and the geologically rapid origin of biological diversity in the fossil record during the Cambrian explosion approximately 530 million years ago.

Intelligent design is not the same as creationism. The theory of intelligent design is simply an effort to empirically detect whether the 'apparent design' in nature acknowledged by virtually all biologists is genuine design (the product of an intelligent cause) or is simply the product of an undirected process such as natural selection acting on random variations. Creationism typically starts with a religious text and tries to see how the findings of science can be reconciled to it. Intelligent design starts with the empirical evidence of nature and seeks to ascertain what inferences can be drawn from that evidence. Unlike creationism, the scientific theory of intelligent design does not claim that modern biology can identify whether the intelligent cause detected through science is supernatural.

For Stanley Jaki, the theory has serious chinks in its armour about which Christians should be fully aware. On no account should they espouse the fallacy of the 'biblical' doctrine of the special creation of each species. This notion flies in the face of sound exegesis and sane theology. The very serious shortcomings of Darwinian theory cannot be remedied with Intelligent Design theory, which philosophically cannot cope with design and purpose. Even worse, as it claims to be a 'scientific' theory of evolution, it implies that design, insofar as it means purpose (and indeed divine purpose) can be the object of measurements, which is the touchstone of truth in science.[47]

However, the concept of Intelligent Design can be readily applied at the philosophical and theological level. Joseph Ratzinger pointed this out when he wrote:

> *The great projects of the living creation point to a creating Reason and show us a creating Intelligence,* and they do so more luminously and radiantly today than ever before. Thus we can say today with a new certitude and joyousness that the human being is indeed a divine project, which only the creating Intelligence was strong and great and audacious enough to conceive of. *Human beings are not a mistake but something willed; they are the fruit of love.*[48]

Later, as Pope Benedict XVI, commenting upon a homily of St Basil, he clearly affirmed the abundant presence of evidence for purpose and true design in the world, and the intelligibility of this design on the part of man:

> I find the words of this fourth-century Father surprisingly up to date when he says: Some people, 'deceived by the atheism they bore within them, imagined that the universe lacked guidance and order, at the mercy as it were of chance'. How many these 'some people' are today! Deceived by atheism they consider and seek to prove that it is scientific to think that all things lack guidance and order as though they were at the mercy of chance. The Lord through Sacred Scripture reawakens our reason which has fallen asleep and tells us: in the beginning was the creative Word. In the beginning the creative Word—this Word that created all things, that created this intelligent design which is the cosmos—is also love.[49]

Concerning the evolution of sub-human life, from ancient times until the eighteenth century, it was thought that living beings could come into existence from inorganic matter, without the intervention of another living being. This theory, known as spontaneous generation, has been discarded as a result of the research of Pasteur and others last century. Up until now, science and technology have not been able to produce life *in vitro* from inanimate material. The principle *omne vivum ex vivo* seems to hold, namely that living beings can only evolve from other living beings. Even if the spontaneous generation of living beings was seen to be possible, this would not be an argument against the existence of God, since He would be responsible for life by directing secondary causes to this particular end. The Church does not oppose a chemical origin to life.[50] However some special divine intervention, even using evolutionary causes, cannot be excluded in the passage from inanimate matter to living being. V. Marcozzi affirmed that there are at least three phases in which God's intervention is necessary and evident: 'The appearance of life, that is of the first living organisms; the evolutionary possibilities with which God imbues these organisms; and finally the coming of man, whose spiritual qualities implicate God's special intervention.'[51] Therefore some would say that life should be regarded as 'God's secret'.[52] It can be seen empirically that while, in the sub-human world, there is a hierarchy in the plant and animal kingdom, nevertheless the distinction between plant and animal is not so sharp, since there are certain primitive organisms which manifest both plant and animal characteristics. The higher species in the animal kingdom are those which are more developed and thus closer to man. The human person, having a spiritual soul, is the apex of the visible creation; he is thus endowed with intellect and free will, and can choose for good or ill and thus is not determined or programmed by his environment so making him essentially distinct from the animals.

Our journey to examine the role of the Church's attitude towards evolution begins with two Church Fathers who were also bishops. The great western Father, Saint Augustine wrote of a certain development within the things which God has created.[53] In eastern Christendom, St Gregory of Nyssa also proposed progress in creation.[54] What medieval and later Christian writers expounded concerning God and the view of the universe does not exclude an evolutionary perspective. God produced the universe by a single creative act of His will, so then its natural development by laws implanted in it by the Creator is to the greater glory of

His Divine power and wisdom. St. Thomas Aquinas wrote: 'The potency of a cause is the greater, the more remote the effects to which it extends.'[55] Furthermore, Suarez pointed out that 'God does not interfere directly with the natural order, where secondary causes suffice to produce the intended effect.'[56] In view of this principle of the Christian interpretation of nature, the history of the animal and vegetable kingdoms on our planet is seen in the light of its origin in the creative act of the Holy Trinity and read in the key of His constant providence.

In the late nineteenth century, there were few instances where the local Magisterium of the Church seemed understandably concerned the evolutionary hypothesis. One of these occurred in Germany. In 1860, the provincial Council of Cologne declared: 'Our first parents were immediately made by God... Hence, we declare openly opposed to Holy Scripture and to the Faith the opinion of those who go so far as to say that man, so far as his body is concerned, was produced by the spontaneous transformation of the less perfect into the more perfect, successively, ultimately ending in the human.'[57] On the other hand there were many Catholic evolutionists who were highly regarded in the Church. In England, St George Jackson Mivart, a leading biologist, was received into the Catholic Church in 1844. He professed a theory of evolution; but he unhesitatingly and consistently asserted the irreconcilable difference between the inanimate and animate, as well as between the purely animal and the rational. By maintaining the creationist theory of the origin of the human soul he attempted to reconcile his evolutionism with the Catholic faith. In philosophical problems, towards which he turned more and more in later years, his attitude was rather that of a neo-scholastic combating the post-Cartesian philosophies; and he opposed with success a critical, or moderate realist, system of knowledge to the widely prevalent agnosticism of his time. In 1876, he was awarded an honorary degree by Pope Pius IX for his scientific work Towards the close of his life, Mivart's philosophical speculations began to verge on an 'interpretation' of theological dogma that seemed to some incompatible with the Faith. The crisis, however, did not become acute before his articles in the *Nineteenth Century* were placed on the Index.[58] The issue of his unorthodoxy did not involve the question of evolution.[59]

Throughout the nineteenth century, the theory of evolution and the possibility of reconciling it with Christian doctrine was a matter of fairly free discussion among Catholics, as evidenced by Knabenbauer who, in 1877, stated that 'there is no objection, so far as faith is concerned, to assuming the descent of all plant and animal species from a few types'.[60] However, abruptly towards the end of the nineteenth century, there was a change of attitude on the part of the Roman doctrinal authorities. Nothing public was done, but theologians, on hearing that their works had been examined in Rome, began to withdraw their books from sale, make public retractions and cease to discuss the subject. In 1998, the archives of the Holy Office were opened to scholars so that it became possible to examine the processes which lay behind these events. It has been proposed that a small group of Roman Jesuit scholars 'were largely responsible for turning back the movement, which was encouraged by Leo XIII, towards making peace with the sciences'.[61] Their influence did not last, for subsequent official documents of the Popes and other official Church teachers 'have reflected a gradual easing of remaining concerns about theories of evolution and their potential impact on Catholic doctrine.'[62]

At the same time, there was a consciousness within the teaching office of the Church that an evolutionist ideology was to be avoided. The *Syllabus* of Pope Blessed Pius IX condemned the application of an evolutionist *ideology* to the deposit of revelation, pointing out the error in saying that divine revelation is imperfect and hence subject to continual and indefinite progress, which ought to correspond to the progress of human reason.[63] In 1870, the First Vatican Council condemned materialism. At the same time it declared that not only can faith and reason never be at odds with one another but they mutually support each other, for on the one hand right reason established the foundations of the faith and, illuminated by its light, develops the science of divine things. On the other hand, faith delivers reason from errors and protects it and furnishes it with knowledge of many kinds. It also proscribed the error that human studies are to be treated with such a degree of liberty that their assertions may be maintained as true even when they are opposed to divine revelation, and that they may not be forbidden by the Church.[64] Pope St Pius X also discouraged an evolutionary ideology applied in the modernist concept of the development of doctrine; he condemned the notion that the progress of the sciences requires that the concepts of Christian doctrine concerning God, creation and revelation be reformed.[65]

In 1909, the Pontifical Biblical Commission expressed no repugnance for evolution as such, but rather was concerned about the historicity of the Genesis account of the origins of the human race. It warned against casting doubt upon the literal historical sense of the first chapters of the book of Genesis, where fundamental truths of the Christian faith are taught, such as the creation by God of all things, the particular creation of man, the formation of the first woman from the first man, and the unity of the human race.[66]

An intervention of the Magisterium took place in 1962 to curb the impact of a wholesale importing of evolutionist ideology into Catholic theology. The occasion was provided by a *Monitum* (warning) issued by the Holy Office in relation to the works of P. Teilhard de Chardin. The document carefully prescinded from a judgement about those points that concern the positive sciences, but made it sufficiently clear that the works of Teilhard de Chardin abound in such ambiguities and indeed even serious errors, as to offend Catholic doctrine.[67]

The rôle evolution may have played in the formation of the human body was a question already considered by Pope Pius XII in 1950:

> The teaching of the Church does not forbid that the doctrine of evolutionism, in so far as it enquires into the origin of the human body from already existing and living matter, be, according to the present state of human disciplines and sacred theology, treated in research and discussion by experts on both sides;

> as to the souls, the Catholic faith demands us to hold that they are immediately created by God.[68]

Most central in a discussion of evolution and the documents of the Magisterium is the *Message to the Pontifical Academy of Sciences* in 1996 of Pope John Paul II. The Pope pointed out that the scientific status of evolution is more developed today than in the time of Pope Pius XII:

> Today, more than a half-century after the appearance of that encyclical, some new findings lead us toward the recognition of evolution as more than an hypothesis. In fact it is remarkable that this theory has had progressively greater influence on the spirit of researchers, following a series of discoveries in different scholarly disciplines. The convergence in the results of these independent studies—which was neither planned nor sought—constitutes in itself a significant argument in favour of the theory.[69]

The Pope went to point out that 'rather than speaking about the theory of evolution, it is more accurate to speak of the theories of evolution'. He explained that the use of the plural is required here, partly because of the diversity of explanations regarding the mechanism of evolution, and partly because of the variety of philosophies involved in the interpretation of evolution.[70] This question of the diversity raises the issue of the relation between the scientific data of evolution and the ideological extrapolation of evolutionism. The theories of evolution tend to ideological extrapolation by their very nature. First, because what is easily observed empirically is *micro-evolution*, or the small changes that occur within a species over time. This kind of evolution is common. An example is that people are generally taller today than they were a hundred years ago. Instead, with no direct empirical evidence, evolutionists claim that over long periods of time these micro-changes could result in *macro-evolution*, which consists of really large jumps, from one species to another like those from amoeba to reptile to mammal. After making this extrapolation, evolutionists may attempt other more daring leaps, like that of making an animal evolve into man. Care must be taken to distinguish between hard scientific fact (obtained in an *a posteriori* manner) in the theory of evolution and an unjustified *a priori* extrapolation of this theory to form an atheist ideology.[71] The fact that materialistic views of evolution easily lend themselves to ideology is illustrated in the connection between a Darwinist perspective and the most repressive totalitarian politics of last century. According to Stanley Jaki: 'The enthusiasm for Darwinism of the advocates of the dictatorship of the proletariat and of a master race is all too understandable. Marx was quick to notice the usefulness of Darwinist theory for promoting class struggle, and Hitler volubly echoed Darwinist views, which were very popular among German military leaders prior to the First World War as a justification of their and his plans.'[72]

In order to avoid this ideological manipulation of new theories at the scientific level in order to take account of the emergence of living beings, one needs a correct method. Here one should not interpret the theories immediately and in the exclusive framework of science.

> In particular, when it is a question of the living being which is man, and of his brain, it cannot be said that these theories of themselves constitute an

> affirmation or a denial of the spiritual soul, or that they provide a proof of the doctrine of creation, or that, on the contrary, they render it useless.[73]

Thus, further interpretation is required, which is precisely the object of philosophy, the study of the global meaning of the data of experience, and therefore also of the phenomena gathered and analysed by the sciences.[74]

In his *Message to the Pontifical Academy of Sciences* in 1996, Pope John Paul II also explained that the Church is interested in the theories of evolution, precisely because of its impact on the vision concerning the human person, who is created in the image and likeness of God.[75] St Thomas observed that man's resemblance to God resides especially in his speculative intellect, because his relationship with the object of his knowledge is like God's relationship with his creation.[76] But even beyond that, man is called to enter into a loving relationship with God himself, a relationship which will find its full expression at the end of time, in eternity. Within the mystery of the risen Christ the full grandeur of this vocation is revealed to us. It is by virtue of his eternal soul that the whole person, including his body, possesses such great dignity. Pius XII underlined the essential point: if the origin of the human body comes through living matter which existed previously, the spiritual soul is created directly by God. Whatever may be said about the creation of the body, be it an immediate creation or a programmed creation through evolution, the human soul is directly created out of nothing by God. Pope Paul VI also pointed out that any application of the theory of evolution becomes unacceptable whenever it fails to affirm very clearly the immediate and direct creation by God of each and every human soul.[77]

Pope John Paul II clearly rejected any evolutionist ideologies which regard the spirit either as emerging from the forces of living matter, or as a simple epiphenomenon of that matter, as incompatible with the truth about man. They are therefore unable to serve as the basis for the dignity of the human person.[78] The Pope also further indicated the link between philosophy and science in the question of evolutionary theory applied to the human person:

> With man, we find ourselves facing a different ontological order—an ontological leap, we could say. But in posing such a great ontological discontinuity, are we not breaking up the physical continuity which seems to be the main line of research about evolution in the fields of physics and chemistry? An appreciation for the different methods used in different fields of scholarship allows us to bring together two points of view which at first might seem irreconcilable. The sciences of observation describe and measure, with ever greater precision, the many manifestations of life, and write them down along the time-line. The moment of passage into the spiritual realm is not something that can be observed in this way—although we can nevertheless discern, through experimental research, a series of very valuable signs of what is specifically human life. But the experience of metaphysical knowledge, of self-consciousness and self-awareness, of moral conscience, of liberty, or of aesthetic and religious experience—these must be analysed through philosophical reflection, while theology seeks to clarify the ultimate meaning of the Creator's designs.[79]

Generally, attempts to conceive the spiritual soul as a product of evolution and thus derived from matter would more or less imply materialism, an evolutionist ideology employed to deny the spiritual nature of man and the work of God the Creator. If one were to maintain, however, that evolution applied only to the body of the human person, preparing it up to a certain point to receive the soul, which then was immediately created by God, this would not necessarily be contrary to Christian belief.

It is one thing to consider the effect of the laws of evolution on the animal kingdom, but it is quite another to apply them arbitrarily to the creation of man. Thus, a discussion of the origin of man in an evolutionist perspective does not mean that Adam was actually generated from an animal as his father. What would be more consonant theologically with Christian tradition is that the programmed creation which may be called evolution gave rise to a species which was then used by God to create man.[80] In the remote preparation, this inferior being was first shaped by God indirectly through evolutionary processes. Next, when this creature was nearly ready, it was shaped by direct divine intervention. The inferior being (which could be called a proto-human) thus arrived at a point where it had been prepared to receive the human soul, then at the appropriate moment, God infused the soul either into an embryo or into an adult member of the species. At the same time God modified the genetic structure of the proto-human under consideration, so that it could indeed accept the soul and become a human being. In this way the genetic structure that the new being possessed was partly inherited from the inferior being and partly due to direct divine intervention. This hypothesis cannot, of course, be checked by scientific investigation. Doubtless, some Christian thinkers would prefer to maintain that even the body of the first human being was, in its totality, the result of a direct divine intervention without any influence of evolution. However, it is not so easy to say that the creation of the first man's body is simply a creation out of nothing, since the Scriptures refer to his formation from the dust of the soil (Gn 2:7). Even if the precise link between what is the contribution of evolutionary processes in the creation of man's body and what is due to direct divine intervention remains a mystery, God is nonetheless ultimately responsible for the creation of the whole Adam and the whole Eve.

So far, science has not been able to prove either polygenism or monogenism. Some scientists proposed on genetic grounds that the human body had a monogenetic origin.[81] However, whereas in theology *monogenesis* means the origin of humanity from one single set of parents, in scientific anthropology monogenesis (or *monocentrism*) only signifies the recognition of the existence of a single centre, from which the representatives of the species *Homo sapiens* developed and spread to other continents.[82] Differences in the colour and form of the human body may be explained in terms of evolutionary adaptation, according to the conditions in different parts of the globe. Assuming that evolution had played a part in the preparation of the proto-human, before the infusion of the soul, and even assuming that science could point to a polygenism in regard to these inferior beings, revelation seems to indicate that

God infused the soul only into one chosen pair among these various hypothetical proto-humans. The act of the infusion of the soul directly by God renders the human being essentially different from the animals. This action lies outside the competence of scientific investigation, which thus cannot really disprove the monogenetic origin of the human person, based as it is upon a divine choice and not merely on evolutionary processes.

The moment of the creation of the first Adam lies in a divine choice; like Christ, the second Adam, he is not the result of 'urge of the flesh or will of man' (Jn 1:13). Because God chose the time at which to infuse the soul into a being which He had prepared, possibly using the evolutionary processes inscribed by Him in the life forms created by Him. In this way, the moment of the creation of the first man is beyond the reach of the empirical sciences. It would be possible for the empirical sciences to find fossil evidence of the first human beings, but it is difficult to tell that these are indeed the very first ones, also because much fossil evidence has now decayed to dust.

> The clay became man at the moment in which a being for the first time was capable of forming, however dimly, the thought of God. The first Thou that—however stammeringly—was said by human lips to God marks the moment in which the spirit arose in the world. Here the Rubicon of anthropogenesis was crossed. For it is not the use of weapons or fire, not new methods of cruelty or of useful activity, that constitute man, but rather his ability to be immediately in relation to God. This holds fast to the doctrine of the special creation of man ... herein ... lies the reason why the moment of anthropogene-

> sis cannot possibly be determined by paleontology: anthropogenesis is the rise of the spirit, which cannot be excavated with a shovel.[83]

Therefore, from the natural sciences it is impossible to affirm that humanity had a polygenic beginning. Monogenism is certainly the safer position, since when the Magisterium has not rescinded the earlier position, that position still stands.[84] This is confirmed in the Catechism which quotes St Peter Chrysologus:

> St. Paul tells us that the human race takes its origin from two men: Adam and Christ. . . The first man, Adam, he says, became a living soul, the last Adam a life-giving spirit. The first Adam was made by the last Adam, from whom he also received his soul, to give him life... The second Adam stamped his image on the first Adam when he created him. That is why he took on himself the role and the name of the first Adam, in order that he might not lose what he had made in his own image. The first Adam, the last Adam: the first had a beginning, the last knows no end. The last Adam is indeed the first; as he himself says: 'I am the first and the last.'[85]

The Catechism effectively teaches that polygenism is not compatible with Catholic Tradition.

8.4.4 A Possible Relationship

In the preceding three examples science and theology had to be careful not to leave their own respective spheres of competence. However what of the cross-fertilization? The modern vision of the cosmos does provide some input to a theology of the creation. However, the relationship between scientific findings and theological beliefs is not one which permits a simple deduction from one to the other. 'It is not possible to use scientific theories, however well supported, to construct an argument for a Creator, and neither can they be used to render existence superfluous'.[86] Rather, the results of the scientific enterprise can be taken as a pointer to the specificity of each part of the cosmos. Because the cosmos is a unity, then the specificity of each part leads to a consideration of the global specificity of the entire universe. Cosmic specificity in turn implies that the universe is dependent on a divine choice making it what it is. Hence the cosmos is not a necessary form of being but rather is contingent. The specificity and interrelatedness of the elements making up the cosmos that science uncovers are indications of *purpose* within creation, which is in turn a particular expression of God's economy of salvation. A concrete example is that small changes in the initial conditions of the physical cosmos would have rendered impossible conditions for life as we know it. It seems that the universe has developed in such a way as to allow human life to be possible; this popular formulation of the so-called Anthropic Principle[87] points to Divine Providence. Nevertheless, this is very different from asserting that man is a necessary outcome of the early conditions in the cosmos. Moreover God's providential plan does not merely furnish what is *useful* for man's existence or continued survival, but also reveals a beautiful world which evokes praise for its Creator.

Finally, as science progresses it uncovers the beauty within the universe. This quality which is more than simple attractiveness,[88] is a reflection, however pale, of God's own beauty and draws the researcher on to ask the question 'What is beyond?' in the spirit of the famous adage of Blessed Niels Stensen: 'Those things which are seen are beautiful, those which are known are more beautiful, those which are not known are the most beautiful of all'.[89] The scientific vision of the cosmos is insufficient to give us a complete picture; the vision of the faith is required as well. Science alone cannot purify human culture of superstition. It seems that in a highly technological society, man's soul has as ever a need for the sacred, which, if not directed towards the only true Creator God, seeks fulfilment in futile approaches to the occult. Science on its own cannot give humanity the progress it desires; it needs the aid of theology and Christian morality in order to avoid ecological disaster, as the next chapter will illustrate.

Fourteen Theses on Relations between Science and Religion

1. There is no intrinsic contradiction between Christian faith and natural science.
2. Science is *of itself* insufficient for human growth in understanding and human development.
3. As science and technology progress, human civilization will not reach a type of earthly utopia.
4. Scientific progress is part of human and spiritual progress. There is a continuity between the progress achieved in this world and the perfection to be received in the world to come, but there is also a discontinuity between the earthly city and the heavenly Kingdom. The continuity and discontinuity is manifested also in the transformation of our human bodies.

5. Just as grace perfects nature in a dynamic partnership, so also is Christian faith like a guiding star which leads science to a deeper and more perfect understanding of its rôle within human experience, without deformation of its nature, but rather a development.[90]
6. Science cannot be regarded as having such autonomy that its applications and philosophy may be followed, even if they contradict faith, morals and the dignity of the human person.
7. The Magisterium of the Church can and should pronounce on scientific issues which have a bearing on faith or morals or have implications for other aspects of the Christian life. Despite the varying historical nature of science, statements can be made concerning the relations of faith and science, since, beyond the progress of science the mind can discern the metaphysics of reality.
8. The Church does benefit from an understanding of the scientific milieu and mentality, and this is necessary for the more efficacious communication and diffusion of the Gospel of Christ.
9. It would be rash, necessarily and immediately to attribute to God that which is still inaccessible to science, for if and when science has achieved a discovery of the said areas, the power of God may appear to be reduced. (This is the 'God of the gaps' error).
10. It is an error to hold that 'in the order of created things there is, immediately manifested to the human intellect, something divine in itself, such that it belongs to the divine nature.'[91]

11. Science arrives at the truth, but not at all of the truth, so that not even all that which is in the natural order is its proper object. Natural science will never be able to penetrate all the secrets of nature to the extent that the cosmos would fail to evoke in man a sense of mystery.
12. Notwithstanding our increasing pure and applied knowledge in science and technology, leading to a greater understanding of the laws of nature and their control, it would be an error to exclude immediate and direct intervention of God in His creation in a miraculous way; for although we are bound by the laws of nature, God is not.
13. The mediation of philosophy, and especially of metaphysics, is required in relating Christian faith and natural science.
14. Among the chief implicit presuppositions of science are that the material entities observed are real, existing independently of the observer, that that these entities have a coherent rationality, and being governed by consistent laws form a consistent whole. The form in which the coherent totality, or universe, exists cannot be considered a necessary form of existence but rather a contingent one.[92]

Further Reading

P. F. Forsthoefel, *Religious Faith meets Modern Science* (New York: Alba House, 1994)

P. Haffner, *Creation and Scientific Creativity. A Study in the Thought of Stanley L. Jaki* (Leominster: Gracewing, 2009)

S. L. Jaki, *God and the Cosmologists* (Edinburgh: Scottish Academic Press, 1989)

E. L. Mascall, *Christian Theology and Natural Science* (London: Longmans, Green and Co., 1957)

Notes

1 This comparison has been adapted from Archbishop Paulos Gregorios, 'Science and Faith: Complementary or Contradictory?', in R. L. Shinn (ed.), *Faith and Science in an Unjust World*, 1 (Geneva: World Council of Churches, 1980), p. 47.

2 See Vatican I, *Dei Filius* in DS 3005; Vatican II, *Dei Verbum* 6.

3 S.L. Jaki, 'Language, Logic, Logos', Chapter V in *Brain, Mind and Computers* (Washington, D.C.: Regnery Gateway, 1989) p. 296. On p. 298, Jaki also notes C. S. Lewis's remark in *That Hideous Strength* (New York: Collier Books, 1962), p. 351, 'They that have despised the Word of God, from them shall the word of man be taken away.'

4 Pope John Paul II, *Discourse to the Plenary Session of the Pontifical Academy of Sciences to commemorate the centenary of the birth of Albert Einstein* (10 November 1979) in *DP*, p. 154. Referring in a note to the life and works of Galileo, the Pastoral Constitution of Vatican II *Gaudium et spes*, 36.1, stated: 'We cannot but deplore certain attitudes (not unknown among Christians) deriving from a shortsighted view of the rightful autonomy of science; they have occasioned conflict and controversy and have misled many into opposing faith and science.'

5 See Pope John Paul II, *Discourse to the Plenary Session of the Pontifical Academy of Sciences* (31 October 1992), paragraphs 6 and 12 in *OR* N.254 (1 November 1992), pp. 6–7. In particular, the Pope cited the adage of Cardinal Baronius: 'Spiritui Sancto mentem fuisse nos docere quomodo ad caelum eatur, non quomodo caelum gradiatur.' (The Holy Spirit wishes to teach us how to go to heaven, but not how the heavens go).

6 See S. L. Jaki, *The Savior of Science* (Washington,D.C.: Regnery Gateway, 1988), pp. 21–22.

7 See *ibid.*, p. 42.

8 See pp. 45, 61, 69, 89 above.

9 S. L. Jaki, *The Road of Science and the Ways to God* (Edinburgh: Scottish Academic Press, 1978), pp. 38, 33.

10 See Jaki, *The Savior of Science*, pp. 46–54.

11 Vatican II, *Ad Gentes Divinitus*, 8.

12 Cf. also Mk 10:29–30; Lk 18:29–30; 1 Tm 4:8. See also Vatican II, *Gaudium et Spes*, 38.2: 'Constituted Lord by His resurrection and given all authority in heaven and on earth, Christ is now at work in the hearts of all men by the power of his Spirit; not only does He arouse in them a desire for the world to come but He quickens, purifies and strengthens the generous aspirations of mankind to make life more humane and conquer the earth for this purpose.'

13 See, for example, the classic article of Lynn White which was the basis for a critique of Christianity by ecologists, who claimed that the Judaeo-Christian idea of man's sovereignty over nature brought about an aggressive abuse of the environment. L. White, 'The Historical Roots of Our Ecological Crisis' in *Science* 155 (1967), pp. 1203–1207.

14 See Vatican II, *Gaudium et Spes*, 22; 1 Tm 2:5.

15 See S. L. Jaki, *Cosmos and Creator* (Edinburgh: Scottish Academic Press, 1980) p. 54. See also my *Creation and Scientific Creativity* (Leominster: Gracewing, 2009), pp. 77–78.

16 Haffner, *Creation and Scientific Creativity*, p. 38. See S. L. Jaki, *The Relevance of Physics* (Chicago: University of Chiacgo Press, 1966), p. 141.

17 S. L. Jaki, 'Physics and the Ultimate' in *The Only Chaos and Other Essays* (Lanham, Maryland: University Press of America, 1990), p. 217.

18 For a definition and discussion of Heisenberg's Uncertainty Principle see section 8.4.1 below.

19 Pope John Paul II, *Crossing the Threshold of Hope* (London: Jonathan Cape, 1994), p. 21. See also Jaki, 'Physics and the Ultimate' who makes a similar statement on p. 227: 'An ultimate unlocking of all the recondite processes of the physical universe should seem a likely event to all who hold two propositions: One is that God created everything according to measure, number, and weight. The other is that it is through his rationality that man is made in the image of God.'

20 See S. W. Hawking, *A Brief History of Time* (London: Bantam Press, 1988), p. 175 and p. 7 above.

21 Jaki, 'Physics and the Ultimate', p. 227.

22 Vatican II, *Gaudium et Spes*, 36.2. See chapter five, §5.4 above.

23 Pope John Paul II, *Discourse at the Congress promoted by the Vatican Observatory on the occasion of the tercentenary of the publication of Newton's 'Philosophiae Naturalis Principia Mathematica'* (26 September 1987), in *OR* 127/231 (27 September 1987), p. 4. See also the Discourse of Pope Pius XII to the Pontifical Academy of Sciences on 24 April 1955 in *DP*, p. 89: 'Can science with the means which are characteristic of it, effect this universal synthesis of thought? And in any case, since knowledge is split up into innumerable sectors, which one, out of so many sciences, is the one capable of realizing this synthesis? Here again We believe that the nature of science will not allow it to accomplish so universal a synthesis. This synthesis requires a solid and very deep foundation, from which it derives its unity and which serves as a basis for the most general truths... A superior force is required for this: unifying by its universality, clear in its depth, solid by its character of absoluteness... That force is philosophy.' See also pp. 20–24 above.

24 Pius XI, Motu Proprio *In multis solaciis* for the erection of the Pontifical Academy of Sciences, *AAS* 28 (1936) p. 421. The original Latin text reads: 'Scientia, quae vera rerum cognitio sit, numquam christianae fidei veritatibus repugnat.'

25 Pope Pius XII, *Discourse to the Pontifical Academy of Sciences*, (22 November 1951) in *DP*, p. 84.

26 Vatican II, *Gaudium et Spes*, 36.1.

27 Jaki, 'Physics and the Ultimate', p. 219.

28 *Ibid.*, p. 220.

29 When given a system whose exact description is not precisely known, the entropy is defined as the expected amount of information needed to exactly specify the state of the system, given what we know about the system. The law of entropy or the second law of thermodynamics is an expression of the universal principle of increasing entropy, stating that the entropy of an isolated system which is not in equilibrium will tend to increase over time, approaching a maximum value at equilibrium.

30 Hawking, *A Brief History of Time*, p. 55.

31 *Ibid.*, p. 136.

32 *Ibid.*, pp. 136–137.

33 *Ibid.*, pp. 140–141.

34 See Pope Benedict XVI, *Discourse to the Pontifical Academy of Sciences* (31 October 2008).

35 See pp. 77–79 above.

36 S. L. Jaki, *God and the Cosmologists* (Edinburgh: Scottish Academic Press, 1989), pp. 81, 208.

37 See B. van Hagens, 'Cosmologia scientifica e cosmologia filsofica,' in *Salesianum* 47 (1985), pp. 555–565.

38 Pope John Paul II, *Discourse to the Pontifical Academy of Sciences* (3 October 1981) in *DP*, p. 162.

39 M. Denton, *Evolution: A Theory in Crisis* (Bethesda, MD: Adler and Adler, 1986), p. 87.

40 Pope Benedict XVI as cited in S. O. Horn & S. Wiedenhofer (eds.), *Creation and Evolution: A Conference With Pope Benedict XVI in Castel Gandolfo*, (San Francisco: Ignatius Press, 2008).

41 Cardinal J. Ratzinger, *'In the Beginning…' A Catholic Understanding of the Story of Creation and the Fall* (Grand Rapids: William Eerdmans, 1995), p. 56.

42 See Pope John Paul II, *Discourse to participants in an inter-*

national symposium on Christian faith and the theory of evolution (26 April 1985) in *IG* 8/1 (1985), p. 1129.

43 See Idem, *Discourse at General Audience* (29 January 1986) in *IG* 9/1 (1986), p. 212.

44 Pope Benedict XVI, *Meeting with the clergy of the dioceses of Belluno-Feltre and Treviso* (24 July 2007).

45 See W. A. Dembski, *The Design Revolution: Answering the Toughest Questions About Intelligent Design* (Downers Grove, IL: InterVarsity Press, 2004); M. J. Behe, W. A. Dembski, S. C. Meyer (eds.), *Science and Evidence for Design in the Universe* (San Francisco: Ignatius Press, 2000); W. A. Dembski, *Intelligent Design: The Bridge Between Science & Theology* (Downers Grove, IL: InterVarsity Press, 1999); M. J. Behe, *Darwin's Black Box: The Biochemical Challenge to Evolution* (New York: Touchstone, 1996).

46 See Cardinal C. Schönborn, *Chance or Purpose? Creation, Evolution, and a Rational Faith* (San Francisco: Ignatius Press, 2008).

47 See S. L. Jaki, *Intelligent Design*? (Port Huron, MI: RealView Books, 2005).

48 Ratzinger, *'In the Beginning'*, p. 56.

49 Pope Benedict XVI, *Discourse at General Audience* (9 November 2005). Cf. St Basil the Great, *On Genesis* 1, 2, 4.

50 Cf. M. Artigas, *Le Frontiere dell'Evoluzionismo* (Milano: Ares, 1993), p. 75.

51 See interview with V. Marcozzi in *Inside the Vatican* 5/1 (January 1997), p. 27.

52 A. Holloway, *God's Master Key. The Law of Control and Direction* (Wallington: Faith Keyway, 1988), p. 18.

53 St Augustine wrote that God created everything together in *De Genesi ad litteram* Book 4, c. 25, 56; Book 5, c.23, 45; Book 7, c.28, 41–42 in *PL* 34, 320, 338, 370–372. Some things were created perfect and complete at the beginning like the angels, the earth, the sea, and the soul of man, as he wrote in *De Genesi ad litteram Liber Imperfectus* Chapter 3, nn.6–10 in *PL* 34, 222–224; *De Genesi ad litteram* Book 6, c.1, 2; Book 7,

cc.23–24 in *PL* 34, 339; 368. However, others, like plants, animals and the body of man (*De Genesi ad litteram* Book 5, c.4, 9–11; Book 5, c.7, 20; Book 6, c.5, 8; Book 6, c.6, 10; Book 6, c.9, 16 in *PL* 34, 324–325; 328; 342; 343; 345–346) required perfection which God brought about in time as was written in *De Genesi ad litteram* Book 4, c.33, 52; Book 5, c.4,11; Book 5, c.20, 41; Book 6, c.10, 17 in PL 34, 318; 325; 336; 346.

54 St Gregory of Nyssa, *In Hexaemeron* in *PG* 44, 71, 77; Idem, *De hominis opificio* c.29 in *PG* 44, 233–240.

55 St Thomas Aquinas, *Summa Contra Gentiles*, Book III, chapter 76.

56 F. Suarez, *De opere sex dierum*, Book II, chapter 10, n. 13.

57 Provincial Council of Cologne, *De doctrina catholica* title 14, n.4 as found in I. M. Dalmau and I. F. Sagüés, *Sacrae Theologiae Summa* Volume II (Madrid: BAC, 1958), pp. 641–642: 'Primi parentes a Deo immediate conditi sunt. Itaque Scripturae sacrae fideique plane adversantem illorum declaramus sententiam, qui asserere non verentur, spontanea naturae imperfectioris in perfectionem continuo ultimoque humanam hanc immutatione hominem, si corpus quidem species, prodiise.'

58 These articles were 'Modern Catholics and Scientific Freedom' in July, 1885; 'The Catholic Church and Biblical Criticism' in July, 1887; 'Catholicity and Reason' in December, 1887; 'Sins of Belief and Disbelief' in October, 1888; 'Happiness in Hell' in December, 1892.

59 His orthodoxy was finally brought into serious suspicion by the articles 'The Continuity of Catholicism' (*Nineteenth Century*, January, 1900) and 'Some Recent Apologists' (*Fortnightly Review*, January, 1900). In the same month January 1900, after admonition and three formal notifications requiring him in vain to sign a profession of faith that was sent him, he was inhibited from the sacraments by Cardinal Vaughan 'until he shall have proved his orthodoxy to the satisfaction of his ordinary'. The letters that passed between Archbishop's House and Dr. Mivart were published by him in the columns of *The Times* newspaper for 27 January 1900.

In March 1900, a last article 'Scripture and Roman Catholicism', repudiating ecclesiastical authority, appeared in the *Nineteenth Century*. Dr. Mivart died of diabetes 1 April 1900, at 77 Inverness Terrace, Bayswater, London, and was buried without ecclesiastical rites, but he was pardoned posthumously. His burial took place in Kensal Green Catholic cemetery on 18 January 1904.

60 See J. Knabenbauer, *Stimmen aus Maria Laach* 13 (1877), pp. 69–86 and especially p. 72.

61 B. Brundell, 'Catholic Church politics and evolution theory, 1894–1902' in *British Journal for the History of Science* 34 (2001), p. 93.

62 *Ibid*., p. 94.

63 See Pope Bl Pius IX, *Syllabus* in DS 2905.

64 See Vatican I, *Dei Filius* in DS 3022 and 3042.

65 St Pius X, Decree *Lamentabili sane* (1907) in DS 3464.

66 See Pontifical Biblical Commission, *De Charactere Historicum Priorum Capitum Geneseos* (30 June 1909) in DS 3512–3519.

67 Holy Office, *Monitum concerning the works of P. Teilhard de Chardin*, 30 June 1962 in *AAS* 54 (1962), p. 166. For an outline of the problems regarding Teilhard de Chardin's concepts in this regard, see chapter one, pp. 9–11 above.

68 Pope Pius XII, Encyclical Letter *Humani generis* 36 in ND 419. Earlier, on 30th November 1941, in a discourse to the Pontifical Academy of Sciences, the Pope had affirmed:
'At the summit of the ladder of all that lives, man, endowed with a spiritual soul, was made by God to be a prince and sovereign over the animal kingdom. The multiple research, be it in palaeontology or of biology and morphology, on the problems concerning the origins of man have not, as yet, ascertained anything with great clarity and certainty. We must leave it to the future to answer the question, if indeed science will one day be able, enlightened and guided by revelation, to give certain and definitive results concerning a topic of such importance.' (From *DP*, p. 43.)

69 Pope John Paul II, *Message to the Pontifical Academy of*

Sciences:on Evolution (22 October 1996), 4. The English edition of *L'Osservatore Romano* at first translated the French original as: 'Today, more than a half-century after the appearance of that encyclical, some new findings lead us toward the recognition of more than one hypothesis within the theory of evolution.' The *Osservatore Romano* English Edition subsequently amended the text to that given in the body of the message above, citing the translation of the other language editions as its reason. It should be noted that a hypothesis represents the preliminary stage of the scientific method, with a correspondingly lower degree of certainty than a theory. Nevertheless, a scientific theory, by its very nature, is still open to verification, correction, and refinement. Of course, regarding the empirical fact of evolution, there is no absolute demonstration, because the process can only be checked indirectly. See R. Pascual, 'L'evoluzionismo nell'attuale dibattito filosofico' in *Il cannochiale* 1/2000 (gennaio–aprile 2000), p. 178.

70 See Pope John Paul II, *Message to the Pontifical Academy of Sciences:on Evolution* (22 October 1996), 4. The Pope referred to materialist and reductionist theories, as well as spiritualist theories.

71 See P. Haffner, *The Mystery of Reason* (Leominster: Gracewing, 2001), p. 172.

72 S. L. Jaki, *Cosmos and Creator* (Edinburgh: Scottish Academic Press, 1980), p. 114 and notes 5 and 6 on p. 160.

73 Pope John Paul II, *Discourse to the Pontifical Academy of Sciences* (31 October 1992) in *OR* (1 November 1992), p. 8.

74 Cf. *ibid.*.

75 See Pope John Paul II, *Message to the Pontifical Academy of Sciences on Evolution* (22 October 1996), 5.

76 See St Thomas Aquinas, *Summa Theologiae* I–II°, q 3, a 5, ad 1.

77 See Pope Paul VI, *Discourse at Symposium on Original Sin*, 11 June 1966, in *AAS* 58(1966), p. 654.

78 See Pope John Paul II, *Message to the Pontifical Academy of Sciences on Evolution* (22 October 1996), 5.

79 *Ibid.*, 6.

80 Pope John Paul II mentioned this idea in a discourse at a General Audience on 16 April 1986 (in *IG* 9/1 (1986), p. 1041), pointing out that there would be no difficulty, from the viewpoint of the doctrine of the faith, to explain the origin of man's body through the hypothesis of evolutionism, which he stressed was a probable possibility and not a scientific certainty. The human body would have been gradually prepared for in preceding living beings. However, the human soul, upon which depends the humanity of man, could not have emerged from matter.

81 For a summary of the scientific arguments in favour of monogenism, see P. F. Forsthoefel, *Religious Faith meets Modern Science* (New York: Alba House, 1994) pp. 29–37; M. Artigas, *Le Frontiere dell'Evoluzionismo* (Milano: Ares, 1993), pp. 35–36, 215–217. See also R. L. Cann, M. Stoneking, A. C. Wilson, 'Mitochondrial DNA and Human Evolution' in *Nature* 325(1987), pp.31–36; E. Watson, P. Forster, M. Richards, H.-J. Bandelt, 'Mitochondrial Footprints of Human Expansions in Africa' in *American Journal of Human Genetics* 61(1997), pp. 691–704.

82 See J. M. Życiński, 'Original sin and recent discoveries in genetics' in P. Barrajón–T. D. Williams (edd.), *Il peccato originale. Una prospettiva interdisciplinare* (Città del Vaticano: LEV, 2009), p. 244.

83 J. Ratzinger as cited by C. Schönborn in his Foreword to S. O. Horn & S. Wiedenhofer (eds.), *Creation and Evolution: A Conference With Pope Benedict XVI in Castel Gandolfo*, (San Francisco: Ignatius Press, 2008), pp. 15–16.

84 In this context, the Catechism twice (*CCC* 28, 360) quotes Acts 17:26–28: 'From one ancestor [God] made all nations to inhabit the whole earth…' This quotation strongly suggests a reference to one person, not plural, but various Bible translations are unclear on this point. That the Catechism refers to a single person is confirmed in the footnote to *CCC* 360 which cites Tobit 8:6, 'You it was who created Adam, you who created Eve his wife to be his help and support;

and from these two the human race was born.' Thus, the 'one ancestor' could only be Adam.

85 See *CCC* 359 and St. Peter Chrysologus, *Sermon* 117 in *PL* 52, 520–521.

86 P. E. Hodgson, 'The Desecularization of Science' in W. Oddie (ed.), *After the Deluge* (London: S.P.C.K., 1987), p. 142.

87 Barrow and Tipler define the Anthropic Principle in two forms, the Weak and the Strong. In the Weak form, it states: 'The observed values of all physical and cosmological quantities are not equally probable but they take on values restricted by the requirement that there exist sites where carbon-based life can evolve and by the requirement that the Universe be old enough for it to have already done so.' The Strong form states: 'The Universe must have those properties which allow life to develop within it at some stage in its history.' See J. D. Barrow and F. J. Tipler, *The Anthropic Cosmological Principle* (Oxford: Clarendon Press, 1986), pp. 16 and 21.

88 See K. Turnauer, unpublished thesis *The Understanding of Beauty According to Joseph Jungmann*. (Rome: Pontifical Institute Regina Mundi, 1995), p. 1, who distinguishes between the 'superficial beauty of "lipstick and rouge"' and 'a much deeper reality, which seems not to be so apparent at first sight'.

89 The original Latin expression is 'Pulchra sunt quae videntur, pulchiora quae sciuntur, longe pulcherrima quae ignorantur.' See F. Sobiech, *Herz, Gott, Kreuz. Die Spiritualität des Anatomen, Geologen und Bischofs Dr. med. Niels Stensen (1638-86)* (Münster: Aschendorff Verlag, 2004) *Westfalia Sacra Band 13*, p. 154.

90 See Pope John Paul II, *Fides et Ratio*, 15.2: 'Christian Revelation is the true lodestar of men and women as they strive to make their way amid the pressures of an immanentist habit of mind and the constrictions of a technocratic logic.'

91 Cf. DS 3201, the error of Rosmini.

92 Cf. Jaki, *Cosmos and Creator*, p. 54.

9

From Assisi to Bikini

The mastery of man over nature reaches from miracle to the experiment, from total inspiration of the heart to complete coldness of intellect, from the sacred hour in Assisi when St. Francis preached to the birds, to the fragmented second in Bikini when a million of God's creatures were torn apart in the sea. The arch which connects St. Francis with the Commander-in-Chief in the Pacific, might be analogous to the range of human possibilities on earth.

Peter Bamm, Ex Ovo

9.1 The Environmental Crisis

The German word *Oekologie* appeared in 1860; some say that a certain W. Reiter coined it. The term derived from the Greek expression for house or dwelling. The word was adopted by the German biologist E. Haeckel in 1866 to indicate the study of an organism's relation to the exterior surrounding world, that is, in a broad sense, the study of the conditions of existence.[1] He developed what was later termed *Haeckel's law of recapitulation* according to the principle that 'ontogeny recapitulates phylogeny', and was first to draw up a genealogical tree relating the various orders of animals. As a philosopher he was an exponent of monistic philosophy, which postulated a totally materialistic view of life as a unity and which he presented as a necessary consequence of the theory of evolution.

Over the past hundred years or more, the science of ecology has developed rapidly in step with environmental problems deriving from a misuse of the fruits of man's technological advances. Particularly over the past thirty years, the mass media have been featuring almost daily the various warning signs in the current environmental crisis. Among these are the problem of deforestation and the disappearance of various animal species. The planet suffers air pollution (for example from car-exhausts), water pollution (such as oil spills from tankers) and ground pollution (for instance from leaks of chemical wastes). Big cities are inundated with refuse, while special difficulties are encountered in the disposal of nuclear waste. Noise pollution is increasingly a nuisance factor in many larger urban centres. Several scientists consider that the the ozone layer has been damaged by fluorocarbons, so lessening the degree of protection afforded against dangerous ultraviolet radiation. These and other problems are the result of the intervention of man in the macro-environment of nature. However, one question is the actual phenomenon of pollution or degradation of the environment, quite another is the evaluation of *how serious* this is in particular cases. Cause and effect are not always so easy to trace when dealing with such a large environment as the earth's atmosphere. Whether or not there really is global warming as a result of the greenhouse effect caused by increased carbon dioxide in the atmosphere is a disputed point.[2] The media have often furnished false, exaggerated or misleading information regarding environmental problems. This pseudo-scientific scare-mongering has often been used to support a particular political or ideological position.[3] Nevertheless, sometimes also governments and industry have sought to cover up the effects of undue interference in the environment for profit motives.

As well as man's manipulation of the macro-environment, he also interferes in the genetic micro-environment of cells of living organisms so provoking various undesirable effects: 'we are not yet in a position to assess the biological disturbance that could result from the unscrupulous development of new forms of plant and animal life, to say nothing of unacceptable experimentation regarding the origins of human life itself'.[4] There is also a great inconsistency in the position of those environmentalists who, while opposing undue interference in the macro-environment of the cosmos, do not object to and even support unjust intervention in the micro-environment of the human body. This incoherence is exemplified in the support which many members of the Green Movement give to population control by artificial means of contraception:

> To pollute the waterways of the human body with chemicals, and block its passages with metal and plastic barriers, deliberately to prevent its functioning in a normal and healthy way, is an extension of the industrial mentality to the most private human sphere. It places woman in the hands of technocrats and the big corporations, totally dependent on them for as long as she wishes to remain the sexual plaything of the men who refuse to take responsibility for her children.[5]

It is thus totally unacceptable to follow the approach of certain ecologists who see the solution of the crisis of man and his environment in terms of population control. These ideological manipulations have at their root an egoistic philosophy which in fact seeks to make life more pleasant for wealthier countries, but disregarding the less well-developed areas. In such poorer states, population control will often rob towns of that very manpower which would be necessary for the development and care of the environment. Systematic family planning campaigns figure among new forms of oppression. 'It is the poorest populations which suffer such mistreatment, and this sometimes leads to a tendency towards a form of racism, or the promotion of certain equally racist forms of eugenics'.[6] In any case, it is not proven that population is really the problem it is made out to be by experts who are often motivated by ideological considerations. A recent editorial in a leading newspaper remained healthily sceptical about ecological speculations concerning so-called over-population:

> Monaco is one of the most populated territories on Earth, with a population of 40,112 to the square mile, followed closely by Hong Kong. Neither is notably less successful or unhappier than the United Kingdom, which has a population density between 25 and 70 times less than theirs. The most sparsely populated territories of the world, from Antarctica to the wilder Highlands of Scotland, are not notable for their quality of life, opportunities for the young or the number of volunteers to live there permanently.[7]

9.2 Ecology and ideology

Alongside the development of ecology, however, there has evolved a pseudoscience based on a reductionist view of man and his environment. It is therefore important to define clearly what actually constitutes the environment for human beings. This definition cannot be reduced to purely physical elements, but should take into account those philosophical and theological considerations which have been delineated in the previous chapters. With respect to the human person, the environment cannot simply be restricted to the physical, plant or animal species which form his surroundings. Thus the environment cannot be thought of as nature in its so-called crude state, but must also include some idea of man's adaptation of nature for good or ill; hence distinction must be made between the *natural* and *artificial* environment. Furthermore, for man, who is a unity of body and soul, the natural world is not his complete milieu, but considerations of human culture must enter in. Moreover, as regards the supernatural calling of man, God and His grace must form part of man's 'surroundings'. However, it is not only the problem of the natural environment that is important but also the 'more serious destruction of the *human environment*, something which is by no means receiving the attention it deserves'.[8] Hence, for the human being, the concept of the environment cannot be reduced to a mere biological chain of vital processes. Any discussion of the natural environment of man must clearly consider the fact that the human person is constituted of soul and body and also has relationships with other human beings. Even as a purely natural being, the human person can arrive at a concept of God. However it is chiefly when we consider the supernatural order that some speak of God as the Environer of the human person.[9] These considerations of the spiritual nature of man and woman are systematically excluded by the materialistic philosophies and political systems of our day, including communism in its various forms, capitalism in many of its varieties, pantheism, and ideas connected with freemasonry. The three main materialistic systems of the past century have been Freudianism (in its reduction of the nature of man and woman), Darwinism (in its distorted view of evolution) and Marxism (in its erroneous socio-political analysis); these and other false philosophies have had their influence on ecological ideology.

9.3 A moral problem

An adequate theology of the environment therefore involves God, the human person and nature; thus problems concerning the environment cannot be resolved in purely socio-political terms, since the ecological crisis is a moral issue.[10] This truth is often ignored by politicians who use 'ecology' as a convenient slogan to obtain credibility[11] or else as a means of promoting their own materialistic ideologies. The Christian moral system which is used to discern the just course of action in the ecological realm must itself be based on the Christian vision of the cosmos:

> We must all learn to approach the environmental question with solid ethical convictions involving responsibility, self-control, justice and fraternal

> love. For believers this outlook springs directly from their relationship to God the Creator of all that exists. For Christians, respect for God's handiwork is reinforced by their certain hope of the restoration of all things in Jesus Christ.[12]

The very picture of the cosmos as a home for man derives from the Judaeo-Christian doctrine of creation. In other cultures, the universe was and is conceived as an object of veneration, of fear, or of simple indifference.

History shows that the Church has always fostered a strong theological tradition which respects the earth and all it contains. Pope John Paul II insisted that it must be our relationship with God to condition our relationship with the environment:

> *It is the relationship man has with God that determines his relationship with his fellows and with his environment.* This is why Christian culture has always recognized the creatures that surround man as also gifts of God to be nurtured and safeguarded with a sense of gratitude to the Creator. *Benedictine and Franciscan spirituality* in particular has witnessed to this sort of kinship of man with his creaturely environment, fostering in him an attitude of respect for every reality of the surrounding world.[13]

Saint Benedict and Saint Francis have taught us, in their different yet complementary ways, to respect God's creation. St. Benedict contemplated the Word of God both in the Sacred Scriptures and in the book of nature.[14] In the Benedictine tradition, the very singing of the psalms and other sacred texts from the Scriptures imbued the monks with a deep sense of the value of God's creation. 'It is precisely this monastic sense of praise, humility, stewardship, manual labour and community that taught Europe and made Europe fruitful and saved Western civilization. It is those things that we now, to our peril, have lost sight of.'[15] St. Francis, with his joyful yet austere approach to the brotherhood of all man and indeed all of creation teaches us that the creatures which surround us can only be saved if seen in the light of Christ who came to set all the creation free.[16] The word 'austere' is used advisedly, since St. Francis is often romanticised and it is forgotten that his brotherhood with fellow human beings and with all creation is achieved by grace, after great penance and self-denial. The Franciscan approach envisages a kind of natural 'brotherhood' of man with creation, which is neither pantheistic nor overly intellectual, but rather concrete. For example, St. Francis speaks of brother sun, sister moon and even sister death. This perception is not in contradiction with the more active approach to creation found in the Benedictine tradition, but rather complements it.

The monasticism of East and West can teach us a great deal through its emphasis on the value of praise, humility, responsible stewardship, manual labour, and community. In this perspective, there is no place for egoism or cosmocentrism. The three religious vows of poverty, chastity and obedience are a remedy against the triple concupiscence. Christians can give a cosmic dimension to their prayer, their listening to the Word, their sacramental life and their asceticism. They can do it by broadly showing the cultural, social and environmental richness that traditional ascetic values possess when opened to history: this involves a voluntary limitation of needs and a profound liking for all forms of life.[17] Religious life, furthermore, indicates that this earthly life of ours is not an end in itself, but leads to our future life in a new heaven and a new earth:

When over the earth the light of the setting sun fades away, when the peace of eternal sleep and the quiet of the declining day reign over all, I see Your dwelling–place like tents filled with light, reflected in the shapes of the clouds at dusk: fiery and purple, gold and blue, they speak prophet–like of the ineffable beauty of Your heavenly court, and solemnly call: let us go to the Father!
Glory to You in the quiet hour of evening,
Glory to You, covering the world with deep peace,
Glory to You for the last ray of the setting sun,
Glory to You for the rest of blissful sleep,
Glory to You for Your mercy in the midst of darkness, when the whole world has parted company with us,
Glory to You for the tender emotion of a soul moved to prayer,
Glory to You for the pledge of our awakening on the day which has no evening,
Glory to You, O God, from age to age.[18]

The Middle Ages, permeated by the living Catholic faith in God who created the world *ex nihilo* and *cum tempore,* formed the matrix of modern science.[19] However, after the Middle Ages, the intimate relation between faith and science was broken down, and this fragmentation was exemplified in the thought of the Enlightenment. The autonomy of science was exaggerated to such an extent that scientists no longer drew upon the moral truths propounded by the Church in order to evaluate rightly the technological applications of science. Precisely this lack of moral consciousness within society lies at the root of current environmental problems, and hence the expression 'From Assisi to Bikini' encapsulates the contrast between the medieval and twentieth century approaches to creation. A moral consciousness is hard to find wherever a pantheistic notion of the cosmos flourishes, as is often the case today, for this idea discourages consistent transcendent laws in the cosmos, whether natural or revealed. In the Christian vision, God is distinct from His creation and so pantheism in its various forms is to be excluded. However, in almost all non-Christian approaches to creation, there is at least a touch of pantheism which features heavily in many secular 'green' ideologies.

9.4 *Stewardship*

Christian ecology considers that the divine command to man and woman to 'fill the earth and conquer it' and to be 'masters of the fish of the sea, the birds of heaven and all living animals on the earth' (Gn 1:28) must be viewed in relation to the injunction to 'cultivate and take care' of the earth (Gn 2:15). In this way, man does not enjoy an absolute sovereignty over creation, but rather a responsible stewardship, in which he is accountable to God the Creator. Human activity should be envisaged as a participation in the divine work of Creation following His laws whether natural or revealed; man's dominion is one which must also extend over himself.[20] Man and woman in their administration of the cosmos must be neither arbitrary nor destructive for they are to participate in God's providential activity towards other creatures.[21] Human stewardship is based on a Christian understanding of man's dominion as service within the cosmos:

> The essential meaning of this 'kingship' and 'dominion of man over the visible world, which the Creator Himself gave man for his task, consists in the priority of ethics over technology, in the primacy of persons over things, and the superiority of spirit over matter. This threefold superiority is maintained to the extent to which the sense of the transcendence of man over the world and of God over man, is preserved.[22]

There is an essential distinction between man and the animals, a fact which is ignored by many ecologists who tend to value animals with the same dignity as human beings. In the book of Genesis, animals are created only from soil (Gn 2:19), while man receives a divine inbreathing (Gn 2:7). Man and woman were to be masters of all the animals (Gn 1:28). This hierarchy among God's creatures is reaffirmed and deepened by Jesus Christ, who teaches that human beings are of greater value than many sparrows (Lk 12:6–7) and more valuable than sheep (Mt 12:12).[23] In secular ecological circles there is often more concern for animal rights than for the rights of the unborn. In some countries there are special cemeteries for dogs, some of which are over one hundred years old, while the starving people of the world are often not properly buried. Certainly, cruelty to animals is to be rejected. Forms of sport (such as hunting) which involve unnecessary suffering for animals are unworthy of the Christian. Often a person who is cruel to animals will also show little regard for his fellow human beings. Recent Christian teaching is very positive concerning to man's treatment of animals:

> *Animals* are God's creatures. He surrounds them with His providential care. By their mere existence

> they bless Him and give Him glory. Thus men owe them kindness. We should recall the gentleness with which saints like St Francis of Assisi or St Philip Neri treated animals. God entrusted animals to the stewardship of those whom He created in His own image. Hence it is legitimate to use animals for food and clothing. They may be domesticated to help man in his work and leisure... It is contrary to human dignity to cause animals to suffer or die needlessly. It is likewise unworthy to spend money on them that should as a priority go to the relief of human misery. One can love animals; one should not direct to them the affection due only to persons.[24]

Nevertheless, the position of the animals has been exaggerated in some recent theological reflection, not least in the statement of one author who states that 'Christ also died for dogs'.[25] Modern vegetarianism also suffers from certain ideological undertones. Nevertheless, some would hold that the position of those who abstain from meat has a basis in Scripture where a case can be made for the thesis that before the Fall of man, the human being as well as the animals all fed on plants: 'God said, "See, I give you all the seed-bearing plants that are upon the whole earth, and all the trees with seed-bearing fruit; this shall be your food. To all wild beasts, all birds of heaven and all living reptiles on earth I give all the foliage of plants for food"' (Gn 1:29–30). It was only after the Flood that God added meat to man's diet (Gn 9:3)! The monastic tradition of Eastern and Western Christendom is one which seems to renounce the eating of meat to some degree. However, Christian asceticism is slow to accept the ideological undertones of modern vegetarianism.

9.5 Ecology, evil and Redemption

Catholic teaching has always affirmed that the beginnings of human history were marked with a tragedy. The cosmic results of this have been described from biblical times: 'How long will the land be in mourning, and the grass wither all over the countryside? The animals and birds are dying as a result of the wickedness of the inhabitants. For they say, "God does not see our behaviour"'.[26] Violence has been introduced into the cosmos as a result of Original Sin. Sin alienates us from God in the first place and also from our fellow human beings, from ourselves and from the natural world. It should be recalled that traditionally man is tempted in essentially three ways: the world, the flesh and the devil. By the 'flesh' is meant the disorder which arises in man as a result of concupiscence.[27] Every form of temptation has an evil influence on man inducing him to make a destructive use of God's creation, no longer for the glory of the Creator, but for man's own selfish and perverted ends. In this context, the devil is in a certain sense the cosmic vandal.[28] Sin has thus had secondary effects on the whole cosmos which is worse off after the Fall. An echo of this is felt even in material creation apart from man: 'It was not for any fault on the part of creation that it was made unable to attain its purpose, it was made so by God' (Rm 8:20). Hence, in a certain sense, the whole cosmos needs to be recapitulated in Christ (Ep 1:10), in order to be freed 'from its slavery to decadence, to enjoy the same freedom and glory as the children of God' (Rom 8:21). This liberation occurs in the Redemption which is actualized through the Church.

The true nature of man and woman within the cosmos is made known in the mystery of Christ, who as well as revealing the Most Holy Trinity also manifests perfect humanity. Indeed, Christ is the Key Who reveals the true meaning of creation; this most specifically Christian theology of Creation presents the way to face the present ecological crisis, as well as other moral problems. This Christocentric perspective, already founded in certain of the Pauline letters,[29] has been developed down the centuries by such theologians as St. Irenaeus and Blessed John Duns Scotus. The doctrine of the Incarnation safeguards the Christian vision of creation; in particular the expression 'only begotten Son' is a powerful barrier against taking the world for another begetting or necessary emanation from the divine.[30] The Incarnation of the Word closes the door upon any type of pantheism and deism, errors which appear in various ecological ideologies.

Consideration of Christ's Redemptive act emphasizes that a healing of the relation of the man to his environment is not a work that can be brought about solely by human hands. Since the damage caused to nature is essentially a moral problem and results from sin, the effects of Christ's Paschal sacrifice need to be applied. This approach is in sharp contrast with the heavily political and ideological notion of man as a self-sufficient being, an idea often found in most secular ecologies of today. On the other hand Christian ecology deals with God healing the cosmos through human instruments.

> The commitment of believers to a healthy environment for everyone stems directly from their belief in

> God the Creator, from their recognition of the effects of personal and original sin, and from the certainty of having been redeemed by Christ. Respect for life and for the dignity of the human person extends also to the rest of creation, which is called to join man in praising God.[31]

The Cross is the tree of life, the Victory of Christ over sin and death and hence over the sinful use which men and women make of their environment. Only through the power of Christ crucified and risen can peace be restored between man and nature. The Paschal Mystery is made present through the ministry of the Church in every age and every place, who in her prayer and sacraments applies the power of Christ crucified and risen so as to restore peace to nature.[32] The Christian, exercizing his kingly rôle, is a mediator of this redemption to the cosmos. Thus spirituality can never regard creation as isolated from the Incarnation and Paschal Mystery. Christ came to restore peace to the cosmos which is like a garden which He tends until it becomes His Kingdom. Some of the great dramas of salvation history have indeed taken place in a garden, from Eden to Gethsemane, and this image has furnished a rich soil for images of the spiritual life:

> When a farmer sets out to till the ground he has to take proper tools and clothing for work in the fields: so when Christ, the heavenly King and the true Husbandman, came to humanity laid waste by sin, He clothed Himself in a body and carried the Cross as His implement and cultivated the deserted soul. He pulled up the thorns and thistles of evil spirits and tore up the weeds of sin. With fire He burnt up all the harvest of its sins. When thus He had tilled

> the ground of its soul with the wooden plough of His Cross, He planted in it a lovely garden of the Spirit; a garden which brings forth for God as its Master the sweetest and most delightful fruits of every sort.[33]

It is exactly the idea of a garden which can be the foundation of a sound ecological spirituality. One starting point for this consists in the words of the Bride from the Song of Songs: 'My Beloved went down to his garden, to the beds of spices, to pasture his flock in the gardens and gather lilies' (Sg 6:2–3).[34] This passage, and indeed the whole of the Song can be interpreted in a *literal* sense as a love poem. It can then be seen in terms of an *allegorical* interpretation in which the Bridegroom represents Christ and the Bride symbolizes the Church. There are also *mariological* interpretations, for 'the Song of Love, Solomon's bridal song, refers in a special and spiritual way to the Church; however it should be applied in a most special and most spiritual sense to the glorious Virgin Mary'.[35] Finally there is the *tropological* or moral interpretation in which the Song expresses the relationship between Christ and the Christian soul. This latter approach furnishes a spiritual interpretation, an image of man's relationship with God in the cosmos. In other words, 'the garden is nature, the prince is God and each of us is the maiden'.[36]

The image of a garden was also adopted by Pope Benedict XVI in his homily at the Mass marking the beginning of his Pontificate:

> The external deserts in the world are growing, because the internal deserts have become so vast. Therefore the earth's treasures no longer serve to

> build God's garden for all to live in, but they have been made to serve the powers of exploitation and destruction. The Church as a whole and all her Pastors, like Christ, must set out to lead people out of the desert, towards the place of life, towards friendship with the Son of God, towards the One who gives us life, and life in abundance.[37]

The aesthetic dimension illustrates the contrast between the desert and the garden in this context. The beauty of nature reminds us that we have been appointed by God to tend and care for this 'garden' which is the earth (cf. Gn 2: 8–17). So, when people live in peace with God and one another, the earth truly resembles a 'paradise.' Unfortunately, sin ruins ever anew this divine project, causing division and introducing death into the world. Thus, humanity succumbs to the temptations of the Evil One and wages war against itself. Patches of 'hell' are consequently also created in this marvellous 'garden' which is the world.[38]

In this Christian spirituality of creation there are many ways of approaching God through His creation: through service and stewardship, through praise, through thanksgiving, through contemplation, through meditation and by seeing the relationship between nature and the humanity of Jesus Christ. Every spirituality of creation must also include an ascetical element. However, renunciation in the Christian perspective does not imply that creation is bad in any sense. In contrast, many non-Christian approaches to creation are at best uncertain about the goodness of creation and are often negative in their attitude to what God has made. Christian moderation in regard to the world around us is based instead on a desire to avoid worshipping and serving 'creatures instead of the Creator' (Rm 1:25). It is also founded on a desire to share earth's goods equitably in a spirit of solidarity. Self-denial also reminds us that the natural order is subordinated to Christ's new creation in grace; it lets the first creation be a pointer to the second: 'For as the earth makes fresh things grow, as a garden makes seeds spring up, so will the Lord Yahweh make both integrity and praise spring up in the sight of the nations' (Is 61:11). As man and woman respond to their kingly vocation in Christ, the cosmos as a home and as a garden is transformed into a sanctuary where thanks and praise are offered to the Father in the Holy Spirit. In every Catholic spirituality of Creation there must be a place for Mary the Mother of God, Queen of all Creation, who intercedes for her sons and daughters as they prepare to inherit the New Creation.

9.6 *Ecology and the Christian vision*

The way forward in an ecological formation 'must not be based on a rejection of the modern world or a vague desire to return to some "paradise lost"'.[39] Some of those who seek an ecological utopia do so in a retrogressive way, by trying to recover an idealized past perfect state of affairs. Others, in a more progressive vein, believe that a utopia is to be found in the future through continual, ongoing scientific progress. Both are false approaches as they attempt to escape the reality of the present moment. Nevertheless, scientific progress could be the key to solving many current ecological problems, not least being the disposal of various forms of waste.

Above all, what is needed to face the current problems in the environment is a clear presentation and proclamation of the Christian truths concerning Creator and Creation. In such a witness, there is much scope for ecumenical collaboration:

> There is an intrinsic connection between development, human need and the stewardship of creation. For experience has taught us that development in response to human needs cannot misuse or overuse natural resources without serious consequences.
>
> The responsibility for the care of creation, which in itself has a particular dignity, is given by the Creator himself to all people, in so far as they are to be stewards of creation. Catholics are encouraged to enter, at various levels, into joint initiatives aimed at study and action on issues that threaten the dignity of creation and endanger the whole human race.
>
> Other topics for such study and action could include, for example, certain forms of uncontrolled rapid industrialization and technology that cause pollution of the natural environment with serious consequences to the ecological balance... An important aspect of joint action in this field is in the area of education of people in the use of resources as well as in the planned use of them and in the care of creation.[40]

Many Christian Churches and ecclesial communities have become aware of the need to give clear ethical guidance on this issue. The Orthodox Churches possess a wealth of spirituality concerning the Christian vision of Creation upon which they are now drawing in the moral education of their faithful.[41] The contribution of Eastern Christendom has a particular liturgical flavour:

> The events of the past find in Christ their meaning and fulness, and creation is revealed for what it is: a complex whole which finds its perfection, its purpose *in the liturgy* alone. This is why the liturgy is heaven on earth, and in it the Word Who became flesh imbues matter with a saving potential which is fully manifest in the sacraments: there creation communicates to each individual the power conferred on it by Christ.[42]

The Orthodox tradition stresses the priestly vocation of humanity, and emphasizes the language of gift and blessing rather than that of dominion and stewardship. The Byzantine tradition stresses that the redemption involves the whole of creation. The priestly calling of man consists in praising and honouring God for His many gifts and blessings in the First Creation and the New Creation. It also involves the cleansing and healing of creation. The human being in his priestly capacity must dispel the power of evil in all things, so as to set creation free. In this context, 'the emphasis in the East has tended to be on cosmology and freedom, the emphasis in the West on morality and obedience'.[43] In the Orthodox tradition, the Church is coextensive with all of the cosmos.[44] Some Eastern Fathers see Noah's ark as a prefiguration of this cosmic ecclesiology, where all creatures were gathered together into safety from the Flood. It is only with the Church, the ark of salvation, that the New Noah, Christ, brings about that vision of peace and harmony in creation, but without any utopian ideology, which Isaiah foresees concerning a redeemed cosmos:

> The wolf lives with the lamb,
> the panther lies down with the kid,
> calf and lion cub feed together

with a little boy to lead them.
The cow and the bear make friends,
their young lie down together
The lion eats straw like the ox.
The infant plays over the cobra's hole;
into the viper's lair
the young child puts his hand.
They do no hurt, no harm,
on all my holy mountain,
for the country is filled with the knowledge of the Lord
as the waters swell the sea. (Is 11:6–9)

A clear and unitary vision of Christian teaching upon Creation and its use to the glory of its Creator is thus most important at this time, and Eastern Christendom could prove of great inspiration in this regard.

The world which had a beginning will also have an end; this consummation will not be brought about by human action. The pessimistic idea that the ecological crisis could provoke the end of the world seems to rob from God's hands dominion over this final point of history. The final transformation of the cosmos, like its creation, is an action of God who is transcendent as well as immanent. Nevertheless the material cosmos is important, because Christ has partaken of it and used it in His sacramental order, above all in the Most Holy Sacrifice of the Mass. There will thus be a continuity between the cosmos of here and now and the new heavens and new earth (Rv 21:1), as will be seen in the next and final chapter.

Further Reading

Pope John Paul II, *Peace with God the Creator, Peace with All of Creation*. Message for the Celebration of the World Day of Peace 1 January 1990

Pope Benedict XVI, *If you want to cultivate Peace, protect Creation*. Message for the Celebration of the World Day of Peace 1 January 2010

P. Haffner, *Towards a Theology of the Environment* (Leominster: Gracewing, 2008)

R. Whelan, J. Kirwan and P. Haffner, *The Cross and the Rain Forest* (Grand Rapids: Eerdmans, 1996)

Notes

1 See E. Haeckel, *Generelle Morphologie der Organismen: Allgemeine Grundzüge der organischen Formen–Wissenschaft, mechanisch begründet durch die con Charles Darwin reformierte Descendez–Theorie* (Berlin: Georg Reimer, 1866), I, p. 238 and II, p. 286.

2 See S. Boyle and J. Ardill, *The Greenhouse Effect* (London: Hodder and Stoughton, 1989) who support the claim of a 'greenhouse effect' and D.L. Ray who in *Trashing the Planet* (New York: Harper Perennial, 1990), pp. 31–48, raises some questions about its validity.

3 See Ray, *Trashing the Planet*, pp. 3–13.

4 Pope John Paul II, *Message for World Day of Peace 1990: Peace with God the Creator, Peace with all of Creation*, 7.3.

5 S. Caldecott, 'Cosmology, eschatology, ecology: Some reflections on *Sollicitudo Rei Socialis*' in *Communio* 15/3 (Fall 1988), p. 313.

6 Pope John Paul II, Encyclical Letter *Sollicitudo rei socialis*, 25.

7 Editorial in *The Times*, 10 August 1993, p. 15.

8 Pope John Paul II, Encyclical Letter *Centesimus Annus*, 38.

9 See E. Holloway, *Catholicism: A New Synthesis* (Wallington, Surrey: Faith-Keyway, 1976), pp. 105–114.

10 See Pope John Paul II, *Message for World Day of Peace 1990*, 6, 7, 15.1.

11 See Episcopal Conference of Lombardy, *La questione ambientale: aspetti etico-religiosi* (Milano: Centro Ambrosiano di Documentazione e Studi Religiosi, 1988), pp. 13–14.

12 Pope John Paul II, *Discourse to Pontifical Academy of Sciences* (22 October 1993) in *OR* 133/245 (23 October 1993), p. 4.

13 *Ibid.*, 4.1.

14 See Pope John Paul II, Apostolic Letter *Sanctorum altrix* for the XV centenary of the birth of Saint Benedict in *IG* 3/2 (1980), pp. 363–364.

15 Sister Joan Chittister OSB, 'Monasticism: An Ancient Answer to modern problems' in E. Breuilly and M. Palmer (eds.) *Christianity and Ecology* (London: Cassell, 1992), p. 73.

16 See Pope John Paul II, Apostolic Letter *Radiabat* for the VIII centenary of the birth of Saint Francis in *IG* 5/3 (1982), pp. 222–229.

17 See Ignatius IV Hazim, Orthodox Patriarch of Antioch, *Trasfigurare la creazione*, (Monastero di Bose: 1994), p. 29.

18 Metropolitan Tryphon, *An Akathist in Praise of God's Creation*, Ikos 4.

19 See pp. 235–237 above and S. L. Jaki, *The Road of Science and the Ways to God* (Edinburgh: Scottish Academic Press, 1978) and Idem., *The Savior of Science* (Washington: Regnery Gateway, 1988).

20 See Pope John Paul II, Encyclical Letter *Veritatis splendor*, 38.1. See also *CCC* 377 which speaks of man's dominion as self-mastery.

21 See *CCC* 373.

22 Pope John Paul II, Encyclical Letter *Redemptor Hominis*, 16 and *Discourse to the Plenary Session of the Pontifical Academy of Sciences* (10 November 1979) in *DP*, p. 152.

23 See *CCC* 342.

24 CCC 2416–2418.

25 See M. Damien, *Gli animali, l'uomo e Dio* (Casale Monferrato: Piemme, 1987), p. 166.

26 Jr 12:4; see also Gn 6:11–12, Ho 4:3.

27 See pp. 180–181 above, and 1 Jn 2:16.

28 See pp. 172–173, 191, 195 above.

29 See Col 1:15–20 and Ep 1:3–14.

30 See pp. 207–208 above and S. L. Jaki, *The Savior of Science*, pp. 72–73.

31 Pope John Paul II, *Message for World Day of Peace 1990*, 16.

32 For the cosmic rôle of the Church see pp. 222–227 above.

33 St Macarius the Great, *Homily* 28, 3 in *PG* 34, 711–712.

34 The idea for this comes from R. Faricy, *Wind and Sea Obey Him* (London: SCM, 1982), pp. 62ff. However, I have used a different passage from the Song of Songs to illustrate the point.

35 Alain of Lille, *In cantica canticorum elucidatio*, Prologue, in *PL* 210, 53.

36 Faricy, *Wind and Sea Obey Him*, p. 62.

37 Pope Benedict XVI, *Homily at the Mass for the Beginning of the Petrine Ministry* (24 April 2005).

38 See Pope Benedict XVI, *Angelus Message* (22 July 2007).

39 Pope John Paul II, *Message for World Day of Peace 1990*, 13.2.

40 Pontifical Council for Christian Unity, *Ecumenical Directory* (1993), 215.

41 See, for example V. Guroian, 'Toward ecology as an ecclesial event: Orthodox theology and ecological ethics' in *Communio* 18/1 (Spring 1991) pp. 89–110; I. Zizioulas, *Il Creato come Eucaristia* (Magnano: Edizioni Qiqajon, 1994).

42 Pope John Paul II, Apostolic Letter *Orientale Lumen* (1995), 11.1.

43 Caldecott, 'Cosmology, eschatology, ecology', p. 318.

44 See pp. 222–223, 225–227 above.

10

The New Creation

As from the power of sacred lays
The spheres began to move,
And sing the great Creator's praise
To all the Blest above;
So when the last and dreadful hour
This crumbling pageant shall devour,
The trumpet shall be heard on high,
The dead shall live, the living die,
And music shall untune the sky!

John Dryden, *A Song for St Cecilia's Day*, 1687

In a very real sense, the Church is already the garden in which grace is causing God's salvific action to flower, since 'for anyone who is in Christ, there is a new creation' (2 Co 5:17). We are 'already children of God but what we are to be in the future has not yet been revealed' (1 Jo 3:2) and so this new creation has not yet come to its full fruition. Practically all the doctrines of the faith relate to events which have already occurred for us (the creation, the Incarnation) or are occurring now (Transubstantiation) or are beyond time (the Most Holy Trinity). However, Christian understanding of the consummation of the world refers to a mystery still to occur. The final mysteries of the faith are those which deal with the death of the human person, the particular judgment, the Second Coming of Christ, the General Judgment, Hell, Purgatory and Heaven. Most books treating this theology of the 'last things,' or eschatology as it is known in technical parlance, would have something to say about the end of the world.

10.1 The End of the World in Art and Science

The way the cosmos is to come to an end has enthralled the minds of artists and scientists. The great Michelangelo in his painting of the Last Judgment in the Sistine Chapel, now magnificently restored, depicts the centrality of Christ in the events which mark His Second Coming in glory. Novelists such as R. H. Benson have tried to describe in literary terms what lies deep in the Christian imagination concerning the end of the world as we know it.[1] Movies have attempted to portray eschatological events.[2] Even modern pop musicians have expressed popular fascination with apocalyptic events.[3]

The scientific community, in its turn, has also reflected upon 'an end of the cosmos'. The idea of an eternal universe is now largely discredited. Our day to day experience is one in which things do not last for ever. Cars get old and end up on the scrap heap. Machinery ceases to function and is too expensive to repair. Electric light bulbs (even the 'long-life' variety) have a finite period of usefulness. Some of the more pessimistic ecologists maintain that life on this planet will be destroyed by man's heedlessness while others think that the end of the *human* world may come about as a result of nuclear war. Taking into account that the sun is a gigantic nuclear reactor, scientists have tried to predict how much longer it would last. At present, the Sun is converting hydrogen into helium at a rate of some 600 million tonnes per second. It is already about 4500 million years old and has used up nearly half of the hydrogen in its core. The sun will continue to burn through the hydrogen for another 5000 million years or so, and then helium will become its primary fuel. The sun would expand to about a hundred times its current size, swallowing Earth and other planets. It will burn as a red giant for another 1000 million years. Finally nothing but iron will be left to burn in the Sun, and since the energy required for that is higher than the Sun can generate, it will gradually dwindle more and more in size until it will become a white dwarf star, about the size of planet Earth.

On these considerations, the biosphere of earth could continue for at least another 100 million years. Recent estimates indicated that in about 1000 million years' time, the earth's climate will become uncomfortably hot as a results of changes in the structure of the sun. However, the end of the solar system as we know it, which could also be occasioned by some other cosmic catastrophe, would not be the end of the universe as a whole. In the nineteenth century, H. von Helmholtz explained that according to the Second Law of Thermodynamics, the universe was using up all its available energy. At a particular finite time within the future, the universe will arrive at a final state of maximum entropy. When this occurs the so called 'Heat-Death' will have been reached where the cosmos and all creatures living in it will 'die.' More recent projections consider that if it contains enough matter, the cosmos will collapse into itself at the end under the force of gravity in what is commonly termed the 'Big Crunch'. It would be fair to say that 'nearly all cosmologists now accept that we live in a universe that had a definite beginning in a big bang, and is now developing toward an uncertain end'.[4]

Practically all scientific approaches to an end of the cosmos have in common that they restrict themselves to considerations of how the cosmos in itself will 'burn out' or collapse. This is consonant with the scientific method which cannot take into account the fact that, from the Christian viewpoint, the end of the universe is its final consummation as an event which is in God's hands. Just as the beginning of the universe depended on a divine choice, so also its final end as we know it is a fruit of God's free decision. Science is similarly unable to tell us anything about what happens 'after' the end of the world.

Not only is the timing of end of the world outside the ken of science, but also the moment of the death of each human person. While medical science can ascertain that death is imminent, and can give sure signs of the fact that a person has passed from this life after the event, the actual moment lies outside its realm of measurement. For, in metaphysical and theological terms, death is defined as the separation of the soul from the body and 'such a separation cannot be perceived by any of the senses but there are visible signs which give moral certainty that it has taken place'.[5]

10.2 The End of the Cosmos in Scripture and Tradition

For the Christian, the *mystery of the beginning of the world* is intimately linked with *the mystery of the end* in which the finality of all creation reaches its fulfilment.[6] The Old Testament teaches that what God created in the beginning will also have an end, which will not be a total destruction, but rather a transformation, using the image of a change of clothing:

> Long ago you founded the earth
> and the heavens are the work of your hands.
> They will perish but you will remain.
> They will are wear out like a garment.
> You will change them like clothes that are changed.
> (Ps 102:26–27)

The End of the World is to take place within the framework of Christ's Second Coming, to judge the living and the dead. We do not know the day or the hour of this Second Coming, and therefore we are ignorant of the timing of the end of the cosmos. Jesus declared: 'But as for that day or hour, nobody knows it, neither the angels of heaven nor the Son; no one but the Father' (Mk 13:32; cf. Mt 24:36). The statement 'nor the Son' has given rise to many interpretations across the centuries, some of them heterodox and implying lack of knowledge in the Son of Man. Among more acceptable ways of understanding the phrase would be the idea that Christ did know the time of His Second Coming in His human nature not however *from* His human nature, but rather from His divine nature.[7] Before His Ascension, Christ reminded His Apostles that it was not for them 'to know times or dates that the Father has decided by His own authority' (Ac 1:7). The Apostle Paul also taught that the time of the Parousia is hidden from us: 'You will not be expecting us to write anything to you, brothers, about "times and seasons", since you know very well that the Day of the Lord is going to come like a thief in the night' (1 Th 5:1–2).

At the same time, both Christ and His Apostles indicate certain signs which are to precede the Second Coming. 'Take the fig tree as a parable: as soon as its twigs grow supple and its leaves come out, you know that summer is near. So with you when you see all these things: know that He is near, at the very gates' (Mt 24: 32–33). The Last Day (1 Co 1:8) is therefore preceded by the last days (1 Tm 4:1). Signs indicated in the New Testament include the preaching of the Gospel to the whole world (Mt 24:14); the incorporation of all Israel into the Kingdom of God (Rm 11:25–32); the coming of false prophets who will lead many away from the faith (Mt 24:4f.); the appearance of Antichrist (2 Th 2:3); severe tribulations which are to include persecutions of the faithful (Mt 24:9) as well as catastophes in nature (Mt 24:29). While it is futile to speculate upon when the end of the world may occur, its coming about may be connected with a kind of 'fullness of time' when the effects of Christ's redemption have reached a certain fruition in all creation. This idea is supported by the Our Lord's indication that the Gospel must be preached to the whole world before the End (Mt 24:14).

A further question concerns what type of end the world will have. Obviously this is veiled in great mystery, but some basic observations are in order. Jesus speaks explicitly about a *destruction* of the world to some extent. Already the great cosmic perturbations listed by Jesus as an proximate prelude to His Second Coming indicate an end of the material cosmos as we know it. 'Immediately after the distress of those days the sun will be darkened, the moon will lose its brightness, the stars will fall from the sky and the powers of heaven will be shaken' (Mt 24:29). Christ also reminds us that 'Heaven and earth will pass away, but My words will not pass away' (Mk 13:31). That there will be an end or consummation of time is indicated when Christ sends out His Apostles: 'And know that I am with you always; yes, to the end of time' (Mt 28:20). If time is to end, then the material reality as we know it must pass away.

Some of the New Testament writers elucidate further how the present world will end. The author of the Letter to the Hebrews affirms that created things are 'going to be changed' (Heb 12:27). In St John's vision, in the presence of the Judge, 'earth and sky vanished, leaving no trace' (Rv 20:11). While St Paul reminds us that 'the world as we know it is passing away' (1 Co 7:31), St Peter foretells the destruction of this world, speaking of the fact that 'the present sky and earth are destined for fire' (2 P 3:7). The Prince of the Apostles adds that 'the Day of the Lord will come like a thief, and then with a roar the sky will vanish, the elements will catch fire and fall apart, the earth and all that it contains will be burnt up' (2 P 3:10). St Peter also affirms that when the Day of God comes, 'the sky will dissolve in flames and elements melt in the heat' (2 P 3:12). This conception of the destruction of the world was also found in the Graeco-Roman world, since fire was the most destructive factor in human experience. It may be asked therefore whether the destruction of the world by fire is to be taken literally or whether it is a way of stating that the world is to be destroyed on the Last Day.

The idea of several ancient sects, such as the Gnostics, Manichaeans and the Origenists, who asserted that the physical world was to be entirely annihilated, is opposed to the Christian vision, which affirms also the restoration of the cosmos. St Thomas Aquinas emphasized that nothing will be annihilated, since the goodness and power of God are shown by the preservation of things in existence.[8] Several philosophical systems of antiquity (such as that of the Stoics) as well as religious ones (such as that of the Hindus and Buddhists) proposed that the cosmos repeated itself in a series of endless cycles. The idea of this or any other eternal world is contrary to Christian faith, which maintains that the end of the cosmos is definitive. Similarly insufficient is a view that the world evolves towards its own destruction in a purely natural way, according to laws immanent within the cosmos. If this were the case, man could eventually predict when the end would come about, which would contradict Christ's words that 'no one knows the hour.' At the same time, it may be asked whether God will destroy the world directly, or through some secondary causality. A certain degree of direct divine intervention would seem to be indicated since the consummation of the cosmos is not merely 'the ripe fruit of evolution and of history.' Moreover, 'a constant battle rages between the kingdom of God and the kingdom of the world'.[9] Despite this struggle, divine Providence guides human existence in the cosmos towards the seventh day rest of creation, which will finally arrive at its fulfilment.[10]

Christian teaching also finds *millenarism* unacceptable; this idea is based upon a mistaken interpretation of the book of Revelation concerning the thousand year imprisonment of Satan (Rv 20:1–3), which holds that there would be a thousand year reign for Christ and His elect here on earth before the General Resurrection. Some exponents of this approach envisaged a 'heavenly Jerusalem' which would come down upon earth as an ideal world, but which would be superseded by a later final heavenly state. The final consummation does not take place simply in history but also beyond history and through the final judgment.[11] Also excluded by the Christian vision is the view, common in Marxism and other materialistic philosophies, that man, through his own efforts, will be able to set up his own earthly paradise in the here and now. Rather, the final consummation of the universe will be an historical event which will lead us beyond history. The end of the world will be a real event and not merely, as some would maintain, an expression of man's daily and continual existential experience of the finite and the imperfect in the cosmos.

The nuanced nature of the Christian position is expressed by St Augustine who affirmed that the present world will not be entirely annihilated, but rather altered: 'The form will pass away, but not the nature'.[12] According to St Irenaeus, the material condition will not be destroyed, but the form will pass away since sin has been committed in it.[13] St Thomas Aquinas wrote of a fire that will cleanse the universe; this was analogous though not identical with the fire that we know.[14] This cleansing is required because 'although corporeal elements cannot be the subject of sin, nevertheless, from the sin that is committed in them they contract a certain unfitness for receiving the perfection of glory'.[15] St Thomas drew a parallel between the Flood which cleansed the world by water, and the fire of the final consummation;[16] he emphasized that 'the entire cleansing of the world and the renewal for the purpose of cleansing will be directed to the renewal of man'.[17] The fire of which St Paul spoke 'would test the quality of each man's work' (1 Co 3:13). The Angelic Doctor affirmed that the cosmos would be renewed.[18] When all is said and done 'we do not know the way the universe will be transformed';[19] it remains a mystery. We do know however that there will be a new heaven and a new earth (Rv 21:1).

The type of destruction the cosmos will suffer is also related to the fate of that last generation who are present at the time of Christ's appearing in glory. In two passages in the Pauline Letters, the Apostle points out that 'we are not all going to die, but we shall all be changed' (1 Co 15:51) and he affirms that 'those who have died in Christ will be the first to rise and then those of us who are still alive will be taken up in the clouds, together with them to meet the Lord in the air' (1 Th 4:16–17). God can grant a special privilege of not dying as happened to Enoch (Gn 5:24; Hb 11:5) and Elijah (2 K 2:1–11; Si 48:9) in the Old Testament. Some theologians have also maintained that Our Blessed Lady did not die.[20] The opinion that the last generation upon the face of the earth will not die is supported by Greek Fathers including St Gregory of Nyssa and St John Chrysostom and

Latin Fathers including Tertullian and St Jerome. As well as the Scriptures, the Creed seems to imply that those who are alive at the Second Coming will not die, for it affirms that Christ will come to judge the *living* and the dead. However some writers would ask whether the opinion that the last generation will not taste death contradicts the words of the Apostle: 'death has spread through the whole human race' (Rm 12:5). Perhaps the catastrophes occurring on the Last Day would be responsible for the death of the last generation, but the above cited passages from the Pauline letters seem to indicate that these people would be swept up to meet Christ so as to avoid the final destruction. It may be that the sufferings which they would have to endure at the end of time would be worse than death itself, and so they would be spared from death's pangs. Clearly, this assumption of a last generation of believers is to be carefully distinguished from the various notions of the Rapture, current in some Protestant and Pentecostal thought.[21]

The very idea that 'we shall all be changed' (1 Co 15:51; cf. Heb 1:12) may furnish an idea of what will happen to the cosmos as a whole, for it will also be transformed. Human beings and the material cosmos must be changed in a way which is mutually compatible. There is a continuity between the body we have now and the resurrected body. The Fourth Lateran Council declared that all human beings 'will rise again with their own bodies which they now bear'.[22] Hence the identity of the human person is not to be found only in the soul but also in the body. The continuity between the body before death and after the resurrection need not be conceived in such a way that all the matter which formed part of a particular earthly body will be present in the risen body. Since the human body always remains essentially the same despite the constantly changing composition of its constituent matter, it is sufficient for the preservation of the identity, if a relatively small portion of matter from the earthly body be present in the risen body.[23] While the cosmos and the human body are of course different, the human person forms part of the cosmos and so it is reasonable to suppose an analogy in what happens to human beings and what occurs in the cosmos as a whole.

The stress which is put on either destruction or transformation of the cosmos is congruent with the respective continuity or discontinuity which is assigned to the human body before and after its resurrection. The degree of discontinuity which is envisaged between the cosmos and the new creation is a function of how 'unsuitable' for glory the present universe would be. Because of the repercussions of original sin, it has to undergo a transformation. In the absence of original sin, perhaps the cosmos would have been transformed into glory in a smooth way; this change would still have been a divine gift. If one is more pessimistic about creation, one tends to emphasize the necessity of at least some destruction of the universe and the human person, while if one is more optimistic about creation, one tends to underline the continuity between the old creation and the new. An optimistic approach to the first creation is supported by the fact that the Lord used images from it to indicate when His new creation would arrive in its definitive fulfilment. In the parable of the fig-tree (Mk

13:28), it is significant that Christ used *summer* in His analogy of when the end would occur. Summer is the time when the light is most powerful, a time of the year when everything comes to its harvest, rather than winter which is the end of all.[24] The renewal in creation carried out by the Holy Spirit, prepares it for its final transformation.

10.3 The New Heavens and the New Earth

The present creation is, in a loose sense, a sign or symbol of the new creation. Once the reality is among us, the sign will no longer be necessary. The new creation is the fulfilment of all that has gone before, all that has been described in these pages and more. However, for the men and women of the present materialistic age, the invisible realm presents a difficulty; thus there is a reluctance to accept the reality of angels, of the human soul and of the world to come.

A glimpse of the restoration or renovation of the world is already seen in the Old Testament. Isaiah prophesies the Lord's words: 'For now I create new heavens and a new earth' (Is 65:17; cf. 66:22). Jesus speaks of the restoration of the world in the context of the Last Judgment: 'I tell you solemnly, when all is made new and the Son of Man sits on His throne of glory, you will yourselves sit on twelve thrones to judge the twelve tribes of Israel' (Mt 19:28). St Paul teaches that the whole of the creation fell in some way under the bondage of sin and awaits its redemption: 'It was not for any fault on the part of creation that it was made unable to attain its purpose, it was made so by God; but creation still retains the hope of being freed, like us, from its slavery to decadence, to enjoy the same freedom and glory as the children of God' (Rm 8:20–21). This passage makes clear that the creation below man has not actually itself sinned but nevertheless suffers the repercussions, damage and contamination of original and actual sin. The redemption of the cosmos is actualized gradually: 'From the beginning till now the entire creation, as we know, has been groaning in one great act of giving birth' (Rm 8:22). For the Christian the restoration of the cosmos has already begun. 'For everyone who is in Christ, there is a new creation' (2 Co 5:17). After all, since the value of the Sacrifice of the Mass is infinitely great, does not its very application also transform the material cosmos for the better?

> Already the final age of the world is with us and the renewal of the world is irrevocably under way; it is even now being anticipated in a certain real way, for the Church on earth is endowed already with a sanctity that is real though imperfect.[25]

However, a final discontinuity will be evident between the world as we know it now and the new heavens and the new earth. St Peter speaks of the destruction of the cosmos by fire and he also stresses that it will be restored : 'What we are waiting for is what He promised: the new heavens and the new earth, the place where righteousness will be at home' (2 P 3:13). St John in his book of Revelation describes the fact that after 'the first heaven and the first earth had disappeared' (Rv 21:1) and 'the world of the past has gone' (Rv 21:4), 'the One sitting on the throne said "Now I am making the whole of creation new"' (Rv 21:5). In other words, after this present Day and the Day of consummation, will come the Third Day on which the whole Body of the Church will rise again, and the temple of the Church will be rebuilt.[26]

On the one hand 'a fundamental continuity' should be affirmed between our present life in Christ and the future life for 'charity is the law of the Kingdom of God and our charity on earth will be the measure of our sharing in God's glory in heaven.' On the other hand there is a 'radical difference between the present life and the future one, due to the fact that the economy of faith will be replaced by the economy of the fulness of life'.[27] The consummation of the cosmos brings it to perfection involving a new creation, a new act on the part of God. The book of Revelation relates the first act of creation and the new creation.[28] The twenty four elders say to the One seated on the throne: '"You are our Lord and our God, you are worthy of glory and honour and power, because You made all the universe and it was only by Your Will that everything was made and exists"' (Rv 4:11; see 14:7). However, the new act of creation is also described. 'Then the One sitting on the throne spoke: "Now I am making all of creation new"' (Rv 21:5). God the Most Holy Trinity is responsible for the old and the new creations. This is emphasized by God's words: '"I am the Alpha and the Omega, the First and the Last, the Beginning and the End"' (Rv 22:13; see 1:8; 21:6). God is the Author of all creative activity. The first creation has a real value. Human beings are already participants in the new creation through their relationships with the old one. However, the first creation must pass away to make way for the world which will last for ever. God's purpose is worked out despite the devil's attempt at a type of 'anti-creation' in the course of history.[29] At the end of time the final victory of God over evil will be realized. The devil and the fallen angels as well as those 'whose name could not be found in the book of life' will be thrown into the 'lake of fire and sulphur' and 'their torture will not stop, day and night, for ever and ever' (Rv 20:10, 15). This place of eternal punishment will involve not only a deprivation of the vision of God but also a positive castigation of the senses for those human beings unfortunate enough to go there. Even the damned will rise again with their bodies and the possession of their bodies will thus allow them to be punished in their senses.

St Paul traces a connection between God's power in creating the universe out of nothing and in raising bodies from the dead; it is God 'Who brings the dead to life and calls into being what does not exist' (Rm 4:17). Furthermore, the Apostle points out the link between the transformation of our bodies and that of the cosmos: 'He will transfigure these wretched bodies of ours into copies of His glorious Body. He will do that by the same power with which He can subdue the whole universe' (Ph 3:21). We see that Christ's risen Body is the model for our own resurrected body. Christ made it very evident in His appearances after the Resurrection that His Body preserved a material aspect. He said '"Look at my hands and my feet; yes, it is I indeed. Touch me and see for yourselves; a ghost has no flesh and bones as you can see I have"'(Lk 24:39). In order to show further the reality of the material nature of His risen Body, Christ asked for something to eat. 'And they offered him a piece of grilled fish, which He took and ate before their eyes' (Lk 24:42–43). St Thomas Aquinas comments on this episode:

> When Christ partook of that meal, His eating was an act, not of necessity as though human nature needed food after the resurrection, but of power, so as to prove that He had resumed the true human nature which He had in that state wherein He ate and drank with His disciples. There will be no need of such proof at the general resurrection, since it will be evident to all.[30]

Thus in the new creation our bodies will be glorified and also the cosmos as a whole. It is a mystery what our future glorified bodies will be like, a mystery which has aroused the interest of Christians in all generations. Already St Paul discourages excessive curiosity in this regard (1 Co 15:35–36). The Apostle simply speaks of 'the things which no eye has seen and no ear has heard, things beyond the mind of man, all that God has prepared for those who love Him' (1 Co 2:9). There will clearly be an identity between our body now and the resurrected body so that we can truly say that it is our own. Yet there will also be a great difference. The body will no longer be subject to sin, suffering and death: what is raised is 'imperishable, glorious, powerful' (1 Co 15:42–43). Exactly what degree of continuity and discontinuity there will be cannot be determined from Scripture or Tradition, but it seems evident that we will have a perfect body.[31] It is generally accepted in the tradition of St Augustine, St Gregory the Great and St Thomas Aquinas that the resurrected body will enjoy sexual differentiation.[32] This idea would further underline the deep roots of the difference between man and woman in the identity of the person's being. However the variety in gender will not have procreation as its object since Christ says: 'For at the resurrection men and women do not marry; no they are like the angels in heaven' (Mt 22:30).

St Augustine taught that the properties of the future world would be just as suited to the immortal existence of the transfigured human body as were the properties of the corruptible existence to the mortal body.[33] It may be asked therefore whether there will be plants and animals as well in the new creation. St Thomas seems to reply in the negative to this question, for according to him they would be incapable of receiving a renewal of incorruption, since 'they are corruptible both in their whole and in their parts, both on the part of their matter which loses its form, and on the part of their form which does not remain actually; and thus they are in no way subjects of incorruption. Hence they will not remain in this renewal'.[34] Nowadays there is a tendency to ask whether in the context of the renewal of the whole of creation, there may not also be a place for plants and animals in a new glorified realm of matter. There would not seem to be any intrinsic reason to exclude inanimate being from the new creation, but rather the presence together of angels, men and women, plants and animals as well as inanimate objects appears to some minds consonant with the completeness of the new heavens and the new earth.[35]

In the New Creation, angels will be present since they are immortal by nature and they enjoy God's glory by gift, human beings will be resurrected by God's power, and animals and plants could be incorporated by God's renewal of material creation. This picture would allow all of the old creation to be represented in some way in the new. Nevertheless, it is hard to make a case for the continuity of any *particular* animal or plant between this life and the next, since these beings do not have a spiritual soul. A relevant issue is also whether the book of Revelation is to be taken literally or figuratively when it indicates that no dogs will be admitted into the heavenly Jerusalem (Rv 22:15). The ontological difference that exists between human beings and animals must always be remembered, since only man is created in the image of God.[36] Above all, the central and essential joy of Paradise will be the beatific vision of God face to face: there will also be a secondary joy in the company of Mary and of all the angels and saints of Paradise, including parents and friends, along with the renewed material universe.[37]

The doctrine that the current universe is going to be destroyed and then renewed, shapes and influences our attitude towards the present world:

> Far from diminishing our concern to develop this earth, the expectancy of a new earth should spur us on, for it is here that the body of a new human family grows, foreshadowing in some way the age that is to come. That is why, although we must be careful to distinguish earthly progress from the increase of the Kingdom of Christ, such progress is vital to the Kingdom of God.[38]

Any denial of the importance of the present world would undermine the true meaning of the Incarnation and so would fall victim to the spiritualism of Eastern world religions. On the other hand, if we lose ourselves in this present world, according to the bias of various historical forms of Western materialism, then the true meaning of the cosmos escapes us. Detachment from creation does not imply a rejection of what God has made. Rather, we moderate our attachment to the cosmos in order to be in harmony with God and His laws, to proclaim God's sovereignty over His creation, and to affirm that all must be renewed and set free, according to His providential plan.

The beginning of this work dealt with understanding the cosmos through human reason and Christian revelation. The full unfolding of the meaning and purpose of creation will be given to us only in the next life. There we shall experience the complete freedom of creation, its perfect relation with God and also its inner synthetic harmony, as Dante declared:

> O grace abounding, Whereby I presumed
> So deep the eternal light to search and sound
> That my whole vision was therein consumed!
> In that abyss I saw how love held bound
> Into one volume all the leaves whose flight
> Is scattered through the universe around.[39]

What God created at the beginning has a great purpose in His all-wise providence, which we gradually uncover as we dwell within the home which is the cosmos. In the final achievement of Sabbath rest, the Holy Spirit will present the Church, in which creation has been gathered up, through Christ to the Father. As we prepare for the new heavens and the new earth we deepen our faith in God the Father, the Son and the Holy Spirit, the Creator of all. We look forward to the Day on which faith will become vision. We reinforce our hope in the promise of the new creation when Christ will be All in all (Col 3:11): then we will experience Him Whom we hope for. Above all we are caught up in the Love of God who is the Lord of the old and of the new creation.

> *In the beginning, God made heaven and earth.*
> One sentence burned upon the formless dark-
> One sentence, and no more, from that high realm.
> The long-sought consummation of all law,
> Through all this manifold universe, might shine clear
> In those eight words one day; not yet; not yet!
> They would be larger, then;
> Not the glib prelude to a lifeless creed,
> But wide as the unbounded realms of thought,
> The last great simplification of them all,
> The single formula, like an infinite sphere
> Enfolding Space and time, atoms and suns,
> With all the wild fantastic hosts of life
> And all their generations, through all worlds,
> In one pure phrase of music, like a star
> Seen in a distant sky.[40]

Notes

1 See R. H. Benson, *Lord of the World* (1907) and *The Dawn of All* (1911).

2 See, for example, *The Omega Code* (Code Productions: 1999), *Megiddo: The Omega Code 2* (Code Productions: 2001).

3 See, for example, Chris de Burgh 'The Vision' in the album *Into the Light* (London: A&M records, 1986):
'And I saw the fire from the sky
I saw fire, and I saw paradise
Fire from the sun, I saw fire
And I saw alpha and omega.'

4 P. Davies, *The Mind of God* (London: Schuster and Schuster, 1992), p. 57. See also Idem, *The Last Three Minutes* (London:

Basic Books, 1994) which deals with scientific theories on the final cosmic scenario.

5 R. J. White, H. Angstwurm and I. Carrasco de Paula (eds.), *The Determination of Brain Death and its Relationship to Human Death* (Vatican City: Pontifical Academy of Sciences, 1992), 'Foreword' p. xiv. See also in the same volume, J. Seifert, 'Is "Brain Death" actually Death?' pp. 132–134. See also R. De Mattei (ed.), *Finis vitae. Is brain death still life?* (Soveria Mannelli: Rubbettino, 2006).

6 See Pope John Paul II, *Discourse at General Audience* (20 August 1986) in *IG* 9/2 (1986), pp. 397–398.

7 See Pope St Gregory the Great, Letter to Eulogius, Patriarch of Alexandria in ND 625: 'What He knew therefore in His humanity He did not know from it, because it is by the power of His divinity that God-made-man knew the day and hour of judgment.'

8 See St Thomas Aquinas, *Summa Theologiae* I, q.104, a.4.

9 W. Kasper, 'Hope in the final coming of Jesus Christ in glory' in *Communio* 12 (1985) p. 379.

10 See Pope John Paul II, *Discourse at General Audience* (30 April 1986) in *IG* 9/1 (1986), pp. 1177–1178.

11 Even mitigated forms of millenarism are unacceptable as can be seen from the decree of the Holy Office (DS 3839) in 1941 which stated that these systems cannot safely be taught.

12 St Augustine, *The City of God*, book 20 chapter 14 in *PL* 41, 679. The original Latin expression is 'Figura ergo praeterit, non natura.'

13 See St Irenaeus, *Adversus Haereses* Book 5, chapter 36, n.1 in *PG* 7, 1221; see also 1 Co 7:31.

14 See St Thomas Aquinas, *Summa Theologiae* Supplement q.74, a.3.

15 *Ibid.*, q.74, a.1.

16 See *ibid.*, q.74, aa. 2 and 5.

17 *Ibid.*, a.74, a.9.

18 See *ibid.*, q.91.

19 Vatican II, *Gaudium et Spes*, 39.1.

20 The dogma of the Assumption of the Mother of God leaves open the question of whether or not she died. A minority of theologians hold that she did not in fact suffer death. Among these was St Epiphanius, *Adversus Octaginta Haereses* Book 3, Tome 2, Heresy 78,11 in *PG* 42, 715–718. See P. Haffner, *The Mystery of Mary* (Leominster: Gracewing, 2004), pp. 209-217.

21 See C. E. Olson, *Will Catholics Be Left Behind?* (San Francisco: Ignatius Press, 2003), which is a thorough critique of the popular Protestant Fundamentalist notion of the 'Rapture'. The term rapture comes from the Latin of the passage 1 Th 4:17, 'simul rapiemur'. The idea among some Protestants is that the rapture is an event whereby God takes a select group of faithful Christians out of the world before or during the tribulation. This concept of the rapture is incorrect and contradicts Sacred Scripture. Saint Paul states that 'the dead in Christ will rise first', and that those 'who are left … shall not precede those who have fallen asleep.' Since the dead rise first, the rapture occurs at the time of the Resurrection. Since those who are left do not precede the dead who rise, the rapture cannot occur before the tribulation, nor anytime before the Resurrection. In summary, the rapture is not an event whereby the faithful are removed from the world before or during a time of suffering. As Christ suffered, so also must the Church suffer. However, there will be a rapture, for Sacred Scripture describes it. The true meaning of this rapture is a sharing in the Resurrection for those faithful who are still alive on earth in those end times.

22 Lateran IV, Chapter 1: On the Catholic Faith, in DS 801; English translation in ND 20.

23 See St Thomas Aquinas, *Summa Theologiae* Supplement, q.79, aa.1–2.

24 See St Bede the Venerable, *In Marci Evangelium Expositio* Book 4, chapter 13 in *PL* 93, 264.

25 Vatican II, *Lumen gentium*, 48.3.

26 See Origen, *Commentary on St John's Gospel* Book 10, n.20 in *PG* 14, 371–372.

27 Congregation for the Doctrine of the Faith, *Letter on certain questions concerning Eschatology*, 17 May 1979, in ND 2317.

28 See U. Vanni, 'L'opera creativa nell'Apocalisse' in *Rassegna di Teologia* 34 (1993) pp. 17–61.

29 *Ibid.*, pp. 43–49.

30 St Thomas Aquinas, *Summa Theologiae* Supplement q.81, a.4.

31 See St Thomas Aquinas, *Summa Theologiae* Supplement q.81, a.1: 'Wherefore that which belonged principally to human nature will be brought to that perfection which it has in the age of youth.'

32 See St Thomas Aquinas, *Summa Theologiae* Supplement q.81, a.3.

33 See St Augustine, *The City of God* book 20 chapter 16 in *PL* 41, 682.

34 St Thomas Aquinas, *Summa Theologiae* Supplement q.91, a.5.

35 Cf. J. Galot, 'Il destino finale dell'universo' in *La Civiltà Cattolica* 152/4 (November 3, 2001), pp. 213–225; G. Cavalcoli, 'La dimensione escatologica del tempo secondo la rivelazione cristiana' in *Sacra Dottrina* 44/1 (1999), pp. 5–46.

36 International Theological Commission, *Communion and Stewardship: Human Persons Created in the Image of God*, 80.

37 Cf. International Theological Commission, *Communion and Stewardship: Human Persons Created in the Image of God*, 76: 'Not only human beings, but the whole of visible creation, are called to participate in the divine life.'

38 Vatican II, *Gaudium et Spes*, 39.2.

39 Dante Alighieri, *The Divine Comedy 3: Paradise* Canto 33, lines 82–87. Translated by D. L. Sayers and B. Reynolds (Harmondsworth: Penguin, 1975) p. 345.

40 A. Noyes, *The Torch Bearers* Vol. II 'The Book of Earth' (Edinburgh and London: William Blackwood and Sons, 1925), pp. 24–25.

Index

From GRACEWING

By the same author

The Sacramental Mystery

The seven sacraments lie at the centre of Christian life and experience, for here God the Holy Trinity touches human lives and hearts. This book is one of the few at the present time to offer a global synthesis of the main themes in the sacramental mystery in which the human and divine, the material and the spiritual realms are intimately intertwined. Paul Haffner outlines how the sacraments are the chief means in the Church through which God's people are reconciled to the Father, through His Son, by the power of the Holy Spirit. The treatise illustrates classical issues like the conditions for the validity and the efficacy of the sacraments, as well as the minister, recipient and effects of these sacred mysteries; it deals with particular topics like the necessity of Baptism, the sacrificial character of the Eucharist, and the nature of Marriage. As he examines each sacrament in turn, the work also explores how new ecumenical questions affect Christian sacramental understanding.

'I warmly commend this work on the subject of sacramental theology.'

Archbishop Csaba Ternyák, Secretary of the Vatican Congregation for the Clergy

ISBN 978 0 85244 476 4

The Mystery of Reason

The Mystery of Reason investigates the enterprise of human thought searching for God. People have always found stepping–stones to God's existence carved in the world and in the human condition. This book examines the classical proofs of God's existence, and affirms their continued validity. It shows that human thought can connect with God and with other aspects of religious experience. Moreover, it depicts how Christian faith is reasonable, and is neither blind nor naked. Without reason, belief would degenerate into fundamentalism; but without faith, human thought can remain stranded on the reef of its own self–sufficiency. The book closes by proposing that the human mind must be in partnership with the human heart in any quest for God.

'This fine work may be seen as a response to the Papal encyclical Fides et Ratio. It is an exploration of the relationship between faith and reason, and in so doing it makes use of a variety of approaches including philosophy, theology and contemplation. It is wholly faithful to the vision of the Church.'

Dr Pravin Thevathasan

ISBN 978 0 85244 538 9

The Mystery of Mary

The Blessed Virgin Mary stands at the heart of the Christian tradition. She holds a unique place in the Church's theology, doctrine and devotion, commensurate with her unique position in human history as the Mother of God. In this book, Paul Haffner offers a clear and structured overview of theology and doctrine concerning Mary, within an historical perspective. He outlines the basic scheme of what constitutes Mariology, set in the context of other forms of theological enquiry, and, working through the contribution of Holy Scripture – in the Old Testament forms of prefiguration and the New Testament witness – he proceeds to examine each of the fundamental doctrines that the Church teaches about Our Lady. From the Immaculate Conception to Mary's continuing Motherhood in the Church as Mediatrix of all graces, the reader will find here a sure and steady guide, faithful to tradition and offering a realist perspective, not reducing the concrete aspects of Mary's gifts and privileges to mere symbols on the one hand, and not confusing doctrine and devotionalism on the other.

The Mystery of Mary, with a foreword by Dom Duarte, Duke of Braganza, was published to celebrate the one hundred and fiftieth anniversary of the definition, by Pope Blessed Pius IX, of the dogma of the Immaculate Conception of Our Lady.

ISBN 978 0 85244 650 8

Mystery of the Church

Mystery of the Church presents a global picture of the main themes of current ecclesiology. First, it deals with the institution of the Church and her essential nature. Subsequently the four hallmarks of the Church are described. Her unity and holiness are guaranteed by the sanctity of Christ her Head despite the sinfulness of her members. The catholicity of the Church is also examined from the perspective of Eastern Christendom. The apostolicity of the Church leads to a description of the Petrine Office. The Church is seen as the instrument of salvation, and her relationship with the State and with science is investigated. Finally the Church is pictured as leading to the Kingdom of God.

ISBN 978 0 85244 133 6

Towards a Theology of the Environment

Pope Benedict said at the beginning of his Pontificate that external deserts in the world are growing, because the internal deserts have become so vast. Therefore the earth's treasures no longer serve to build God's garden for all to live in, but they have been made to serve the powers of exploitation and destruction. This book is a theological investigation of the environment, and takes in scientific, biblical, moral and spiritual themes, all addressed by recent Church teaching on the subject. Starting with a detailed analysis of the various problems assailing the environment at present, a distinction is made between the science of ecology and the ideological overtones often associated with this area. An overview of Christian teaching on ecology is presented as an antidote to both New Age pseudo-mysticism and political ideology. The formulation of a Christian theology of the environment has direct consequences for both our moral life and our prayer.

ISBN 978 0 85244 368 2

Creation and scientific creativity
A study in the thought of
Stanley L. Jaki

Father Stanley Jaki (1924-2009) was one of the greatest thinkers of the twentieth century and his contribution to Catholic thought and culture has been profound, especially regarding the relationship between science and religion. This work focuses on the close link joining science and Christianity, despite the differences between them. Through his study of modern science, theology and history, Stanley Jaki showed that faith and reason are not mutually exclusive. The problems arise because of those ideologies which seek to eliminate God from the ultimate equation. Jaki highlighted the Christian origins of the modern natural sciences. He showed that the concept of the cosmos as both contingent and rational, together with the acceptance that God could work through secondary causes, provided the unique environment for the natural sciences to flourish, from the Middle Ages onwards. He explored the crucial role played by belief in creation out of nothing and in time, reinforced by faith in the Incarnation, in enabling this birth of science.

'Haffner's work offers an excellent synthesis of Jaki's thought, with an elegant and fluid style' — Mgr Mariano Artigas

ISBN 978 085244 454 2

Lightning Source UK Ltd.
Milton Keynes UK
12 February 2010

149986UK00002B/2/P